Applied Marketing Research

Applied Marketing Research

Luiz Moutinho
University of Wales

Martin Evans
University of Glamorgan

ADDISON-WESLEY PUBLISHING COMPANY

Wokingham, England · Reading, Massachusetts · Menlo Park, California
New York · Don Mills, Ontario · Amsterdam · Bonn · Sydney · Singapore
Tokyo · Madrid · San Juan · Milan · Paris · Mexico City · Seoul · Taipei

The programs in this book have been included for their instructional value. They have been tested with care but are not guaranteed for any particular purpose. The publisher does not offer any warranties or representations, nor does it accept any liabilities with respect to the programs.

Many of the designations used by manufacturers and sellers to distinguish their products are claimed as trademarks. Addison-Wesley has made every attempt to supply trademark information about manufacturers and their products mentioned in this book. A list of the trademark designations and their owners appears on p. xii.

Cover designed by SPL Design & Marketing and
printed by The Riverside Printing Co. (Reading) Ltd.
Typeset by Colset Private Limited, Singapore.
Printed in Great Britain by Mackays of Chatham plc, Chatham, Kent.

First printed 1992.

ISBN: 0 201 56504 8

British Library Cataloguing in Publication Data
A catalogue record for this book is available from the British Library.

Library of Congress Cataloging in Publication Data
Moutinho, Luiz.
    Applied marketing research / Luiz Moutinho, Martin Evans.
        p.   cm.
    Includes bibliographical references and index.
    ISBN 0-201-56504-8
    1. Marketing research.   I. Evans, Martin (Martin J.)   II. Title.
HF5415.2.M69   1992
    658.8′3 — dc20   92–17238
                                                              CIP

Dedicated to:
My parents (LM)
Anne and my father (MJE)

Preface

A glance at the contents page of this book should confirm the 'Applied' approach we intend – coverage of Marketing Research techniques, yes, but even greater coverage of applications of techniques and methodologies within the marketing mix elements.

We also include 'reader participation' in the form of short case studies, problems and topical 'clippings from the press'. These – and the text more generally – are supported by an Instructor's Manual.

The book is intended for those undergraduate and postgraduate students taking a course on marketing research and information. It is also aimed at post-experience students and practitioners in marketing research and indeed at those in marketing management because the 'buyer' or 'user' of reasearch has a need to be able to more fully evaluate what they are buying and using.

Our aims, then, are to provide students with a concise and reasonably comprehensive explanation of marketing research methodologies and techniques in the applied contexts of the marketing decision making areas. Additionally, it is an objective to provide the practitioner with a concise work of reference.

We would particularly welcome feedback from readers and adopters of the book – this market research is important to us, we want to practise what we preach!

Before you 'read on' into Chapter 1, we offer grateful thanks to Maggie Pickering at Addison-Wesley for her help and encouragement, to Karen Trigg and Louis Jones for slaving over a hot word processor, to our colleagues and students for their ideas, suggestions and inspiration – and last, but not least, to our friends and families for putting up with our hiding away from them while researching and writing this book.

Luiz Moutinho and Martin Evans
Cardiff, January 1992

Contents

Trademark notice

Andrex™ is a trademark of Scott Limited
Ariel Liquid™ is a trademark of Proctor & Gamble Limited
Domestos™, Persil™, and Radion™ are trademarks of Lever Brothers Limited
Ecover™ is a trademark of Ecover of Belgium
Flake™ is a trademark of Cadbury Limited
Kattomeat™ is a trademark of Dalgety Spillers Foods Limited
Kit Kat^R is a registered trademark of Société des Produits Nestlé SA
Kodak™ is a trademark of Eastman Kodak Limited
Marlboro™ is a trademark of Philip Morris Products Inc.
Minitab^R is a registered trademark of Minitab Inc.
Mr Sheen™ is a trademark of Reckitt & Coleman Products Limited
Rice Krispies^R is a registered trademark of the Kellogg Company
Shake 'N' Vac™ is a trademark of Johnson Wax Limited
Vanish™ is a trademark of Benckiser Limited

Part I

The Marketing Research Process: Designs and Techniques

1

Marketing, Marketing Information Systems and Marketing Research

Marketing research is one component of a Marketing Information System (MKIS). This book is primarily concerned with this marketing research element, but also covers closely related components. So before delving into marketing research specifically, it is worth spending a little time overviewing the marketing information system.

This (MKIS) has been variously described by different writers, for example:

> 'A designed set of procedures and methods for generating an orderly flow of pertinent information for use in marketing decisions, providing management with the current or conditional future states of his market and also providing indications of market responses to company actions as well as the actions of competitors.' (Boone and Kurtz, 1971)

> 'A marketing information system is a continuing and interacting structure of people, equipment and procedures to gather, sort, analyse, evaluate and distribute pertinent, timely and accurate information for use by marketing decision makers to improve their marketing planning, implementation and control.' (Kotler 1989)

Jobber's and Fletcher's definitions of the marketing information system are perhaps especially helpful as they go on to quantify the diffusion of the MKIS in the UK on the basis of their definitions in studies that took place six years apart, in 1977 and 1982.

Jobber defined the MKIS as:

> 'a system in which information was formally gathered, stored and distributed to managers in accord with their informational needs on a regular, planned basis'.

He took the *Times Top 500* as a sample base and received 440 responses from these firms in 1977. Of the respondents 50% had a MKIS that conformed to Jobber's criteria.

Fletcher defined the MKIS as:

'a formalized and systematic procedure for the handling of all the firm's market intelligence'.

Fletcher again used the *Times Top 500* as a sample base for his study, but this time obtained 117 responses from 200 companies approached. His figure of 54% of companies with a MKIS that conformed to his criteria would seem to confirm Jobber's findings and suggest that there had been little change in penetration over the six-year period.

These analyses of large, sophisticated companies highlight a number of points:

(1) Size does not necessarily mean sophistication, especially in marketing.

(2) Relying on a single, narrow definition of a MKIS would not be helpful.

(3) The problems identified by Jobber of implementing a MKIS, such as poor quality of data, defining managers' and users' needs, educating users as to the potential of such systems or assessing the technical problems, may well be a feature of smaller enterprises as well.

(4) The implementation barriers are important. Jobber's 'barriers' can be summarized as
   (a) no real need
   (b) lack of staff appreciation
   (c) budget constraints.

(5) Fletcher's 'barriers' were
   (a) no benefits, marketing information not important
   (b) marketing information not formally integrated and
   (c) market was small, no need for formal information system.

The MKIS can be seen, therefore, to contain many different sources and types of information – internal, operational data, market intelligence data, market research data and external data. As well as the data there are the functional aspects of the MKIS, and their role in support of information gathering, evaluation, processing, dissemination, analysis and control.

A helpful model is that of Piercy and Evans (1983), as illustrated in Figure 1.1.

One very useful feature of this model that is not present in, say, Kotler's original, is the distinction made between Data and Information, (Kotler, 1989).

Studies of MKIS have blossomed since Information Technology (IT)

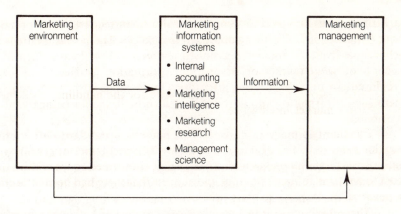

Figure 1.1 Components of the marketing information system. (*Source*: Piercy and Evans (1983))

became a significant factor, especially during the 1980s. More is said about IT and its impact in the last chapter of this book, but it is worth reporting at this stage that, according to Fletcher:

> 'Information technology has three main strands – computing, microelectronics and telecommunications – which are combined to provide a wide variety of products and services. It is difficult therefore to create a simple definition of IT which will combine all these elements. One definition is that information technology is the acquisition, processing, storage and presentation and transmission of information in all its forms.'

This definition he describes as the 'wider interpretation of IT', in contrast to the narrow definition of IT as referring simply to computers or information systems.

Of equal importance as the basis for assessment of marketing information within a business is the basis for assessing the use of information technology in support of marketing activities and objectives. The mere presence of computer hardware is not evidence of its usefulness or appropriateness. Indeed, in a qualitative study Kench and Evans (1991) found significant differences between *strategic* versus *tactical* uses of computer and IT systems. Some of the most sophisticated *on line* database technology is perhaps often only employed on a relatively low level, day-to-day, tactical basis.

Marketing research is clearly a key element in the MKIS and is increasingly using recent and new information technology.

What marketing research is specifically concerned with is the provision of information about markets and the reaction of these to various product, price, distribution and promotion policy actions.

It is not, however, concerned with the provision of information *per se*, marketing researchers tend to somewhat fear a client request 'for information' about a market, an advertising approach and so on. The problem here is that such vague requests are not decision orientated – they do not help in the selection of *what* market or advertising information is relevant or *why* it is required. In turn this creates difficulties in deciding how, when and from where such information should be collected, how it should be analysed and interpreted.

The point is made quite clearly in numerous standard definitions of marketing research. For example, the one by Tull and Hawkins (1976), which states that 'Marketing research is a formalized means of obtaining information to be used in making marketing decisions'. A classical definition was put forward by the American Marketing Association as long ago as 1960, 'The systematic gathering, recording and analysing of data about problems relating to the marketing of goods and services'. These serve to reinforce the point that marketing research is about specific marketing problems – not the collection of information *per se*.

Marketing research has a relatively 'immediate' focus, in that the decision context is not usually more than several months into the future. A later chapter discusses 'Marketing intelligence and environmental scanning' as being more concerned with longer term marketing planning.

The immediacy of marketing research can be seen from Figure 1.2. The 'boxes' provide examples of the main concerns of marketing research.

Less decision orientated dimensions of marketing information are shown as marketing's various 'environments'. The scanning of these is discussed in Chapter 14 and comprises the marketing intelligence MKIS component.

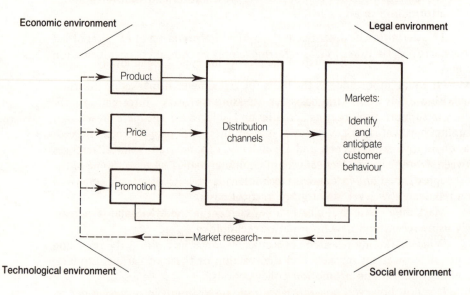

Figure 1.2 Marketing, marketing research and marketing intelligence.

In the same way that marketing is concerned with providing appropriate product, price, distribution and promotion offerings to target markets, so marketing research includes market research, product research, price research, distribution research and promotion research – and this provides the structure for Part II of this book. Table 1.1 overviews the wide range of such marketing research contexts. There is, therefore, a distinction between *marketing research* and *market research*, the former being far more inclusive than the latter.

Another significant dimension of many definitions of marketing research (including the ones quoted above) refers to its being systematic or formalized. Chapter 2 expands upon this point.

Table 1.1 Types of marketing research.

Types	*Examples*
Market research	Identifying customer requirements
	Studying customer groupings and market segmentation studies
	Measuring size and potential of markets
	Examining competitive positions and market share analysis
Product research	New product development programmes
	Concept and product tests
	Test marketing
	Packaging research
	Research of the product life cycle – brand loyalty
	Brand switching research
Pricing research	Measuring price awareness of buyers
	Analysing price sensitivity
	Examining brand perception–price relationships
Distribution research	Testing the effectiveness of marketing channels
	Measuring buyer behaviour toward manufacturer and retailer branding decisions
	Retail location studies and other retail marketing research
Promotion research	Research to help determine promotional objectives
	Promotional copy testing
	Promotional media research
	Measuring buyer response to promotional campaigns

REFERENCES

Boone L. E. and Kurtz D. L. (1971). Marketing information systems: Current status in American industry proceedings. *National Conference of the American Marketing Association*, New York

Fletcher K. (1982). Marketing information systems: A lost opportunity. *MEG Conference Proceedings*, Lancaster

Jobber D. (1977). Marketing information systems in United States and British industry. *Management Decision*, **15** (2), 297–304

Kench R. and Evans M. (1991). IT: The Information Technology dichotomy. *Marketing Intelligence*, **9** (5), 16–22

Kotler P. (1989). *Marketing Management Analysis, Planning, Implementation and Control* 6th edn. Englewood Cliffs NJ: Prentice-Hall

Piercy N. and Evans M. (1983). *Managing Marketing Information*. Croom Helm

Tull D. S. and Hawkins D. I. (1976). *Marketing Research: Measurement and method* 2nd edn. Collier Macmillan

2

The Marketing Research Process

To continue, then, with the last point made concerning marketing research being 'systematic' and 'formalized', the definition offered by Zaltman and Burger introduces a sequence of research events, from diagnosing marketing information requirements through data collection to data analysis:

> 'Marketing research involves the diagnosis of information and the selection of relevant inter-related variables about which valid and reliable information is gathered, recorded and analysed.' (Zaltman and Burger, 1975)

This leads to the structuring of research programmes around a series of stages in the research process as shown in Figure 2.1.

Such stages can be of great help both in the *planning* of research programmes and in the *control* and *evaluation* of them. The iterative 'feedback loop' implies that the process can continue, with 'answers' leading to more, and better, questions and in this way the marketing research process may be endless.

The research process

Stage 1: Defining and clarifying the marketing problem

It is suggested here that of all the stages in the total process it is often this one at the beginning of a research programme that in practice can be riddled with error and bias.

A research programme is manifested in its final research report and it is usually possible in this, to some extent, to be able to evaluate other stages of

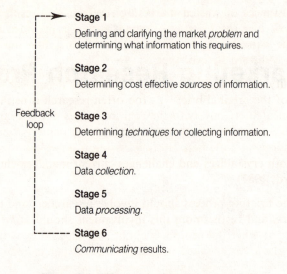

Figure 2.1   The marketing research process.

the process. For example, any questionnaire used should usually appear in an Appendix and the reader can scrutinize this – as will be seen later it is relatively easy to criticize a questionnaire, its wording, structure, sequence and so on, but it is not so simple to construct one. Also, the sample design and size should be explained and again the reader is given the opportunity to evaluate this. The manner in which the data has been analysed and reported can also be studied in the report, but even if the project objectives *appear* reasonable to a reader who is not the person responsible for making decisions, they may be wholly inadequate for the actual decision area concerned.

The point, then, is that although error and bias can occur at any stage of the process, if the first stage is not fully explored and agreed between decision maker and researcher, the entire programme can waste time and money.

To illustrate this we refer to an advertising research programme which was commissioned by Vaux Breweries to evaluate a poster advertising campaign for a new beer. Levels of awareness were evaluated and attitudes measured using a questionnaire and street interviewing, and the results were gratefully received by the brand manager concerned. However, later feedback from the organization revealed that the decision maker resided in general marketing management and while the research results were relevant and useful, they had their limitations. The problem materialized as poor communication: while the brand manager briefed the researchers in line with his perception of the problem, the marketing manager wanted to use the information to decide whether to launch a new lager using, predominately, a poster campaign. The point is that the initial research problem is broader than the evaluation of one campaign.

Other instances of wasted marketing research as a result of faults in problem analysis and the briefing of researchers are provided by England (1980), and the dangers are generalized by Millward, the joint managing director of the Millward Brown Agency:

> 'The utility of any research project is critically dependent upon the quality of the original brief . . . too often research is neither communicated effectively to the decision takers nor relevant to their decisions . . . make sure that the real decision makers attend key presentations . . . the best briefing session is a two-way discussion which both crystallizes and challenges current management thinking.' (Millward, 1987)

Thus, the briefing process should involve researchers and their clients' decision makers, and furthermore this involvement should often lead to not only agreement of what the project is about, but also an evolution through the project to allow for changed circumstances and perceptions. The 'brief' should, according to Edwin Smith, managing director of IFF Research, contain:

> 'A statement of the problem facing the client, other areas in which information is required . . . details of the background leading to a request for research . . . the purposes to which research will be put . . . the date by which results are required . . . an indication of the budget available for the work.' (Smith, 1987)

The 'problem definition' stage should lead naturally to the listing of appropriate informational requirements (the 'data list') in the context of the decision areas concerned.

Exploratory versus conclusive research

Developing a clear formulation of the scope and nature of a research problem may be referred to as *exploratory research* which explores the parameters of the problem, in order to identify what should be measured and how best to undertake a study.

Exploratory techniques are usually relatively unstructured, sometimes merely discussions of the problem with knowledgeable people, or the study of case histories of similar projects which could suggest a methodology.

Group discussions with consumers are popular, as they are not constrained by highly structured questionnaires and enable the problem to be seen from a 'consumer' perspective. Indeed, in the practical setting exploratory research may provide enough information for the decision maker's needs (or perhaps all he or she can afford). Certainly, there have been increases in the use of qualitative research, such as the employment of group discussions with small samples without any large scale follow-up (Krauser, 1981).

In contrast, *conclusive research* is conducted through the main research design and is aimed at measurement of the variables identified from the exploratory exercises. It provides the information, specified on the data list, which management requires. Chapter 7 discusses data collection techniques, so for the present, it should be noted that there is a logical progression from exploratory to conclusive research.

Stage 2: Determining cost effective sources of information

The list of specific informational requirements (the data list) should have been built up in problem definition and it is necessary to determine where the data can be found. There is a popular misconception that marketing research is no more than an interviewer in the street with a questionnaire and clipboard. While this image *is* appropriate to some research programmes, there are others where the interviewing is conducted in a hall, or a person's home, others that require no interviewer at all (for example, postal surveys) and some that involve no questioning (such as observation studies) and yet others that rely exclusively on existing reports or other documentation (that is, secondary data sources).

Secondary versus primary data sources

The range of data sources can be broadly categorized under the headings of secondary and primary. *Secondary* sources involve information that already exists, such as company records or previous reports, government statistics, newspaper and journal articles and commercial market research agency reports. Figure 2.2 lists some examples of the wealth of information that exists.

This point serves to demonstrate that it is always worth exploring the possibilities of using secondary sources – as a *first* resort – before commissioning what would usually be a more expensive and time consuming programme of collecting 'new' information using 'primary' research methods.

In fact, the major area of research, which precedes buying agency research or starting an in-company research project, involves secondary data and because of the heavy use of such sources, there is a need to adopt a critical perspective in using them. First, the researcher evaluates secondary sources for *impartiality*, as far as this is possible, to be reasonably sure that there is no slant or bias in the information resulting from the provider or compiler attempting to make a case for or against something. Secondly, the researcher checks that sources are *relevant*, that is, whether the information is what the researcher wants to know and thirdly, that sources are *reliable*, that is, whether the information is representative of the group it purports to describe (for instance a sample of twelve consumers is unlikely to reflect all consumers in a national population), and fourthly, that sources provide information with internal *homogeneity*, that is the consistency of, for example, a set of figures.

Many of these are free (either because they are to be found in most public libraries or because they are available free from government departments). Even some of the expensive commercial reports can be found in some libraries.

KOMPASS – gives names and addresses of companies (that is, possible competitors) by country and by product category.

Kelly's Guide – lists industrial, commercial and professional organizations in the UK, giving a description of their main activities and providing their addresses. Listings are alphabetical according to trade description and also according to company name.

Key British Enterprises – a register of 25,000 top UK companies which provides company name and address and also some basic financial data such as sales, number of employees and the Standard Industrial Code (SIC).

UK Trade Names – lists trade names and the parent company.

Who Owns Whom – lists firms and their parent organization.

Business Monitor – gives statistics for different products e.g., numbers of manufacturers, industry sales and import levels.

Family Expenditure Survey – gives average weekly expenditure on many products and services according to: different regions, size of household, age of head of household, household income levels. Useful for estimating market size and potential sales levels.

Regional Trends – plots population size and structure trends through the regions, together with more on regional income and expenditure.

Henley Centre for Forecasting – projects future social attitudes, lifestyles, income and expenditure.

Market Intelligence (MINTEL) – monthly reports on profile of different markets (both customers and competitors).

Retail Business – monthly reports on profile of different retailing markets (both customers and competitors).

The Retail Directory – gives details of retail trade associations and lists retail companies according to type (co-op, multiple, department store and so on) and according to geography (for example, the retail outlets within many towns are listed).

Target Group Index (TGI) – annual profile of most product markets in terms of who buys what, 34 volumes each year.

National Readership Survey – profile of readers of newspapers and magazines (for advertising media selection). Match with profile of target market.

BRAD (British Rate and Data) – gives costs of advertising in press, radio, poster, cinema, television and all other mass media.

MEAL (Media Expenditure Analysis) – provides information on competitors' advertising expenditure on specific brands per month. Also gives advertising agency concerned.

Trade Associations – usually have information on numbers of competitors and size of market.

Local Chambers of Trade – have statistics on companies in their trading area and information on trading conditions.

Electoral Register – can be used to help define the catchment areas of retail outlets and the number of potential customers. Also used to draw samples for market research.

Viewdata – (e.g. Prestel) general purpose on-line databases, including some market and company information. Others are more specialized, for example, TEXTLINE provides a 'key word' search of many newspapers and journals for information and articles on the topic concerned.

Figure 2.2 Secondary data sources.

So great is the amount and variety of secondary sources that sizeable books are published which do nothing other than list possible sources of information to do with certain topics and areas of concern. Indeed, the government's Statistical Service annually publishes its booklet *Government Statistics: A brief guide to sources*, together with another guide *Profit from Figures*, which illustrates some of the main uses of government statistics.

Primary sources, on the other hand, involve collecting new information, first hand, for the particular research programme. Figure 5.5 provides only an overview of the approaches here, because Chapter 3 provides a more complete discussion.

Without pre-empting the following chapter too much, Table 2.1 distinguishes primary data collection techniques in a framework which suggests an increase in the ease of creating control, that the researcher can exert over the variables being measured, when progressing from *observation* through *interview* to *experimentation*.

Table 2.1 Primary data overview.

Observation	*Interview*	*Experimentation*
Personal observations Watching customers/ consumers; monitoring competitors' new product launches, changes in prices, packaging, advertising, etc.	*Types of interview* • postal • telephone (including CATI, see pages 27 and 267) • personal (including computer interviewing, see page 28)	*Nature of experiments* Holding some variables constant and changing other variables to measure their effects.
Traffic counts • of customers in store • of vehicles/people passing poster sites, etc.	*Interview structure* • unstructured, such as group discussions • structured, with highly specific questions, many of the multiple choice type	*Examples of experiments* Changing an advertising campaign and comparing sales after the campaign with those before ('Before–After' experiment).
Recording devices E.g., using in store surveillance equipment (CCTV) to improve store layout and displays; TV set meters; eye camera.	*Direct/indirect questions* Used to uncover 'motives', may need to avoid a direct question, and ask 'Why would someone?' rather than 'Why do you?'	By also comparing sales in another area (one that is not exposed to the new campaign) can identify the effects of 'uncontrolable' variables ('Before–After with control group' experimental design). The 'test market' is perhaps the ultimate marketing experiment.

Ad hoc *versus continuous research*

Another distinction worth making within primary data collection methods is between *ad hoc* and *continuous* research. When the same respondents are observed or interviewed repeatedly over a period, then this is referred to as continuous research, as opposed to an *ad hoc* study that collects data on one occasion only from given respondents.

An example of this is the consumer panel (not to be confused with a group discussion). Here, respondents – often in the form of 'households' – agree to report on their buying behaviour over a period of time, perhaps completing a type of diary every week or so and posting this to the research agency concerned. More on this in later chapters.

Cost effectiveness

The criteria of impartiality, validity, reliability and homogeneity, discussed earlier, are important in determining the appropriateness of specific research outcomes, whether by someone else, as in the case of secondary sources, or in the case of one's own primary study.

In addition, there are practical, but constraining influences of time and money – and indeed, expertise and politics – and research designs are really based on a compromise of some sort.

Secondary sources are often cheaper and less time consuming than primary ones, though some are very expensive in absolute terms. If secondary sources only provide exploratory results, or if there are problems due to, say, invalidity or reliability, then first hand data collection is likely to be the next stage, if time and money warrant.

A rule of thumb in assessing cost effectiveness is the extent to which research results provide benefits exceeding their costs and this approach has been refined by the use of Bayesian Analysis (see Churchill (1987) and Figure 2.3) which helps by using probability theory to estimate the value of decisions made without research information, compared with decisions made with information derived from different types of research design, sample size variations and so on.

The presentation of research alternatives in the form of decision trees is useful to both researcher and research user. As discussed earlier, the more the decision maker is involved in the preliminary stages of research programmes, the more likely is the resulting programme to produce information which is appropriate to the specific decision context.

Some managers use subjective probability scales to help them in their decision making process. One scale measures the level of combined disagreement among them, with regard to a final decision on a specific project. Another, the profit consequences scale, is intended to measure the expected monetary value in terms of the overall profitability of the project. Combining these two 5-point subjective scales (combined disagreement and profit

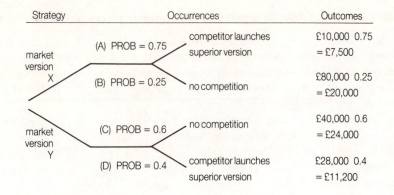

Strategy	Occurrences	Outcomes
market version X	(A) PROB = 0.75 — competitor launches superior version	£10,000 0.75 = £7,500
	(B) PROB = 0.25 — no competition	£80,000 0.25 = £20,000
market version Y	(C) PROB = 0.6 — no competition	£40,000 0.6 = £24,000
	(D) PROB = 0.4 — competitor launches superior version	£28,000 0.4 = £11,200

Four possible occurrences: financial value of each:

A = £10,000 B = £80,000 C = £40,000 D = £28,000

From the 'outcomes' column it can be seen that the *expected value* of marketing version X is £7,500 + £20,000 = £27,500, while the expected value of marketing version Y is £24,000 + £11,200 = £35,200. Thus, marketing version Y *would appear to be* the more favourable course of action.

Figure 2.3 Decision tree.

consequences) in a summated 10-point scale will help managers in the process of choosing a decision alternative.

Where there is a situation where the management disagreement level/ profit consequences scores suggest delaying a decision to obtain additional information, to increase the likelihood of selecting the correct alternative, increased costs become a factor to consider. Decision delay is not without some cost; the reduction of uncertainty is not free of charge. This cost must be compared to the expected gain resulting from increasing the probability of selecting the best course of action; that is to say, the cost of such added information should not exceed its value.

If additional information is deemed necessary, how can the decision makers determine the amount of money to allocate to the marketing research unit that will gather it? If marketing research is the only cost associated with decision delay, the marketing manager could, in theory, allocate any amount that does not exceed the estimated profit consequences of a wrong decision. In other words, if additional research data improves the chances for a more profitable decision, then the maximum amount that should be expended for such data is the difference between the expected profit consequences of the decision taken without additional data and the expected profit consequences of the decision taken with additional data. This difference is sometimes referred to as the expected value of added information.

The cost of marketing research is only one cost element in decision delay. Opportunity cost is another. For example, delaying the introduction of a new

Table 2.2 Pay-off table for decision on introduction of a new soft drink product.

Predicted sales	Marketing alternative pay-offs (millions of pounds)		Do not introduce product
	Probability of outcome	Introduce product	
£40 million	0.3	£4.0	£0
£20 million	0.7	−£2.0	£0
Expected profit:	(0.3) (£4) + (0.7) (− £2) = £0.2		£0

product pending the results of extensive consumer research may improve the chances of making the right decision. However, the expected benefits from such a decision should be compared to the amount of predicted sales revenue that would be lost during the testing period.

A third cost which may be incurred as a result of decision delay stems from the reduction of lead time over competitive counteraction. Less and less frequently do companies enjoy long periods of competitive product advantage. A new product, even when a competitor is caught by surprise, can often be quickly duplicated, or a highly similar product soon introduced. To test a contemplated product line addition in the marketplace over a long period of time will alert competitors. They can purchase test products, analyse them and produce similar products in quantity while the originator is still seeking additional data for the reduction of uncertainty.

Table 2.2 is a pay-off table for a marketing decision on the introduction of a proposed new product by a soft drinks manufacturer. The marketing alternatives in Table 2.2 have been evaluated in terms of the established monetary criterion, namely, expected profit. The expected profit for each alternative was obtained by multiplying the probabilities of the outcomes by the pay-offs for each alternative and summing up as follows:

Alternatives	Expected profit in pounds (millions)
Introduce product	$(0.3) \times (£4.0) + (0.7) \times (−£2.0) = −£0.2$
Do not introduce product	$(0.3) \times (£0) + (0.7) \times (£0) = £0$

At this point, the principal decision maker was reluctant to pass up a chance to make £4 million and was wondering if more information should be gathered before taking action, thus incurring delay. In terms of the combined disagreement (say, level 3) and profit consequences (say, level 5) on the 10-point (combined disagreement and profit consequences) scales used by the top management of the company, this situation 'scored' between 8 and 9.

These 10-point scales are designed to measure (initially on a separate basis): (1) the degree of combined disagreement achieved by a group of managers when evaluating a specific issue related to a particular problem-solving situation, and (2) the estimated profit consequences attached to the assessment of the same managerial issue confronted by the company. The scales range from low level of combined disagreement (1) to high level of combined disagreement (10) and from low profit consequences (1) to high profit consequences (10).

The subsequent stage of analysis involves merging the rating scores derived from both scales into a final 10-point scale, which should reproduce the final assessment rating of the managers' combined disagreement and perception of profit consequences associated with a particular decision-making area.

Due to the composition of the group of decision makers and intra-group variability, different weights can be placed alongside the rating scores in order to maximize the effectiveness of this scaling procedure.

It would thus meet the criterion for deciding to delay the marketing decision and gather more information.

In the context of the decision analysis framework, the following could be noted regarding the marketing decision situation shown in Table 2.2.

(1) The agreed-upon marketing alternatives are

   (a) to introduce the product
   (b) not to introduce the product.

(2) The criterion may be stated: if the expected profit is greater than some specified amount, say £0.1 million, then the new soft drink product will be introduced.

(3) Profit consequences are high for a decision to introduce the product (a £2 million loss on sales of £20 million) and high for a decision not to introduce the product (£4 million foregone).

(4) The estimate of 0.7 for low sales and 0.3 for high sales is decidedly stronger for low sales, but the high sales estimate may come from the most experienced members of the decision group.

(5) The expected monetary result (−£0.2 million) indicates that the appropriate action is to abandon the project, that is, not to introduce the product.

Since the indicated values of the expected profit criterion are zero and negative for the two alternatives, the proper decision is clearly not to introduce the new product.

If the marketing manager authorized an expenditure of £0.2 million for a market survey and the results of this survey convinced the decision makers to revise their original estimates of the probabilities of the outcomes given in Table 2.3 to 0.6 for high sales and 0.4 for low sales, then the expected profit for the product introduction alternative would be £1.6 million as illustrated in Table 2.3. Based upon the evaluation of the alternatives in this case, the decision is plainly indicated to introduce the new product, since the expected

Table 2.3 Pay-off table for decision on introduction of a new soft drink product after market survey.

| Expected sales | Marketing alternative Pay-offs in pounds (millions) | | |
	Revised probability of outcome	Introduce product	Do not introduce product
£40 million	0.6	£4.0	£0
£20 million	0.4	−£2.0	£0
Expected profit:	(0.6)(£4) + (0.4)(−£2) = £1.6		£0

profit is £1.6 million. When the cost of the survey, which was stated to be £0.2 million, is included, the net expected profit is £1.4 million. Since this is preferable to the zero profit from not introducing the soft drink product, the decision is to introduce the new product. Of course, one does not know in advance which direction the probability revisions will take, but conducting the research produces a known out-of-pocket cost.

Stage 3: Determining techniques for collecting information

Once it has been determined *what* information (Stage 1) should be collected and from *where* it should be found and indeed whether it should be pursued (Stage 2), it is then necessary to determine *how* it should be collected.

This stage is concerned with the instruments and procedures for data collection; secondary data has to be found, interpreted and summarized, so the main focus of discussion in this stage is on primary data collection.

The following elements of a research design are the major concerns here, though not all of these will be part of every research programme. Firstly, the techniques of observation, interview and experimentation (and some of these have been listed in Table 2.1), secondly, questionnaire and observation form design, and thirdly, sample design.

These elements, as with aspects of all other research process stages, are sources of error and bias which may invalidate the whole programme: an inappropriate research instrument, for example asking interview respondents for information they cannot or will not give accurately; or an inappropriate sample asking questions of the wrong people – or too few of the right people – will seriously affect the utility of research results.

These issues are further explored in Chapters 3, 4 and 5.

Stage 4: Data collection

In the actual collection of data the main types of error and bias during this 'fieldwork' stage are due to poor interviewing or observation procedures.

Interviewing techniques are also covered in Chapter 4, where some attention is given to the potential error and bias which may occur at this stage. For example, it is known that interviewers can start to make mistakes towards the end of long spells of interviewing and bad weather can sometimes lead to short cuts such as the interviewing of 'non-quota' respondents, or even interviewing anyone who happens to be in the dry and warmth of the nearest public house! If names and addresses of respondents are taken at the time of the interview, then a supervisor can contact a proportion of them as a control, to confirm that they were indeed interviewed and that their characteristics match the sample requirements. Even the threat that supervisors might do this may be reasonably effective.

The same maxim also applies to the need for thorough training of the fieldforce. Lectures and traditional classroom techniques play a minor role here – mainly in setting the scene for fieldwork in the context of marketing research and marketing decision making. The best way to learn interviewing skills is through practice. Mock interview situations can be created, and perhaps these can be recorded on video and played back for group analysis. Trainees can accompany experienced interviewers during live research programmes, perhaps followed by the trainee conducting some interviews – with the experienced interviewer observing, to later discuss his/her performance.

Stage 5: Data processing

Once the data has been collected it has to be analysed, edited and tested, before communication to the decision maker. It is all too easy for the planning stages of a research programme to revolve around designing samples and questionnaires and little else. When this happens the researcher will be shaken by the problems of data analysis – perhaps hundreds of questionnaires have been returned, how should they be analysed? What should happen to open-ended questions – there appear to be as many different ways of answering these as there are respondents?

The key is to plan in advance, indeed this is another reason for this general division of the whole research process into a series of stages.

A valuable discipline is to list all the data processing requirements in Stage 1, at the time of compiling the data list. It is more likely, then, to be reasonably sure that the data list is accurate. These problems and other aspects of data processing, such as statistical analysis and illustrative data sets from case histories, for computer analysis will be discussed in Chapter 6.

Stage 6: Communicating results

In the same way that it was suggested in Stage 1 that communication between decision maker and researcher is important for the objectives of the research programme to be clarified and agreed, so the same applies at the end of the process. Results have to be communicated for the users of research in such a way that their meaning is not distorted and so that they answer the brief as originally agreed.

The following chapters (in Part I) pursue this framework in more detail by examining the techniques involved with designing, implementing and analysing research programmes.

REFERENCES

Churchill G. A. (1987). *Marketing Research: Methodological foundations* 4th edn. Illinois: Dryden Press

England L. (1980). Is research a waste of time? *Marketing*, 16 April, 5–7

Krauser P. (1981). Research: A safe bet for the fight against product failure. *Campaign*, 31 July, 33–5

Millward M. (1987). How to get better value from your research budget. *AMSO Handbook and Guide to Buying Market Research in the UK*, pp. 6–10

Smith E. (1987). Commissioning a research project. *AMSO Handbook and Guide to Buying Market Research in the UK*, pp. 18–21

Zaltman G. and Burger P. C. (1975). *Marketing Research*. Illinois: Dryden Press

FURTHER READING

Crimp M. (1990). *The Marketing Research Process* 3rd edn. London: Prentice–Hall International

Easton G. (1982). *Learning from Case Studies*. Englewood Cliffs NJ: Prentice–Hall, pp. 156–194

Jay A. (1970). *Effective Presentation*. London: Management Publications

Little P. (1971). *Communication in Business*. Harlow: Longman

Shipman M. D. (1972). *The Limitations of Social Research*. Harlow: Longman

3

Primary Data Collection: Observation – Interview – Experimentation

When primary data are to be collected there are a number of key decisions in the research design – the data collection methodology, including the design and use of questionnaires, if these are appropriate to the research problem and the choice of sampling protocol.

In the case of data collection methods, the framework for choice is summarized in Table 2.1 as a continuum reflecting the degree of control that the researcher can exert over the variables being studied. In this way, observation, interview and experimentation can be modelled as a methodological sequence.

Indeed, there are variations of approach within each of these categories, such that each may itself be regarded as a continuum – for example, some interviews are freer than others, reflecting different degrees of structure and required control. This continuum provides the structure for this chapter.

Observation techniques in marketing research

Much information for marketing decision making can be collected without asking a single question, but rather by observing the behaviour of customers or competitors.

Observation design

Observation techniques can be used in a number of different ways as outlined below.

Structured or unstructured

In a formalized research programme, observation may be used in an unstructured form to record, for example, general purchasing behaviour, as opposed to the more structured observation of such factors as the sex of purchasers of a specific brand of toothpaste. Indeed, a fairly unstructured observational approach may serve as exploratory research in attempting to explore and clarify the focus that is needed in conclusive research.

Natural or contrived

It is usually more realistic to observe in actual or real conditions, such as recording the number of people who look at a poster, although this is not always possible. For instance, when evaluating new store layouts, customer flows can be observed using a hall as a simulated store to test alternative designs without disrupting the real stores.

Disguised or undisguised

Perhaps the greatest potential problem of observation is that of modified behaviour – people who know they are being watched may not act as they otherwise would. For example, some continuous studies record respondents' television viewing habits and record the grocery products they purchase. It has been found that some respondents watch different programmes, or buy different products, during the first few weeks of such recording, until reverting to their more normal habits.

A study of the demand for taxis in Newcastle upon Tyne in the late 1970s, illustrates disguised and undisguised observation and the problem of modified behaviour. This study involved observation of taxi ranks to calculate the average time taxis had to wait before picking up passengers, and the average time that passengers had to wait for a taxi. The taxi drivers knew that research was to be carried out, with the aim of deciding whether to increase the number of taxi licences in the city. Observers were positioned at all the ranks, including the two most popular. Observers at one main rank were positioned openly and were noticeable to anyone in the vicinity (not by design, but as a result of the topography of the area). Although there were several taxis at this rank at the beginning of the first observation period, within minutes there was a mass influx of taxis, far more than arrived at any other similar length of time over the next fortnight.

When the results were later analysed it was found that the same number of taxis that arrived at the first rank in the first 15-minute period, had departed from the second main rank. The striking difference was that the observers at the second rank were positioned in a hidden location and it was concluded that as soon as the observers were themselves seen by the taxi drivers at the first

Observer: _____			Rank: _____	
Date:_____ Time on:_____			Time off:_____	
Taxi			Passenger	
Taxi number	Time in	Time out	Time in	Time out

Fifteen minute count: ☐ ☐ ☐ ☐ ☐

P/T   P/T   P/T   P/T   P/T

Comments/Weather conditions:_____

_____

Signature_____

Figure 3.1 Newcastle taxi observation form.

rank, they contacted their colleagues by radio and called them from the rank which (to the taxi drivers) appeared not to be under observation.

The rationale was that the drivers did not want the number of licences increased and wanted, therefore, to give the appearance of plenty of taxis! See Figure 3.1 for the observation form that was employed here.

Human or mechanical observation

Various mechanical and electronic devices offer alternatives to a human observer watching an event.

It is possible to use closed circuit television cameras for such applications as monitoring a new retail store layout. For monitoring the television viewing habits of respondents in consumer panels, meters attached to their sets have been used for many years and cable television effectively makes such meters common to all those households receiving cable output.

The set meter records whether the set is on or off at regular intervals and if it is 'on', which channel has been selected. This does not measure how many people are watching – just which channel the set is tuned to.

Another type of continuous research is the retail audit where sales of specific brands are recorded. Often this used to be by means of physical stock checks by observers at regular intervals. The replacement of manual stock and shelf counts by laser scanning has been discussed elsewhere in this book, but a dramatic example of the change in method of data collection toward higher technology is given by the winning, by Gallup, of the contract to compile the record charts (the previous agency, the British Market Research Bureau used a somewhat slow and cumbersome physical diary system).

A further illustration of observation techniques in continuous research concerns those consumer panels that rely on respondents to place the packaging of relevant products consumed in a special audit bin, for the observer to count during regular visits.

Mechanical observation techniques may use devices like the psychogalvanometer, or lie detector, one version of which records changes in perspiration rates as a result of emotional reaction to stimuli such as test advertisements. Similarly, the tachistoscope allows an object, such as an advertisement or a product package, to be illuminated for a fraction of a second to test the advertisement or package for initial impact, legibility, recognition, and so on.

The advantage of observation is that it can be more objective because what actually happens is recorded, compared with the subjectivity of questioning approaches, which, as will be shown shortly, by the very nature of question wording and interviewing, can introduce some bias.

However, as discussed above, such objectivity is lost if subjects are aware of the observation and modify their behaviour. In practice, the researcher may be unable to even approach the ideal of effective data collection through observation. The fact that the researcher does not have to gain respondent cooperation poses an ethical problem, as exemplified by Crawford (1970). Crawford discusses the use of (unknown to those being observed) one-way mirrors in ladies' changing rooms in American department stores to observe how bras were put on and taken off! This was part of a new product development programme by an American women's underwear manufacturer and was employed because it was thought less provocative than asking women direct questions about this sort of intimate product. It was, of course, a totally unethical research approach, but it does beg the question of where the line should be drawn regarding what to observe – and it also raises the ethical issue of whether respondents' cooperation should first be gained. If it should, then we return to the problem of modified behaviour. In any case respondent cooperation may be essential as in the continuous research mentioned earlier.

Indeed, it would be inappropriate to attempt to observe such intimate behaviour as washing, brushing teeth or other personal habits, and some topics themselves are not susceptible to observation – such as attitudes and motivation, which require verbal responses to specialized questions. More mundanely, some simply take too long to be exhibited, so fieldwork would be too time consuming and costly.

It should also be noted that observation requires the design of forms, in much the same way that interview surveys require questionnaires. For example, Figure 3.1 shows the observation form used in the Newcastle taxi observation study discussed earlier.

Interview survey methods

There are, in fact, various types of interview used in research surveys, and typically a distinction is made between postal, telephone and personal interviews. Further distinctions can be made between structured and unstructured interviews, and the personal interview can be of a depth or group type. Indeed, new technology provides another kind of interviewing, where the computer provides a vehicle for asking questions and collecting responses, in some cases using the Viewdata facilities of domestic television sets. Each form of interviewing merits a brief outline, as the basis for a choice of methodology.

Postal interviews

Postal questionnaire studies have the obvious advantage over personal interviews of being able to cover a very large geographic area, usually with little increase in postal costs. The major characteristic of postal surveys is the absence of an interviewer, which eliminates interviewer bias but at the same time provides little scope for respondents to query the meaning of the questions. The lack of personal contact also means that when a questionnaire is sent to an address there is no guarantee that the respondent is the addressee, since the questionnaire may be completed by another member of the family or another member of the organization.

However, on the positive side, where a survey requires the respondent to consult with others, or with filed information, the postal survey provides the necessary time and freedom, and another result of there being no interviewer is that some respondents may be less inhibited about answering certain questions. On the other hand, without an interviewer, misunderstood questions cannot be explained, open questions cannot be probed and the non-verbal communication of the respondents (facial expressions, intonation and the like) cannot be observed.

However, the single most significant problem usual in postal surveys is a low level of response – it is all too easy for the respondent to ignore a postal questionnaire. Without a carefully constructed covering letter, emphasizing such factors as how useful (and confidential) the respondent's replies will be, or without a reminder, response rates can be as low as single figures. Even with these and the obvious enclosures such as stamped addressed return envelopes, response rates may be so low as to be unrepresentative of the selected sample. The point is, of course, that non-response may not be a random factor – the characteristics of those who *do* respond may be significantly different from the characteristics of those who do *not* respond – a factor for which survey results should be tested where possible.

Once such limitations have been identified for a particular study then avoidance may be planned. Despite the important problems, postal surveys are used extensively in practice, perhaps often because it is an acceptable compromise between reliability and validity, and cost considerations.

Telephone interviews

Although not used as much as other interviewing approaches, nor as much in the UK as in the USA, the telephone interview is becoming more important and merits consideration in research design, as long as the sampling can be restricted to those with telephones.

As in the case of postal surveys, there is a geographical advantage, although it is less pronounced than with postal questionnaires because of long-distance telephone rates, time-related call charges, and the inability in many cases to make use of cheap rate times (phoning companies at the weekend or in the evenings promises little success). This method can be more expensive than a postal survey.

Telephone interviews are often appropriate for industrial or organizational surveys because most companies have telephones and the chances of contacting someone from an organization during office hours are reasonably good – although it may be more difficult to contact the relevant respondent *within* an organization.

Once the problems of organizational switchboards are overcome, telephone interviewing can be the quickest of all the interviewing methods because the interview is made from the researcher's desk, so no fieldwork travel is involved, and the replies are immediate. This said, there are clearly some questions that cannot be asked over the telephone, such as those asking the respondent to look at something like a product or package, or the type of attitude scales discussed below, and telephone interviews are of necessity restricted to questions which are capable of instant reply. On the other hand, the telephone can sometimes hide the existence of a questionnaire and the interview can appear more like a conversation to the respondent, who may feel more relaxed and less inhibited.

There is certainly increased interest in the form of interviewing, as demonstrated by the coverage received in the marketing research literature, for example, by Collins (1981), White (1982) and Weitz (1982), who offer additional commentary on the use of the technique.

Telephone interviews and new technology

There have been many calls to use applications of new information technology in marketing research, and Hyett (1982) points to the link between telephone interviewing and the use of minicomputers and mainframe computer terminals. He suggests that the computer be used to store the questionnaire and as the interviewer goes through the interview over the telephone, the computer can select and display the appropriate questions for each respondent. The replies can be keyed directly into the computer store, for immediate analysis.

The more sophisticated Viewdata technology, being interactive, will allow questions to be sent down the line to households possessing such a system. After being displayed on people's television sets, their answers can be keyed in via a Viewdata keypad, or via a home computer keyboard, and sent back along the line to the researcher for analysis. Such systems are as yet in their infancy and Viewdata is not a technology in wide ownership as yet. However, already tested and used is a compromise between the above approaches, involving the use of a computer visual display unit, presenting the respondent with a self completion questionnaire. Such work has been reported by Shugan and Hauser (1977).

Personal interviewing

The distinguishing feature of personal interviewing is, of course, face to face communication between respondent and interviewer, which poses problems of bias and error, as well as offering flexibility and control. However, it is the fieldwork cost of interviewing that provides the main disadvantage of this type of data collection. In fact, the sample design employed is of some importance here, because different fieldwork problems occur when using different sampling methods. For example, with a quota sample, the interviewer has to select respondents who possess the required characteristics, while with random sampling, the interviewer must contact a specific name and address.

The presence of an interviewer offers the opportunity for varying degrees of structure. For instance, questions might be open-ended to allow the respondent to answer in his or her own words, without the constraints of predetermined optional answers in *closed* questions, and the interviewer can ask the respondent to expand on a point with various probing techniques. In unstructured interviewing, there is more of a conversation because, although certain broad topics are to be explored, there is no set sequence of pre-worded questions. This is sometimes referred to as a *depth interview* and is an example of qualitative, as opposed to quantitative, research. The latter would usually contain a number of pre-worded and sequenced questions to which there may only be pre-coded, multiple-choice answers. The former allows more freedom on the part of the respondent to reply to more generalized questioning, and indeed to allow respondents to reply in *their* terms rather than the questioner's predetermined terms.

A variation is the *group discussion (or focus group)*, which is generally unstructured and qualitative. With this method several respondents (possibly between six and ten in number) are brought together (perhaps at a coffee morning in one of the respondents' homes) and the interviewer guides the discussion through relevant topics, leaving most of the talking to members of the group. This method is widely used to pre-test advertisements. While the costs per respondent may be high with group discussion work, as a result of the degree of skill required by the interviewer and the time that a group discussion takes, if a research programme relied on, say, four groups exclusively, then overall costs would be lower than if a shorter, more structured, questionnaire were used on a sample of, say, 500 respondents.

However, since groups revolve around the sociology of group dynamics, it is not surprising that the interviewer, as group leader, must possess social skills in dealing with such problems as respondents who emerge as group dominators. Interviewees may adopt the roles de Almeida (1980) describes: 'the competing moderator, the choir, the super ego, the compiler, the rationalizer, the conscience, the rebel, the pseudo-specialist and so on'.

A number of important issues have been generated by the assessment of interview survey methods above. First, there is the need to clarify the nature of the other survey methods to which reference has been made; second, there is the field of questionnaire design which is implicit in planning interviews and in the question of interviewing techniques. Sample design as a constituent of the research plan is another major topic to be dealt with.

Other survey approaches

Omnibus surveys

Omnibus, or shared, surveys are becoming increasingly popular in the UK. The research design of an omnibus survey is constant, but the questions included vary according to which clients 'buy in', thus providing a quick and inexpensive survey approach. As long as the research design and methods are satisfactory, the advantage is that costs are shared among all clients.

Omnibus surveys vary in the specialization of their samples, different operators offering, for example, samples of 4000 adults nationally, 1000 motorists nationally or 2500 managers of small businesses. Clearly the operators do not alter their published designs for a single client, but repeat a survey of the same design at regular intervals. Because the research design is the constant there is a minimum of administration in planning and fieldwork, and it is claimed that the major sources of error and bias will have been reviewed over time – and most of them 'ironed-out'.

Omnibus surveys can be used in a number of ways. For example, if the same questions are asked in consecutive surveys, the results can either be combined to give a larger sample size, with the aim of reducing sampling error, or analysed to measure change over time. However, this last example should not be equated with continuous research since the same respondents would not be interviewed in consecutive surveys, in spite of the same sample design being used.

Most of the opinion polls reported in the national media are omnibus surveys, and the clients are normally paying something between £100 and £600 per question, depending on the operator.

Consumer panels

The panel does not involve group discussions, but is a form of continuous research, reporting on the behaviour of the same respondents over time. Households are recruited to the panel and provide information on their buying behaviour in certain specific, or general product, categories and on their media habits – such as television, radio and print exposure.

The reporting of behaviour is often by means of a diary, which is completed and either posted to the research agency concerned, or collected by a researcher. For example, in a panel for media studies, the radio stations listened to would be noted on a pre-printed chart for each day of the week. A grocery panel would require the brands, pack sizes, prices paid and stores used to be recorded, for the product categories being studied. This often does not involve face to face interviewing, but the use of, for example, a special audit bin in which the packs of products are placed for a researcher and the set meter to measure television viewing. These data collection approaches have been discussed under 'observation' earlier.

Households are commonly selected on the basis of random sampling (using electoral registers and multi-stage sampling of the type discussed shortly) rather than quota sampling, which provides a further distinction between the methodologies used for continuous as opposed to *ad hoc* research. The major problem with panels is the high mortality rate of panel members, that is, the withdrawal rate due to boredom (and indeed because of members moving home, invasion of privacy and so on) is high – perhaps up to 40% after the first interview. Clearly, the aim is that replacements should be as representative as possible. However, the problem of recruiting replacements, together with the need to offer members some form of inducement or payment, provides a constant danger of panel composition being unrepresentative. For example, once recruited new members sometimes change their behaviour, so it might be appropriate to exclude the results from these households for some time until their behaviour reverts to normal.

The basic working of the panel system is that operators compile reports of consumer profiles and other aspects of their buying behaviour, such as stores used, brands preferred, times of purchase and so on, and sell these to their clients. These firms can thus monitor their competitors' marketing, as well as their own, with the additional advantage that a time series of information is built up, allowing the identification of trends and change over time.

Retail audits

The other major form of continuous research is the retail audit, using a representative sample of retail outlets that agree to provide information over a period of time.

The information provided is usually on sales of various products. For example, as discussed on page 24, the record charts were compiled by the

British Market Research Bureau using a retail audit. BMRB used to collect weekly diaries from their panel members, which contained lists of records sold, and the research agency computed totals for each. The major problem was the representativeness of the retail panel:

> 'it is of course a fairly simple matter to select a list of record shops that is fully representative of the business in Great Britain, by size of shop, area, type of shop and so on. It is quite another matter to persuade all those shops to provide detailed information to BMRB about their sales each week. Fortunately most dealers are willing to carry out this quite onerous task. However, two important multiples, Boots and W. H. Smiths, do not at present provide sales information, but there are hopes that both may contribute to the charts in the near future.' (BMRB, 1980)

In addition to producing the 'charts' these data are further analysed to give sales by record company, as a service to manufacturers, whose despatches of records to shops frequently bear little relation to sales over the counter in a given week. Manufacturers receive information on sales, market shares and the performance of different types of outlet.

Other agencies – principally Nielsens and Attwoods in grocery and pharmaceuticals, for example – run retail audits covering a range of different products, with some variations in data collection methods. Typically the data is collected by a regular visit by a researcher, who makes a physical stock check of the product categories being studied and compares this with stock levels at the previous visit and with records of what has been bought-in in the meantime. Thus, past stock plus purchases, minus present stock, equals sales (weighted for pilferage, returns and other loss). As noted in Chapter 2, new technology is changing the nature of the retail audit.

Experimental design

The third form of data collection, having considered observation and interview studies, is experimentation. A simple example demonstrates the nature of marketing experimentation.

Suppose a marketer believes sales are low because of inefficient advertising and wants to establish what will happen if some change is made in advertising. A new advertising campaign is developed and launched, and sales are monitored and compared with sales before the new campaign. In terms of experimentation this would be a *simple before–after design*, which has been summarized by Boyd *et al.* (1977) in the following manner:

Before measure	Yes (initial sales = $X1$)
Experimental variable	Yes (new advertising)
After measure	Yes (new level of sales = $X2$)

The difference between the two levels of sales is taken to be the effect of the new campaign. So, if $X1$ is 5000 units per month and $X2$ is 6000 units per month, the organization might conclude the new campaign to be effective. Clearly, this may not necessarily be valid. If, for example, competitors' distribution systems delayed delivery of competing products to the shops during the time of this new campaign, the customers may be purchasing the test product, not because of an effective advertising campaign, but because of the lack of availability of alternative brands.

It is clearly impossible to control competitors' marketing activity when conducting marketing experiments, and there are many other uncontrollable variables to take into account when designing and analysing experiments. For example, there might be a general trend of increasing sales and, perhaps, sales might have been even higher if the old campaign had continued!

There are dangers in simply comparing sales before and after the introduction of an experimental variable. The effect of time has to be considered and it might be, as for example with poster advertising, that the time delay before achieving any influence might be substantial.

Another problem with the experiment above, is that the wrong dependent variable (that is, the variable that is measured to judge the effect of the experimental variable) may be selected. Much depends on what the advertising campaign is trying to do of course, and it may therefore be more valid to measure changes in attitudes or perceptions rather than sales.

Another way of improving an experimental design like the one above would be to include a control group, that is, to measure the same dependent variables in the control group in the absence of the experimental variable. This allows some degree of assessment of uncontrollable variables. For example, in the illustration above, if for the experimental group (that is, those exposed to the experimental variable) the before–after calculation showed increased sales from 5000 to 6000 units per month, but for a control group sales rose from 4000 to 4800 per month, then the 20% increase for both groups might mean that there had been little effect from the experimental variable.

This type of design is a *before–after with control* (Boyd *et al.*, 1977) as shown below:

Experimental control	Group	Group
Before measure (initial sales)	$X1$	$Y1$
Experimental variable (new advertising)	Yes	No
After measure (new level of sales)	$X2$	$Y2$
Therefore, effect of experimental variable = $(X2 - X1) - (Y2 - Y1)$		

Marketing experiments can use data from consumer panels or retail audits, with the advantage of being able to demonstrate changes over time more effectively than *ad hoc* research. This topic is further discussed in Chapter 8 in terms of the use of test marketing in new product development. The test market is the largest marketing experiment because the whole mix is tested, rather than just one variable. Panel data is particularly useful in test markets, because not just sales, but customer profiles, new and repeat buying levels, attitudes, retail preferences and so on are analysed over a period.

In fact, it is not always necessary to take before measures. For example, the Mason Haire (1950) study of instant coffee usage was an *after-only with control* design. No before measure was taken, but the sample divided into experimental and control groups given the different shopping lists. After measures were made for both groups, that is, all were asked to describe the sort of housewife who would have compiled the list.

One reason why a before measure might not be appropriate is that the very existence of one could produce bias. For example, consider the case where a new advertisement for a perfume is being pre-tested using a research design that involves asking a sample of women which brands of perfume they normally consider purchasing, and then showing a film which has an advertisement break where the new advertisement is shown. A repeat of the first question could be taken as the after question, and any change in the number of women preferring the test brand of perfume is a crude measure of the effectiveness of the new advertisement.

A problem with this sort of design is that people often repeat their first answer in order to appear to be consistent. Others, however, may realize what the test is attempting to do and this could distort perceptions and responses. This example identifies two further considerations to take into account when planning an experimental design: first, a before measure may bias the after measure (for example, when respondents try to remain consistent); and second, the nature of questioning, especially for before measures, may destroy any attempt to disguise the experimental variable, so that the interaction produces further bias. The aim should be to design an experiment that facilitates the identification, and preferably quantification, of all variables that can account for differences between before and after measures so that there can be an acceptable isolation of the effects of the experimental variable. Lastly, in operating test markets there is always the problem of experimental discipline, that is maintaining realistic test conditions rather than 'making' the test work at any cost.

This chapter has reviewed the general options of primary research methodology. We now turn to the techniques of designing questionnaires and administering them.

REFERENCES

de Almeida P. M. (1980). A review of group discussion methodology. *European Research*, **8** (3), 114–20

BMRB. (1980). *The Charts*. British Market Research Bureau

Boyd H. W., Westfall R. and Stasch S. F. (1977). *Marketing Research*: *Text and cases* 4th edn. Ontario: Irwin

Collins M. (1981). Telephone interviewing: A solution or a new set of problems? *Market Research Society Newsletter,* **180** (5)

Crawford C. M. (1970). Attitudes of marketing executives toward ethics in market research. *Journal of Marketing*, **34** (2), 42–46

Haire M. (1950). Projective techniques in marketing research. *Journal of Marketing*, **14** (2), 649–56

Hyett P. (1982). Should we be having more of IT? *Market Research Society Newsletter,* **196** (3)

Shugan S. M. and Hauser J. R. (1977). *P.A.R.I.S. – An interactive market research information system*. Discussion paper 292. Northwestern University: Center for Mathematical Studies in Economics and Management Science

Weitz J. (1982). Getting our lines crossed. *Market Research Society Newsletter,* **197** (3)

White G. (1982). Telephone research without tears. *Market Research Society Newsletter*, **196** (12)

FURTHER READING

Cox K. K. and Enis B. M. (1973). *Experimentation for Marketing Decisions*. Glasgow: Intertext

Davis E. J. (1970). *Experimental Marketing*. London: Nelson

4

Primary Data Collection: Questionnaires and Interview

The nature and design of questionnaires varies enormously between projects and involves some considerable skill, but there are a number of general points worth outlining.

Guidelines for questionnaire design

The data list, or information needs, drawn up in the first stage of the research process provides the logical basis of the questionnaire. However, caution is needed to avoid writing one question for each discrete item of required information, since it has to be remembered that a questionnaire is going to be used by the interviewer, the respondent, and the programmer and data analyst who are likely to be different people. In essence, questionnaires have to be designed for the understanding of the various users rather than that of the designer. To illustrate the implications of designing for the several users of the questionnaire, the questionnaire must instruct the *interviewer* how to use it, since, for example, many interviews require certain questions to be asked of some respondents, while other questions will be relevant to other respondents. Thus the route through a questionnaire varies for different respondents, depending on their characteristics and responses.

For example, a survey was conducted to determine whether people in the broadcasting area of a local commercial radio station would be interested in listening to the station if it extended its broadcasting hours. The first question was 'do you listen to the radio?' and the next 'which station(s) do you listen to?' It is evident that if the answer to Question 1 is 'no' then Question 2 is not relevant, so an instruction to the interviewer should be added after Question 1 along the lines of 'if "no" go to Question 6'.

The next issue is how the respondent should be considered when designing questionnaires. One aid could be the use of show cards, so for Question 2 above providing a complete list of radio stations can help respondents' memories and speed up questions and replies.

In the radio study mentioned a card was handed to each respondent, at this point in the interview, listing:

BBC Radio 1
BBC Radio 2
BBC Radio 3
BBC Radio 4
BBC Radio 5
BBC Local radio
Local commercial radio
Any other (please state)

This device is useful for many questions that are likely to have a finite number of responses – that is, *closed questions*, such as multiple choice (or multi-dichotomous) questions, where several alternative answers are provided – or dichotomous questions where the answers are 'one or the other', such as 'yes' or 'no'.

The respondent should be the central consideration when wording and phrasing questions, with the aim of ensuring that each question means the same to every respondent, and indeed the same to the researchers. *Ambiguous questions* are a recurring difficulty. For example, in introducing an interview, if the interviewer asks 'Would you mind answering a few short questions?' some respondents might be positive towards the interview and reply in the affirmative with a 'yes' or nod of the head. However, 'yes' to this question strictly means 'I do mind answering questions', hence potential confusion. 'Would you answer . . .?' might be a clearer opening.

As well as ambiguities, *leading questions* are another trap. For instance, questions such as 'You do think that . . . don't you?' should not be asked because they suggest the required answer. Another danger concerns the asking of *more than one* question at a time, such as 'Do you enjoy television and poster advertising?'

Some subdivided questions can act as filters, to ensure that only relevant questions are asked, and in this area flow charts are sometimes useful since they can highlight groups of questions relevant to some respondents and not to others. Figure 4.1 provides a demonstration of this approach, which does not provide precise question wording (see Appendix 1), but aids in the sequencing and routing of questions as well as providing instructions to the interviewer – in short, in designing the questionnaire.

A third wording problem is that of *unclear questions*. For example, it is easy for questions including double negatives to be confusing to all concerned, even though they provide subtle and important nuances of meaning. Double

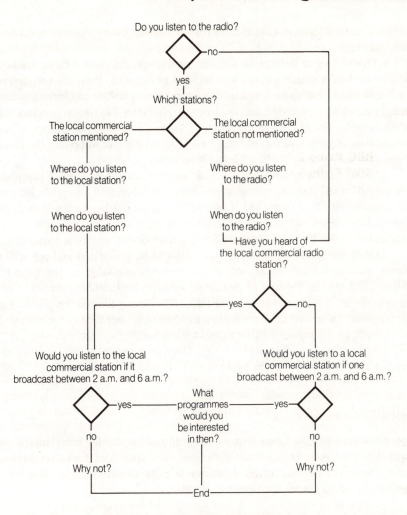

Figure 4.1 Flow chart questionnaire.

negatives should generally be avoided – for instance, consider the problems with the following questions: 'Do you not use non-stick pans?' and 'Is it not uncommon for you to buy unbranded products?'

Questionnaires have typically to include *profile questions* of some kind, for example, when quota sampling is used and the interviewer must select those respondents who fit the given quota characteristics. Obvious profile details should not be in question form, for example, the sex of the respondent (generally) merely requires noting by the interviewer, although other characteristics need to be in multiple choice form. Age categories, for instance, can be put onto a show card allowing respondents to point to their appropriate category, rather than risking the refusal to answer a direct question on something like age.

There is some debate on whether profile details should be at the beginning or end of a questionnaire – if located at the end, then the respondent's confidence has been gained and questions answered before any intimate details on age, income, occupation and the like are requested. On the other hand, when quota samples are used, it is necessary to select those who possess appropriate characteristics at the outset, although such questions risk annoying the respondent, who may not proceed with the interview.

Most questionnaires also include *reference information*. Examples of this would be the identity of the interviewer and when and where the interview was conducted. This is needed if checks are to be made to ensure that interviewers have been carrying out the given instructions, and to identify those interviewers who have not been following the correct question sequence.

Once designed, the questionnaire should be pre-tested and piloted, not merely among fellow researchers or whoever is available at the time (pretesting), but among the sort of people in the proposed sample. Ideally, a small subsample of the main sample (perhaps 5% or so) should be selected and interviewed, in order that problems of question wording, sequencing and interviewer performance can be noted and subsequently revised.

Appendix 1 at the end of this chapter includes a few examples of questionnaires used in recent surveys.

Specialized questions

Some research programmes require the study of particular behavioural characteristics and this section briefly reviews two such forms of measurement. First, the ways of measuring attitudes will be described, followed by the methods used to reveal consumer motivations.

Attitude measures

Attitude measurements require special consideration because it is far too easy to ask a respondent questions like: 'What is your attitude towards Smith's Department Store?', only to receive a reply along the lines of 'I like it', or 'It's all right'. While such feelings may be important, it would be of greater use to uncover the reasons for such feelings, and the type of actions in which they are likely to result.

This perspective views an attitude as more than emotions and considers its structure to be composed of the following:

(1) the *cognitive* component, which includes what is known about the topic concerned, even if part of this is misconception;

(2)   the *affective* component, which is the feelings and emotions resulting from what is known about the topic;

(3)   the *conative* component which includes the likely intentions resulting from (1) and (2).

If intentions are emotions based on specific elements of knowledge, then those emotions need to be discovered if the results can be meaningfully used. Furthermore, such dimensions are perceived by respondents with varying degrees of strength, so that the concept of degree in measuring attitudes is unavoidable. While some form of scale is required, the straightforward like/dislike continuum would be of only limited value. A more useful approach is to compile a series of scales, each measuring a different component of the same attitude. For the Smith's Department Store example, Figure 4.2 offers an improvement. The technique used here is known as the *semantic differential* and was developed by Osgood *et al*. (1957). One advantage is providing a convenient way of comparing attitudes to different topics (for instance, to different stores) on the same dimensions, and on the same pictorial representation.

However, using the semantic differential requires some way of identifying the dimensions that are of importance to customers/non-customers, to

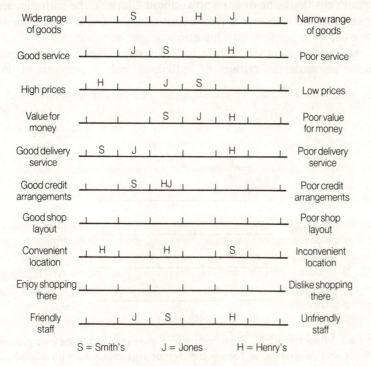

Figure 4.2   Semantic differential.

avoid including unimportant dimensions. Group discussions can be used for this purpose, as could another technique which is called the **repertory grid**. This technique involves asking the respondent how he or she perceives two items of a triad to be similar and different from the third. In Figure 4.3 reasons for similarity are shown by a tick and the different item with a cross. While some of the reasons given are likely to be of little use, some might provide bi-polar adjectives that the researcher would not otherwise have considered, for the semantic differential. This method is adopted from work by Kelly (1955) on personality constructs.

Alternative attitude measurement techniques use statements rather than adjectives, and the scaling is in terms of either the strength of each statement (Thurstone Scales), or the strength of respondent's agreement with each statement (Likert Scales).

Likert Scales (Likert, 1932) consist of presenting respondents with a series of statements about the topic concerned and asking them to indicate their degree of agreement with each, according to a scale ranging from 'strongly agree' to 'strongly disagree'.

It is important, though difficult in practice, for the range of statements offered to cover the range of cognitive, affective and conative dimensions that the topic involves. In Figure 4.4 the first four dimensions are cognitive (what the respondent thinks he or she knows about Glogg's), the fifth dimension is affective (how the respondent feels about Glogg's) and the last dimension is conative (how the respondent's intentions might be reflected).

As well as the analysis approach shown later in Figure 4.6, it is sometimes useful to 'summate the ratings' of individual scale dimensions in order to

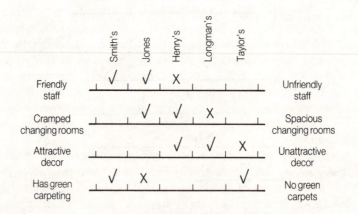

Figure 4.3 Repertory grid. Each respondent comes up with their own reasons for similarity and difference, so for another respondent presented with Smith's, Jones and Henry's, there may be a totally different reason – as there can be for another respondent when presented with Jones, Henry's and Longman's – and so on.

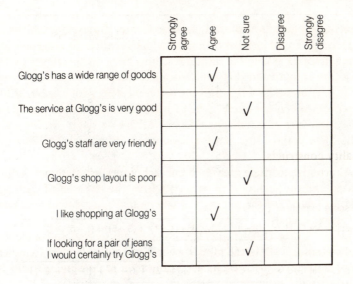

Figure 4.4 Likert scale.

produce an overall score for the resulting aggregate rating. Figure 4.4 shows a version of the Likert scaling technique, where a mixture of positive and negative sentiments allows respondents' consistency to be checked.

Both the semantic differential and the Likert scale can be used quantitatively by assigning values to each scaling position, and average scores for all respondents' replies can be calculated, either for each scale, or in an overall summation.

In Figure 4.2 for example, if each scale position is scored from 1 to 6 for each dimension (that is, for the first dimension, 'S' is scored 2, 'H' is scored 4 and so on), then the positioning of 'S' by all respondents can be averaged and shown pictorially for each dimension. Alternatively, the overall average can be calculated for all dimensions – for 'S' here, it would be $(2 + 3 + 4 + 3 + 1 + 2 + 3 + 5 + 2 + 3)/10 = 2.8$. The latter approach would not be universally applicable because it assumes equivalence between scale dimensions and also implies that every scale is scorable in the same terms, while in fact some dimensions will be descriptive and it will not be possible to evaluate them.

A third way of quantifying the semantic differential is to calculate 'distance-scores', as Osgood originally did. These show how close the topics researched are in terms of the semantic differential dimensions. Figure 4.5 illustrated D scores for the similarity between 'S' and 'H', and between 'G' and 'J'.

The Likert approach of Figure 4.4 could be scored 1 to 5 for the 'strongly agree' to 'strongly disagree' positions for each statement. As with the semantic differential, an average for all respondents for each statement could

Dimension		Scale values for	
	G	H	J
1	2	4	5
2	3	5	2
3	4	1	3
4	3	5	4
5	1	5	2
6	2	3	3
7	3	4	4
8	5	1	3
9	2	6	4
10	3	5	2

Distance score formula $= \sqrt{\Sigma d^2}$

Distance score for G–H $= \sqrt{(2-4)^2+(3-5)^2+(4-1)^2+(3-5)^2+(1-5)^2+(2-3)^2}$
$$+(3-4)^2+(5-1)^2+(2-6)^2+(3-5)^2 = 8.7$$

Distance score for G–J $= \sqrt{(2-5)^2+(3-2)^2+(4-3)^2+(3-4)^2+(1-2)^2+(2-3)^2}$
$$+(3-4)^2+(5-3)^2+(2-4)^2+(3-2)^2 = 4.9$$

Figure 4.5 'D' score calculation.

be calculated, or the overall ratings summated (which was Likert's original approach). For many marketing research programmes it is more convenient to merely calculate the percentage of respondents who gave each response, as demonstrated in Figure 4.6.

As an alternative to Likert scales, the *Thurstone* method of measuring attitudes is worth a brief mention. It presents respondents with a series of statements and requires them to pick out the one statement that most accurately reflects their attitude. The difference between statements should be of a uniform degree to allow the scaling approach to be effective.

The following statements could be presented to respondents:

'I think Smith's is the best store in town.'
'I think Smith's could be improved?'
'I have no feelings one way or the other about Smith's.'
'I don't think Smith's is the best store in town.'
'I think Smith's should close because it is so bad.'

The scoring here could value the first statement +2, the last −2 and the others accordingly. It is often difficult to compile a series of statements that easily facilitate the choice of just one by the respondent, while at the same time maintaining the same distance between them, though the compilation of such statements appearing at equal intervals has been developed and tested (Thurstone and Chare, 1929).

	SA	A	(%) NS	D	SD
Glogg's has a wide range of goods	5	7	50	36	2
The service at Glogg's is very good	9	34	29	18	10
Glogg's staff are very friendly	20	10	8	37	25
Glogg's shop layout is poor	8	17	20	12	43

Figure 4.6 Likert analysis.

Motivation studies

Another behavioural dimension requiring special types of question is that of motivation. The separation of attitude and motivation is perhaps only partially valid, though convenient, because to some extent it is possible to uncover motivating factors from some of the attitude measurement techniques described above, and indeed it is possible to study attitudes through the following motivation research methods.

Many motivation studies employ *projective techniques* which in essence ask the respondent to reply through some third party. The rationale is that there are both 'good' and 'real' reasons for behaviour. While the former will probably be given in response to a direct questioning approach (such as, 'Why did you buy this?') such an answer may only be partially true. There may be a *real* reason for behaviour that either the respondent is unwilling to admit, or unable to recognize. An indirect question (for example, 'What sort of people buy this?' or 'Why do people buy these?') might be sufficient to reveal *real* reasons for behaviour.

The widely quoted Haire (1950) study of instant coffee usage illustrates this last point. Here, an indirect questioning approach was employed where women were asked what sort of housewife would have compiled the shopping lists shown in Figure 4.7. One half of the sample had the list which differed only by having instant coffee included. The instant coffee shopping list was seen to have been drawn up by a lazier, less well-organized woman, who was described as not being a good housewife. Direct questioning, on the other hand, revealed *good* reasons for preferring real coffee, which revolved around the product not tasting as good as drip-grind coffee.

Other examples of projecting respondents' real motivations through some third party medium are given in the following. *Sentence completion*, where respondents are given an incomplete statement and asked to finish it. For example, the stem might be 'The person who shops at Smith's is . . .', and the way it is completed may reveal more than the answer to 'Why do you shop at Smith's?'

Cartoon completion, which asks the respondent to complete the speech balloons of a situation presented in cartoon form. Two women might be

Shopping list 1	Shopping list 2
$1\frac{1}{2}$ lb hamburger	$1\frac{1}{2}$ lb hamburger
2 loaves Wonderbread	2 loaves Wonderbread
Bunch of carrots	Bunch of carrots
1 can Rumfords baking powder	1 can Rumfords baking powder
1 lb Nescafé instant coffee	1 lb Maxwell House drip-grind coffee
2 cans Del Monte peaches	2 cans Del Monte peaches
5 lb potatoes	5 lb potatoes

Figure 4.7   Mason Haire shopping lists. (*Source*: Mason Haire. Projective techniques in marketing research. *Journal of Marketing*, April 1950)

pictured outside Smith's Department Store, the speech balloon over the first containing the words 'My next door neighbour thinks Smith's is for snobs', and the respondent's true feelings are thought to be revealed by the way she completes the cartoon with what the second woman might say.

A picture depicting a situation could be presented and respondents asked to say what led up to what is shown, and what might happen next. This is a *Thematic Apperception Test* (the TAT is a particular test developed by Murray), but in practice the difference between this and cartoon completion may be limited.

A variation on the sentence completion method is to present respondents with the first part of a *story* and ask them to complete it. The rationale for this extension is that more details can be given, allowing replies to comment on several points.

When selecting names for new products or organizations, the *word association* test may be useful. If spontaneous replies consistently produce undesirable associations and connotations, then the name may be inappropriate.

Another technique available is to allow respondents to act out the role of someone else (this version of *role playing* is referred to as *psychodrama*). The role could be of another type of shopper, or even that of a salesperson, and again the idea is to elicit real, hidden feelings. In addition to the above, it is often appropriate to use some form of *unstructured interview* perhaps in the group form discussed earlier.

Interviewing techniques

The parallel to designing a clear and appropriate questionnaire, is the preparation and the development of interviewing skills.

Kahn and Cannell (1968) propose three conditions necessary for successful interviewing: *accessibility* of the interviewer to the respondent, and of the information to the respondent (both physically and psychologically);

cognition on the respondent's part, in understanding what is required and *motivation* on the part of the respondent to answer and to answer accurately. They also describe five symptoms of inadequate response that can occur during interviewing:

(1) *partial response*, where the respondent gives a relevant but incomplete answer;

(2) *non-response*, which is either refusal to answer or a silent response;

(3) *inaccurate response*, which is a biased or distorted answer;

(4) *irrelevant response*, where the question asked is not answered;

(5) *verbalized response problem*, where a respondent explains why he or she cannot answer the question.

To encourage respondents to reply more fully and accurately, experienced interviewers develop skills such as using neutral questions, like 'What exactly do you mean?' and 'Could you say more about that?' Sometimes aided recall (indicating some of the possible answers) can be used, as can the explanation of questions to respondents. The danger of explanation, however, is that the interviewer actually changes the meaning of questions, so there is a thin line between interviewer bias and interviewer help.

Non-verbal behaviour can be exploited during interviews, with interviewers employing 'expectant pauses, glances and nods' to elicit more information. Indeed, non-verbal communication is two-way because respondents' intended meanings can be interpreted through their gestures and intonation. However, interviewers should be aware of the dangers of misinterpreting what respondents are trying to say. For this reason it is usual to require interviewers to record verbatim everything a respondent says.

This last point introduces further interviewing problems, since responses have to be recorded as well as questions asked. Open-ended questions especially, create recording difficulties because each word of sometimes lengthy replies has to be taken down unless the replies are pre-coded following a pilot.

Interviewers have to repeat their task with many different respondents but with the same questionnaire, so the resulting boredom and fatigue should be taken into account when setting the number of interviews, or interviewing time, for each interviewer. The repetition of asking the same question in the same way over and over again can eventually lead the interviewer to take short-cuts by, for example, paraphrasing questions, which provides another source of interviewer bias.

As already stated, interviewers should be properly trained and then given time to become acquainted with the questionnaire before using it, to avoid errors over question sequencing and poor recording of answers.

Interviewers have responsibilities beyond asking questions and recording answers, for example there is the initial task of making contact with appropriate respondents, and also the need to gain sufficient cooperation for the interviewer to proceed. When quota sampling is used, interviewers are provided with a list of the characteristics they must look for in potential respondents, and errors often occur when interviewers become tired of waiting for the 'right' people to come along. Close supervision can go some way to overcoming this problem, for example by checking up that some of those interviewed did indeed possess appropriate characteristics. This encourages interviewers to select more carefully and, if a quota cell is difficult to complete, to discuss this with a supervisor rather than attempting to cover it up. An alternative interviewing point might be decided upon, or they merely may need to try again later. The same could apply in poor weather when people do not want to stop to be interviewed.

When a survey uses random sampling, interviewers will work from a list of names and addresses of the relevant population (such a list is called a 'sampling frame'). When the named respondent is not at the listed address at the time of call, no one else should normally be interviewed. Instead – again the threat of checks can discourage such a short cut – up to three call-backs are usually made and if there is still no success, another respondent may be randomly selected.

For some surveys, especially those using an electoral register sampling frame, some addresses may be out of date, either because the respondent has moved (or died), or indeed, because the whole street no longer exists. Again, another respondent should be selected from the sampling frame at random, (rather than the interviewer choosing the most convenient person).

Often only about a third of the interviewer's time is spent actually interviewing, due to the time needed for travelling to interview points, waiting to contact appropriate people, possibly editing questionnaires at the end of an interviewing period and certain general administrative functions.

The problem of gaining the cooperation of respondents can be eased by explaining the purpose of the survey and providing evidence of being a bona fide interviewer. This has been made easier for those organizations that have joined the Market Research Society's scheme of allocating identity cards to interviewers. One obstacle that this can overcome is the equation of market researchers with salespeople, which is usually due to salespeople posing as researchers. If respondents can remain anonymous then this can be emphasized to gain their cooperation, together with encouragement that their replies will be greatly valued and respected.

If interviewers are asked for their opinions on the questionnaire and its design and on general interview and survey procedures, then because of this extra trust and consultation the interviewer may feel more involved and respected and therefore be more diligent and enthusiastic.

Having discussed questionnaires and interviews we now continue our coverage of marketing research techniques and approaches to issues of sampling and sample design.

APPENDIX 1: QUESTIONNAIRE EXHIBITS

Radio research questionnaire

Interviewer number ☐

Date of interview ☐

Area code ☐

Time of interview ☐

Good morning/afternoon, Sir/Madam, I am doing some research into radio audiences. Would you mind answering a few short questions?

Question 1:

Do you listen to the radio?   Yes ☐

(if 'No' go to Question 6.)   No ☐

Question 2:

Which station(s) do you listen to?

BBC Radio 1   ☐

BBC Radio 2   ☐

BBC Radio 3   ☐

BBC Radio 4   ☐

BBC Radio 5   ☐

BBC Radio Newcastle   ☐

Metro Radio   ☐

Luxembourg   ☐

Others (please state)   ....

Question 3:

Do you listen to the radio (a) at home   ☐

(b) at work   ☐

(c) in the car   ☐

(d) other places (state)   ☐

Question 4:

What times during the day do you listen to the radio?

(show card) 2 a.m.–6 a.m. ☐

6 a.m.–12 noon ☐

12 noon–6 p.m. ☐

6 p.m.–10 p.m. ☐

10 p.m.–2 a.m. ☐

Question 5: (Only ask this question if Metro is named in Question 2. If not, go to Question 6.)

What times during the day do you listen to Metro?

(show card) 6 a.m.–12 noon ☐

12 noon–6 p.m. ☐

6 p.m.–10 p.m. ☐

10 p.m.–2 a.m. ☐

Question 6: (Only ask this question if Metro is *not* named in Question 2, *or* if the answer to Question 1 is 'No'.)

Have you heard of Metro Radio?   Yes ☐

No ☐

(If 'Yes' go to Question 7.)
(If 'No' go to Question 8.)

Question 7:

Would you listen to Metro Radio if it broadcast between 2 a.m. and 6 a.m.?

Yes ☐

No ☐

Don't know ☐

(If 'No', end interview)

Question 8: (Only ask this question if the answer to Question 6 is 'No'.)

Would you listen to a *local* radio station if one broadcast between 2 a.m. and 6 a.m.?

Yes ☐

No ☐

Don't know ☐

(If 'No' end interview)

Question 9:

What types of programme would you listen to between 2 a.m. and 6 a.m.?

(record answer in full) ....

....

....

....

....

Age of respondent: 15–34 ☐

35 and over ☐

Name ....

Address ....

....

....

Newspaper research questionnaire

I'm doing a survey about newspapers, radio and TV and would like your help.

		OFFICE USE ONLY	
		COL.	CODE

(1) Which newspapers have you read or looked at in the last week?

Any others?

PROBE UNTIL ANSWER IS 'NO'

TICK BOX(ES). ✔

		COL.	CODE
(National Dailies)	*Financial Times*	1	1
	Times	2	
	Guardian	3	
	Daily Telegraph	4	
	Daily Express	1	2
	Daily Mail	2	
	Daily Mirror	1	3
	Daily Star	2	
	Sun	3	
(National Sundays)	*Sunday Times*	1	4
	Sunday Telegraph	2	
	Observer	3	
	Sunday Express	1	5
	Mail on Sunday	2	
	Sunday Mirror	1	6
	Sunday People	2	
	News of the World	3	

					OFFICE USE ONLY	
					COL.	CODE

			✔		
(2) Now thinking of other sources of information, when did you last go to a cinema?	In the last 7 days			1	7	
	Up to 1 month ago			2		
	Up to 6 months ago			3		
	Over 6 months ago/can't remember			4		
(3) Do you have a TV in the house?		Yes		1	8	
		No		2		
IF NO GO TO QUESTION 7						
(4) Do you have a video cassette recorder in the house?					9	
		Yes		1		
		No		2		
(5) How often do you watch TV/video these days?						
PROMPT IF NECESSARY	5 or more days a week			1	10	
	3 or 4 days a week			2		
	Less often			3	9 = N/A	
(6) Which channel would you say you watched most often?		BBC 1		1	11	
		BBC 2		2		
		ITV		3		
		C4		4		
		Video		5		
		Don't know		6	9 = N/A	
(7) Have you listened to the radio anywhere in the last week?						
		Yes		1	12	
		No		2		
IF 'YES' Which station would you say you listen to most?		BBC Radio 1		1	13	
		BBC Radio 2		2		
		BBC Radio 3		3		
		BBC Radio 4		4		
		BBC Radio 5		5		
		Radio Newcastle		6		
		Metro Radio		7		
		Other		8	9 = N/A	
		WRITE IN				
		....				
		....				

Classification questions

			OFFICE USE ONLY		
(8) How many adults are there in the household, including yourself?	0	✔	0	COL.	CODE
	1		1		
	2		2		
	3		3	14	
	4		4		
	5+		5		
And how many children?	1		1		
	2		2		
	3		3	15	
	4		4		
	5+		5		
(9) Is there a car in the household? IF 'YES' ASK: Just one, or more than one?	No		0		
	YES, 1		1	16	
	YES, 1+		2		
(10) Is the house owned or rented? IF RENTED: Is it from the council or from someone else?	Owned		1		
	Council		2	17	
	Other		3		
(11) Is there a telephone in the household? IF YES, ASK FOR NUMBER	Yes		1	18	
	NO		2		
(12) What is the occupation of the head of the household? WRITE IN			A 1		
			B 2		
			C_1 3	19	
			C_2 4		
			D 5		
			E 6		
(13) Which age group are you in? SHOW CARD B	Under 25		1		
	25–34		2		
	35–44		3	20	
	45–54		4		
	55–64		5		
	65 & over		6		
CODE MALE OR FEMALE	Male		1	21	
	Female		2		

Name of respondent ....

Address ....

....

ASK FOR POSTAL CODE AND WRITE IN: ....

START POINT ....

Signature of interviewer ....

Evening wear survey

I'm from .... doing a survey on evening, wear, can you help me?

(1) What evening activities do you ever participate in?
READ OUT:

	TICK	COL.	CODE
Dinner parties		1	
Theatre/cinema		2	
Dances/balls		3	
Night clubs		4	
Special parties		5	
Eating out		6	

Any others?
WRITE IN ....

	COL.	CODE
	7	
	8	

(2) FOR EACH MENTIONED:
How often do you attend ....

	Once a month (code 1	Several times a month 2	Once every few months 3	Less often 4)	COL.	CODE
Dinner parties					9	
Theatre/cinema					10	
Dances/balls					11	
Night clubs					12	
Special parties					13	
Eating out					14	
Others	....	....	....	....	15	
....	....	....	....	....	16	

(3) FOR EACH MENTIONED:
What do you usually wear for ....

	evening dress (code 1	dress 2	top & skirt 3	top & trs. 4	suit 5	adapted day wear 6)	COL.	CODE
Dinner parties							17	
Theatre/cinema							18	
Dances/balls							19	
Night clubs							20	
Special parties							21	
Eating out							22	
Others							23	
....							24	

(4) Do you usually buy outfits specially for the evening?

		COL.	CODE
YES	1		
NO	2	25	
SOMETIMES	3		

	COL.	CODE

(5) For a special evening event would you buy a special outfit?

YES	1	
NO	2	26
SOMETIMES	3	

(6) Generally, how many times would you wear an evening outfit?

ONCE	1	
A FEW TIMES	2	27
MANY TIMES	3	

(7) What sort of fabric do you prefer to wear in the evening?

NATURAL	1	
SYNTHETIC	2	28
NATURAL/SYNTHETIC	3	
NO PREFERENCE	4	

(8) Do you prefer patterned or plain fabrics for evening wear?

PATTERNED	1	
PLAIN	2	29
NO PREFERENCE	3	

(9) What colours do you prefer for your evening wear?
READ OUT:

PASTEL	1	
BRIGHT	2	
DARK	3	30
WHITE	4	
NO PREFERENCE	5	

(10) Which one of these would best describe your preference for evening wear?
READ OUT:

Romantic	1	
Feminine	2	
Sexy	3	31
Sophisticated	4	
Fashionable	5	

Anything else? WRITE IN .... | 32 |

(11) For evening dresses which length would you prefer?
READ OUT:

Full	1	
Ankle	2	
Calf	3	33
Knee	4	
Mid-thigh	5	
Mini	6	

(12) Generally, how much do you spend on an evening dress or separates?

UP TO £20	£20–£34	£35–£49	£50–£99	£100 or more		
					34	
(Code 1	2	3	4	5)		

		COL.	CODE

(13) From which shops would you expect to buy evening wear? — COL. 35

WRITE IN .... — 36

.... — 37

.... — 38

IF LAURA ASHLEY MENTIONED GO TO QUESTION 16

(14) (ONLY IF LAURA ASHLEY NOT MENTIONED)

Would you ever consider buying evening wear from Laura Ashley?

		COL. 39
YES	1	
NO	2	
DON'T KNOW	3	

(15) (ONLY IF LAURA ASHLEY NOT MENTIONED IN QUESTION 13)

Have you ever shopped for clothes in Laura Ashley?

		COL. 40
YES	1	
NO	2	

(16) (ASK ALL)

How do you feel about Laura Ashley clothes ... in terms of ...

the range of garments available?

SHOW CARD:

			COL.
Wide range		narrow range	41
Too frilly		too plain	42
Fashionable		traditional	43
Expensive		inexpensive	44
Good quality		poor quality	45

(Code   1   2   3   4   5)

(17) Which of these age groups are you in?

SHOW CARD:

		COL. 46
15–19	1	
20–29	2	
30–39	3	
40–49	4	
50 or over	5	

(18) Are you employed?   YES ☐   NO ☐

IF SO, What is your occupation?

WRITE IN .... — COL. 47

(19) What is the occupation of the head of your household?

WRITE IN .... — COL. 48

THANK YOU, YOU HAVE BEEN MOST HELPFUL.

REFERENCES

Haire M. (1950). Projective techniques in marketing research. *Journal of Marketing*, **14** (2), 649–56
Kahn R. L. and Cannell C. F. (1968). Interviewing. *International Encyclopaedia of the Social Sciences*, **2** (2), 118–35
Kelly G. A. (1955). *The Psychology of Personal Constructs*. New York: Norton
Likert R. (1932). A technique for the measurement of attitudes. *Archives of Psychology*, No. **140**. New York: Columbia University Press
Osgood C. E., Suci G. J. and Tannenbaum P. H. (1957). *The Measurement of Meaning*. Urbana: University of Illinois Press
Thurstone L. L. and Chare E. J. (1929). *The Measurement of Attitudes*. Chicago: University Press.

FURTHER READING

Belson W. A. (1981). *The Design and Understanding of Survey Questions*. Farnborough: Gower
Hoinville G., Jowell R. and Associates (1978). *Survey Research Practice*. London: Heinemann
Macfarlane-Smith J. (1972). *Interviewing in Market and Social Research*. London: Routledge and Kegan Paul
Moser C. A. and Kalton G. (1973). *Survey Methods in Social Research*. London: Heinemann
Oppennheim A. M. (1972). *Questionnaire Design and Attitude Measurement*. London: Heinemann
Payne S. (1957). *The Art of Asking Questions*. Princeton: University Press

5

Primary Data Collection: Sampling and Sample Design

There is an inevitably close relationship between the choice of data collection method and research instrument, and the selection of respondents, or sample design.

One approach would be to include all relevant people in the study, which would make the study a census. Indeed, this is sometimes possible if the relevant population is small and perhaps geographically concentrated, as is sometimes the case in industrial markets. It is more usual, however, for populations to be larger and thus less suitable for a census. In these circumstances, something less than the whole population will be observed or interviewed, and it is necessary to select a sample from the total population.

Sample size

The most important sampling decisions concern how many should be in the sample, and how they should be selected.

For sample size, clearly in the practical world the cost effectiveness criterion is of paramount importance in determining how many people should be interviewed or observed. The fact is that while decision makers want research results to be accurate, generally increased accuracy comes with increased sample size (for the same sample design). Indeed, there is normally a trade-off between some increases in research costs and increased research accuracy or other benefits.

According to Bayesian principles, the difference between research benefits (in expected financial payoffs) and research costs provides the criterion for deciding whether or not to proceed and theoretically this yardstick can be used to assess whether extra benefits from a larger sample are worth the extra cost.

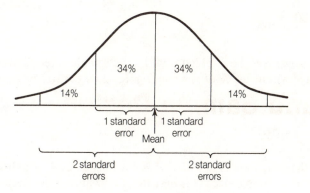

Figure 5.1 Normal distribution.

However, even so, resources other than finance such as time and human resources are also important, if a larger sample cannot be staffed, or if it would push the estimated completion date too far, then the smaller sample may be acceptable.

Where levels of research accuracy are important in determining sample size, the relationship can be summarized in the following way. If research aims to reveal results in percentage terms, for example, when measuring the percentage of consumers who have tried a new product, then the formula for helping to determine sample size is

$$\text{sample size} = \frac{pq}{S_p^2}$$

where p is the estimate of what the population percentage might be (q is $100 - p$), and S_p reflects the degree of accuracy desired in the estimated percentage. It might be worth noting that pq is maximum when $p = 0.5$. This model is based on the characteristics of the normal distribution which are explained more fully in Chapter 6. Briefly, if many samples are taken from a population their results (that is, the percentage of consumers with the characteristic measured) would vary but would be normally distributed. For such a distribution, about 34% of items would be one standard error away from the mean on either side. Adding these divisions together, it can be seen that 95% of the items will be between ±2 standard errors. See Figure 5.1.

An item in this context would be what each sample estimates the population percentage (with the characteristic of interest) to be. If the true population percentage is 20%, most samples taken to estimate it would produce a figure close to this, and the 'average' of a great many samples would be what the mean of this distribution is, that is 20%.

If we want to be 95% confident that our estimate from the sample will be within ±2% of the true value, then the size of sample required to give this level of accuracy is

$$\frac{20 \times 80}{2^2} = 400$$

If accuracy is to be doubled, that is, the sample is required to estimate the percentage within ±1% of the true figure, then the size of sample would have to be

$$\frac{20 \times 80}{1^2} = 1600$$

Note that when working with a 95% confidence level, doubling accuracy involves squaring sample size. This may be of relevance to the accuracy versus cost debate discussed on page 15.

When the study has to estimate an average as opposed to a percentage, the following formula is used:

$$\text{sample size} = \frac{s^2}{S_{\bar{x}}^2}$$

For example, a research programme may aim to estimate the average number of cigarettes bought in a month by smokers, and it is considered likely that 300 cigarettes ±40 (that is, the estimated standard deviation) are bought. The sample is intended to find the figure within 5 cigarettes of the true one, so, the sample size should be:

$$\frac{40^2}{2.5^2} = 256 \tag{5.1}$$

In this case, 2 SEs would be 5 cigarettes, so 1 SE (s) is 2.5.

These examples assume a 95% level of confidence is wanted, but if a 99% level of confidence is desired, then because 99% of items under a normal curve are approximately ±3 standard errors from the mean, then the sample sizes would be as follows: (a) for the new product example, 3 SE = 4% therefore 1 SE = 1.3, and the sample size is then

$$\frac{20 \times 80}{1.3^2} = 947 \tag{5.2}$$

(b) for the smoking example, 3 SE = 5 cigarettes, therefore 1 SE = 1.7, and the sample size is then

$$\frac{40^2}{1.7^2} = 554 \tag{5.3}$$

Many books on statistics expand the above and provide appropriate formulae for other types of sampling exercise (see Further Reading at the end of the chapter).

Sample design

Probability versus non-probability sampling

Choice in sample design is between those based on the laws of probability (introduced in the section above on sample size), and those based more on subjectivity and referred to as non-probability sampling. The latter includes: *convenience sampling*, which selects those who are easily and readily accessible; and *judgement sampling*, where those considered relevant and representative are selected; while *quota sampling* is the most widespread type of non-probability sampling.

Random sampling

When a complete list exists of all individuals or items in the relevant population (that is, a sampling frame), it is possible to design a sample that gives a calculable chance of each being selected. This principle provides the basis of random sampling. There is a popular misconception that 'random' means something rather vague and haphazard, like interviewing anyone available in the street, while in fact it is extremely precise.

In Simple Random Sampling, a population composed of, say, 12 items, could be used to select a sample of, say, 3. The following methods could be used to select the 3 items – each of which has a calculable probability of being selected. First, the lottery method, where 12 disks (or equivalent) are placed in a receptacle, each disk being labelled to represent one of the 12 items and a blind draw of 3 is made; second, by reference to mathematical tables of Random Sampling Numbers, 3 are selected, for example 5, 6 and 8 – items labelled 5, 6 and 8 would then be the sample; third, with a large sample a more convenient approach would be to divide the population size by the sample size to calculate the sampling interval (n) and every nth item can be selected. In the example above, the sampling interval would be $12/3 = 4$. Thus, every fourth item could be taken: 4, 8, 12 or 3, 7, 11 or 2, 6, 10 or 1, 5, 9. This is referred to as *systematic random sampling* and provides a practical method of selecting random sample items.

When there are subdivisions in a population (strata) there are four ways of designing a random sample. Take, as a common example for all four, the catchment area of a small store which has been defined as one ward of a

Table 5.1 Population distribution in an electoral ward.

| | Polling districts | | | | | Ward total |
	A	B	C	D	E	
Population size	50	300	50	100	500	1000

parliamentary constituency, where the ward contains 1000 people divided among five polling districts, as shown in Table 5.1. Assume that a random sample of 100 people is to be taken. The alternative approaches would be as follows.

First, select the same number from each polling district (PD), that is, twenty from each of A, B, C, D and E. Selection could employ the systematic approach described above. This is referred to as disproportionate stratified random sampling.

A second method would be to select that proportion of the sample from each PD that reflects the proportion of the ward that live in each PD. Thus, half of the ward's population live in E (500/1000) so we select 50 people (50% of 100) from E. On this basis, 5 people (50/1000 of 100) would be selected from A, 30 from B, 10 from D and 5 from C. This is again a stratified sample, but this time this is a proportionate random sample.

Third, it is not always essential to include respondents from each PD, and it may not be convenient if, for example, fieldwork costs of covering all five are high. Then, it is possible to randomly select only some of the PDs and the choice of which to select is itself based on random sampling. It might be decided, for example, to concentrate the fieldwork in just two PDs, where a random selection of 2 from 5 has identified B and D. Then, either 50 people from each would be selected (disproportionate random sampling) or 75 from B and 25 from D (proportionate random sampling). This approach is referred to as *multi-stage sampling* and there can be many more stages than in this example. In a larger geographic area, for instance, there may be several parliamentary boroughs with only some being selected, and within those selected only some constituencies chosen and so on, as illustrated in Figure 5.2.

Fourth, further concentration of fieldwork is possible if only a very few PDs are selected, but the sample includes everyone in these PDs. In the example, if PDs A and C are selected, the sample of 100 would be fulfilled by interviewing everyone in A and C. This is referred to as *cluster sampling* and can again be implemented through selection at two or more levels. However, it is probably better suited to a situation in which the strata are equal in size, since a *random* selection of just two PDs which, when combined, produce exactly the desired sample size, is unlikely to occur.

Cluster sampling tends to have a higher sampling error factor since there are likely to be more similarities among those in PDs A and C (after all, they are just two local areas and could be two very similar local areas) than if, say, 10 PDs were selected from a wider geographical area covering more variation in household type.

ACORN

ACORN is a development by Webber (1977) which is offered commercially by CACI as a sampling approach, as well as for locating territory for direct mail shots, retail outlets and so on. ACORN (A Classification of Residential

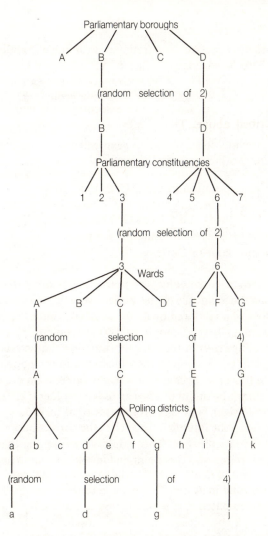

Figure 5.2 Multi-stage sampling example.

Neighbourhoods) is based on classifying households in terms of residential type – for example, Type A includes modern family housing for manual workers, Type B includes modern family housing and higher incomes, and Type I includes high status, highly educated people with a large proportion of educated young single people with a hedonistic lifestyle.

Some studies suggest ACORN is a better discriminator of buyer behaviour than the more traditional demographic characteristics of age, sex, socio-economic groups and so on. CACI state: 'the selected sample areas can be printed out in terms of constituent postcodes and street addresses eliminating the need for electoral registers' (CACI, 1979).

Quota sampling

With many marketing research programmes no suitable sampling frame exists, for example, there is no complete list of baked beans buyers or other fast moving consumer goods. Typically, such markets are segmented according to characteristics like age, sex and socio-economic groupings, where there is no accessible sampling frame.

Quota sampling allows for such factors, as the following example demonstrates. Assume that a market is segmented according to age and socio-economic group, producing four segments:

(1) 15–34-year-olds in socio-economic group ABC1

(2) 15–34-year-olds in C2DE

(3) 35 years and older in ABC1

(4) 35 years and older in C2DE.

Sufficient data is available for marketing regions (for example, ITV areas) to estimate the incidence of these characteristics in regional populations. For example, 70% of an ITV region might be C2DE, and 67% might be 35 years and older. Assuming that a sample of 500 is required, this type of sample design would produce *cells* of the relevant sampling characteristics with *quotas* allocated to each in proportion to their incidence in the population, as shown in Figure 5.3. In this case, because 70% of the population are C2DE and 67% are 35 years or older, the quota of 35-year-olds and older C2DEs is 70% of 67% of 500 (the sample size), and this produces a total of 235.

It is then up to the interviewer to select the correct quotas of respondents with each set of characteristics. This would very often be the basis for street interviewing and reimpress the point made earlier that selecting people at

Cell A	Cell B
ABC1 (30% of region)	C2DE (70% of region)
15–34 years old	15–34 years old
(33% of region)	(33% of region)
Quota = 50	Quota = 115
(30% of 30% of 500)	(70% of 33% of 500)
Cell C	**Cell D**
ABC1 (30% of region)	C2DE (70% of region)
35 years and older	35 years and older
(67% of region)	(67% of region)
Quota = 100	Quota = 235
(30% of 67% of 500)	(70% of 67% of 500)

Figure 5.3 Quota sample cells.

random in the street is actually not random sampling but more often quota sampling according to respondent characteristics.

At this point we have discussed research approaches from general research design and sampling, to questionnaire construction and data collection. We now move on to examine what happens once data has been collected, in the 'analysis' stage of the process.

REFERENCES

CACI (1979). *ACORN – A new approach to market analysis.* London: CACI Market Analysis Group

Webber R. (1977). *Parliamentary Constituencies: A socio-economic classification. OPSC Occasional Paper*, 8

6

Data Analysis

This chapter examines the 'processing' of marketing research data, once it has been collected using the methods discussed earlier. A summary of the process for handling a batch of questionnaires produced in such a research study is as follows:

(1) Edit the completed questionnaires to check for accuracy and obvious errors in use.

(2) Code the responses for processing.

(3) Tabulate the responses to each question. Once in this form the data can be analysed, using various statistical tests, and conclusions drawn. Recommendations can perhaps be made.

(4) Communicate both the nature of the research programme and the results to the sponsors of the research.

Data processing

Typically a computer package would be used to process such data and this section is concerned with data entry (from completed questionnaires onto a computer file) and its subsequent analysis – using the widely available MINITAB statistical package. This package was originally available for main-frame and mini computers but is now available for use on desk top micros as well. It is widely used in marketing research as are other popular packages such as SPSSX, MARQUIS, SWAP, SAS and so on.

For the following section on data processing, the only assumption made about your computing knowledge and experience is that you know how to 'log-on' to a computer system that has the MINITAB package. You are encouraged to work through this while at an appropriate computer terminal.

To begin, once you have 'logged-on' to the computer system you should see the appropriate 'prompt' sign, that is, the sign that informs you that the system is ready for your next command.

To access MINITAB, type

MINITAB ⟨R⟩

(Note ⟨R⟩ means pressing the RETURN or ENTER key.) MINITAB will have been accessed when, after a few lines of text saying things like MINITAB Release, you see the prompt:

MTB⟩

this tells you that a MINITAB command is now awaited.

The questionnaire used here (Figure 6.1) is very simple and is not put forward as a good example of questionnaire design but rather as representing the most simple form for computer coding purposes. The respondent is presented with a series of questions and for each question the respondent is asked to select one answer from a choice of three. The issue of giving multiple responses is discussed towards the end of this coverage of MINITAB and serves to reinforce the point that this questionnaire is poor in design terms but merely used to demonstrate computer coding.

The numbers to the right of the questionnaire are the appropriate computer codes. A different column is used for each answer given and the various codes *within* each column summarize what the actual response was. Thus, the first respondent might have preferred Bryan Adams in Q1 (code 3), U2 in Q2 (code 1), Tina Turner in Q3 (code 3), Soul 2 Soul in Q4 (code 3), American football in Q5 (code 1), racket sports in Q6 (code 1) and clothes from Top Shop/Top Man (code 1) in Q7.

To enter this data, with the MTB⟩ prompt on the screen, a MINITAB command is awaited and the one used here is READ. Type

READ C1−C7; ⟨R⟩

(Note '−' is the minus sign) the prompt changes to SUBC⟩. Type

FORMAT(7F1.0). ⟨R⟩

(Note that the ';' sets up a subcommand request (shown by SUBC) and the '.' is important because it signifies the end of the subcommand.)
This tells MINITAB to expect 7 columns of data and the confirmation of its expectation to receive data (rather than another command) is seen in the DATA⟩ prompt rather than the MTB⟩ prompt. The subcommand FORMAT(7F1.0). tells MINITAB that all 7 columns are single whole digits with nothing to the right of the decimal point (the (7F1.0) part of this command).

Had the questionnaire run to 28 columns and the codes used were numbers like 22.9 and 54.2 then the FORMAT statement would have been

Complete the following questionnaire by ticking the appropriate box by each question – make a choice even if you don't particularly like any of the alternatives given.

			CODE	COLUMN	
(1)	Which of the following do you prefer?				
	Bruce Springsteen	☐	1		
	Shakin Stevens	☐	2	1	
	Bryan Adams	☐	3		
(2)	Which of the following do you prefer?				
	U2	☐	1		
	Dire Straits	☐	2	2	
	Michael Jackson	☐	3		
(3)	Which of the following do you prefer?				
	Madonna	☐	1		
	Kim Wilde	☐	2	3	
	Tina Turner	☐	3		
(4)	Which of the following do you prefer?				
	Bob Dylan	☐	1		
	Cliff Richard	☐	2	4	
	Soul 2 Soul	☐	3		
(5)	Which of the following do you prefer?				
	Watching American football	☐	1		
	Watching football	☐	2	5	
	Watching snooker	☐	3		
(6)	Which of the following do you prefer?				
	Participating in racket sports	☐	1		
	Participating in water sports	☐	2	6	
	Participating in athletics	☐	3		
(7)	Which of the following do you prefer?				
	Clothes from Top Shop/Man	☐	1		
	Clothes from Marks & Spencer	☐	2	7	
	Clothes from Next	☐	3		

Figure 6.1 Questionnaire.

FORMAT(28F2.1) – meaning that all 28 columns were double digit numbers to one decimal place.

The data is entered, after the DATA⟩ prompt, in the following manner (for the first respondent's replies, as given above):

DATA⟩3133111 ⟨R⟩

MINITAB has accepted this row of numbers and the DATA⟩ prompt asks for some more data and each row of numbers typed in this way represents a different respondent.

The DATA⟩ prompt will continue until you type

DATA⟩END⟨R⟩

which changes the prompt back to the one which asks for a command.

If you logged-off the system at this point, the data just entered would be lost, so to enable you to save the data so it can be accessed at some later date, type

MTB⟩WRITE 'FILE' C1−C7 ⟨R⟩

You can use a more meaningful filename such as 'project' or 'survey' or whatever – note that the quotation marks are the *single quotes*. If your coded questionnaire runs to, say, 24 columns, then you would save it with MTB⟩WRITE 'FILENAME' C1−C24 (if in that case you typed write FILENAME C1−C7 only the first 7 of your 24 would be saved).

When MINITAB has saved the data in the file filename it should respond with the now familiar MTB⟩ prompt. To confirm that this file exists, leave MINITAB by typing

MTB⟩STOP⟨R⟩

and this takes you back to the computer 'system'. To get back into MINITAB type

MINITAB⟨R⟩

and wait for the MTB⟩ prompt. If the data had not been saved you would not be able to reaccess it at this point, so see if it has been saved by typing

MTB⟩READ 'FILE' C1−C7 ⟨R⟩

After a short time – though with very large files this can take a few minutes – the file should appear.

Here it says

1 ROWS READ

and you should see the 7 columns representing the answers to the 7 questions by the first respondent. Only up to the first 4 rows of data appear on the screen when a file is accessed, whatever size of file you have – so don't panic if you have a file of 34 respondents and you wonder where your other 30 rows have got to.

If you now want to add more respondent replies – say the survey is completed in batches – you can do this by typing (after you have accessed the file (in this case called 'FILE')) the following

MTB⟩INSERT C1−C7; ⟨R⟩
SUBC⟩FORMAT(7F1.0). ⟨R⟩

The DATA⟩ prompt tells you that data rather than a command is expected and you can type in more rows of data, in the same way as before. Thus, the next respondent might have gone for Shakin Stevens (code 2 in C1), Michael Jackson (code 3 in C2), Madonna (code 1 in C3), Bob Dylan (code 1 in C4), watching snooker (code 3 in C5), participating in water sports (code 2 in C6) and clothes from Top Shop (code 1 in C7). To enter this data, type

    DATA⟩2311321⟨R⟩

Further entries can be made from this new batch and then when you have completed the batch, type

    DATA⟩END⟨R⟩

to get back to the MTB⟩ prompt. To update the file, save it again with

    MTB⟩WRITE 'FILE' C1−C7 ⟨R⟩

This process can continue so that consecutive batches of completed and coded questionnaires can be added to the file – but do remember to resave the file after every session of additions.

If you want to add more information to each respondent's replies then MINITAB has a command to enable you to do this. Thus, if the two responses already saved to the file 'FILE' came from respondents on different courses, then these courses can be coded in the next unused column (in this case column 8).

Thus, if the file is accessed, with

    MTB⟩READ 'FILE' C1−C7 ⟨R⟩

you should see the response

```
2 ROWS READ
Row     C1    C2    C3    C4    C5    C6    C7
  1      3     1     3     3     1     1     1
  2      2     3     1     1     3     2     1
MTB⟩
```

To add data to a new column (column 8), type

    MTB⟩SET C8⟨R⟩

The prompt will change to

    DATA⟩

You can now type in a code for each respondent according to which course they were on (say code 1 for the MBA course and code 2 for an undergraduate business studies course).

    DATA⟩2 1⟨R⟩

This would add code 2 to column 8 for the first respondent and code 1 to column 8 for the second respondent. To update the file with this additional information you would resave the file with

    MTB>WRITE 'FILE' C1−C8 ⟨R⟩

Note that you now need to state C1−C8 (not C1−C7) because of the additional column of data to be saved.

    To confirm that the data has been saved, and to see the difference that the 'course' code makes to the file, type

    MTB>READ 'FILE' C1−C8 ⟨R⟩

the response should be:

```
2 ROWS READ
ROW     C1    C2    C3    C4    C5    C6    C7    C8
 1       3     1     3     3     1     1     1     2
 2       2     3     1     1     3     2     1     1
MTB>
```

(Code 2 in C8 refers to an undergraduate respondent and code 1 in C8 refers to an MBA respondent.)

Data analysis

Using the data set that appears in Appendix 1, the following describes some basic analysis commands.

    The data set refers to 95 student responses to the questionnaire referred to above. You might find it useful to enter this data into a MINITAB file (using the data entry procedure described above).

Histograms

It might be useful in most survey analysis to have straightforward counts of the number of people who gave each of the alternative responses to each question.

    If you type

    HIST C1⟨R⟩

the histogram for C1 is produced. Ignore the asterisks, they merely give an indication of where the greatest response is (each asterisk refers to 2 observations in this case). The numbers 1, 2 and 3 under the 'midpoint' heading are the codes 1, 2 and 3 for column 1 (that is, Question 1 in this case) and therefore the number of respondents who gave Springsteen (code 1), Shakin Stevens (code 2) and Bryan Adams (code 3) can be read. The same applies to the HIST command for other columns.

However, it is not necessary to enter the HIST command separately for every column, instead if you type

HIST C1 − C7⟨R⟩

all of the histograms will be produced. You will note that only a screenfull of information is shown at one time and at the bottom of the screen the message

continue?

appears. If you want the next screen of histograms either type y for 'yes' or just press the enter key.

If you do not want it to scroll round to the next screen, type n for 'no' and it will revert to the

MTB⟩ prompt.

Tabulations

The next command of analysis is TABL, short for tabulate (all MINITAB commands can be abbreviated to 4 letters).

What the tabulate command does is to provide a sort of cross-referencing of the number of people who said one thing to one question and who also said something else to another question. For example, if we wanted to find out how many respondents had chosen Springsteen in Q1 and watching American football in Q5, you could type

TABL C1 C5⟨R⟩

Use a space between C1 and C5 here, rather than the '−' (minus sign) as used in commands so far.

This produces a table with the first column in the tabulate command, in this case the C1 codes, down the left of the screen and the second mentioned column (C5, here) across the top. Thus, down the left we have 1, 2 and 3 referring to Springsteen, Stevens and Adams, and across the top, 1, 2 and 3

	C5 CODES			
		Watching		
	American football	Football	Snooker	
C1 CODES	(1)	(2)	(3)	Totals
Springsteen (Code 1)	20	20	12	= 52
Shakin Stevens (Code 2)	6	3	5	= 14
Bryan Adams (Code 3)	14	10	5	= 29
Totals =	40	33	22	95

Figure 6.2 Cross-tabulation.

refer to watching American football, watching football and watching snooker. The numbers in the table give us the cross-referencing, so it can be seen how many chose Springsteen (code 1 in col 1) and also for American football (code 1 in col 5). See Figure 6.2.

Percentages

Usually it is useful to produce results in percentage terms. To express the histograms in percentages, we can use a variation of the tabulate command, so if you type

TABL C1;⟨R⟩

the ';' tells MINITAB that you have not finished giving the command, that there is an additional subcommand to follow. You can see that the prompt summarizes this with

SUBC⟩

The subcommand to add here is

COLP. ⟨R⟩

short for column percentage. The full point '.' is important because it signifies the end of the subcommand.

The same data as for HIST C1 appears but now as percentages of the total sample – that is, showing the percentages of the total sample that preferred Springsteen, Stevens and Adams, respectively.

There are various ways of looking at a cross-tabulation in percentage terms. The first is to express all results as a percentage of the total sample, thus, if you go back to the tabulation of C1 and C5, type

TABL C1 C5; ⟨R⟩

the ';' prompts for a subcommand, confirmed with the response

SUBC⟩

The subcommand to use in this case is

TOTP.⟩

(short for total per cent). The full point again tells MINITAB that it is the end of the subcommand.

We now get a table with the same data as that from the TABL C1 C5, but now all the numbers are expressed as percentages of the total sample.

Other ways of looking at the same data use the 'COLUMN %' subcommand and the 'ROW %' subcommand.
If you type

TABL C1 C5; ⟨R⟩

and for the subcommand type

COLP. ⟨R⟩

you will get another table with the same data but this time the percentages are expressed as percentages of the column totals (that is, of the codes in C5). Thus, reading down each column you will see (in the first column) what percentage of all those who gave the code 1 response in C5 (watching American football) also gave each of the codes in Q1 (Springsteen, Stevens and Adams, respectively) and so on for the other two columns. The 'ALL' column and row are the totals for each column and row.

The 'ROW %' can also be produced if you type

TABL C1 C5; ⟨R⟩

and for the subcommand type

ROWP. ⟨R⟩

short for ROW %. Then, the resulting table again uses the same data but this time shows what percentage of all those who gave code 1 in Q1 also gave codes 1, 2 and 3 in Q5 (shown in the first 'row') and what percentage of all those who gave code 2 in Q1 also gave the various codes in Q5 (the second 'row') and so on.

It is worth looking at both ROWP. and COLP. – they *do* show different things. But be careful about percentages – you may find 66.66%, although looking to be an important and high figure, is really only 2 out of the subsample of 3!

Print-outs

To get a print-out you need to access MINITAB and the appropriate file before creating a temporary file to which you send the commands and types of data analysis required. For example, if you wanted all the histograms and two tabulations of the 'interest' data you would work through the following, assuming you are 'in' MINITAB and have the appropriate file accessed:

```
MTB⟩OUTFILE 'W1' ⟨R⟩
MTB⟩HIST C1 − C8 ⟨R⟩
MTB⟩TABL C1 C4⟨R⟩
MTB⟩TABL C3 C6⟨R⟩
MTB⟩NOOUTFILE⟨R⟩
MTB⟩STOP⟨R⟩
```

Everything between the two 'OUTFILE' commands is sent to the temporary file 'W1' which can be printed after leaving MINITAB (with 'STOP'). You will then need to follow the 'printing' instructions for the type of computer system you are dealing with. The 'W1' file is ready for printing.

Statistical analysis

Statistical tests of research data are based on the characteristics of sampling distribution and on the laws of probability, as introduced in the discussion of random sampling earlier.

If a research programme is undertaken to test some hypothesis or belief and the results are not entirely consistent with this hypothesis or belief, then there are two possible explanations. First, that the hypothesis or belief is wrong or, second, that the hypothesis is likely to be true, and the fact that the research results are different from the hypothesis is due to statistical variation – or chance. Only if the differences between the research results and the initial hypothesis cannot or could not be explained in this second way by statistical, chance variations, are the differences said to be statistically significant.

The following section describes a number of tests of significance. It should be pointed out, however, that these tests are strictly applicable only to research based on some form of random sampling, because only this is in turn based on the laws of probability. Indeed, it is generally taken by purists that only simple random sampling allows such testing, but in practice most surveys use some other sampling method, and many depart from the random and employ non-probability techniques such as quota sampling. In this connection, Koerner (1980) has discussed the compromises that can be made in order to conduct data tests. He suggests that once the standard error has been calculated according to the appropriate statistical test, it should be weighted by a design factor – for example, this would be 1 for a simple random sample and perhaps 1.5 for a quota sample.

Testing a population percentage

> 'Last year your market share was 20%. This year, you carry out a random sample of 600 consumers and this suggests that your market share has risen to 21%. Has there been a significant increase in market share?'

To answer this basic question, a significance test can be used to provide information on the chances of 20% still being the true market share. That is, we test the population percentage (not the 'sample' percentage of 21%). If the test suggests that 20% is not likely to be the true percentage then the true market share is said to be significantly different from 20%.

For instance, if (say) 100 different surveys, of the same size, were taken to find the true market share, then, from such a large number of separate surveys, it could be expected that although some are likely to estimate market share to be a little more than it really is and some a little less than it is, due to sampling variations, the average of these 100 surveys could be taken to be sufficiently close to the true figure.

The distribution of the market share measurements in these 100 surveys could be described as in Figure 6.3, with the mean being 20, if the true population percentage is 20. The distribution of sample results does not, however, give any indication of how much of a spread there is of individual sample results. For this, the standard error is required. One standard error away from the mean (that is, one 'Z') would contain approximately 34% of all the sample results. (This figure is taken from normal distribution tables – when reading the figure in the table against one 'Z', 0.3413 is identified, which means that the probability of an item in the distribution, taken at random, being between the mean and one standard deviation away from the mean is 0.3413.)

The standard deviation is the measure of the spread of a normal distribution and normal distribution tables provide the size of the area under the curve between the mean and various numbers of standard deviations away from the mean. When dealing with distributions of sample results, the same tables and logic apply, but the measure of spread is referred to as the standard error.

For the example given at the beginning of this section, the mean of the sampling distribution is taken to be 20, and its standard error (SE) is calculated by

$$SE = \sqrt{\frac{\pi(100 - \pi)}{n}} = \sqrt{\frac{20 \times 80}{600}} = 1.63 \qquad (6.1)$$

π is the population percentage being tested, which is 20% in this case, and n is the size of sample taken, given in the example as 600. This has converted one standard error into market share percentages. Thus, if Z is 1.63 market share per cent, it can be useful to label the $+Z$ as (from left to right) 18.37 and 21.63, respectively.

The results so far can be summarized as follows: if 20% is still the true market share, 34 out of every (similar sized) 100 surveys would probably suggest market share to be something between 20% and 21.63%.

It is necessary to calculate how rare our sample result of 21% is, if the true percentage is 20%. To do this we need to relate it to the probabilities as

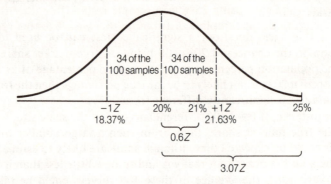

Figure 6.3   Distribution of sample results.

described by the sampling distribution in Figure 6.3. The approach is to position our 21% somewhere along the horizontal axis. That is, we must convert our 21% into standard errors and this is done by employing the following calculation

$$Z = \frac{p - \pi}{SE} \tag{6.2}$$

Here, p denotes the sample percentage as found by our survey and Z is used to denote the number of standard errors that our sample percentage figure (21%) is away from the mean (20%) of the sampling distribution. The logic of this calculation is that it is not merely the actual difference between the two percentages (21–20) that matters – but this difference relative to the sampling distribution as described.

In this case

$$Z = \frac{21 - 20}{1.63} = 0.6 \tag{6.3}$$

Therefore, 21% is 0.6 of a standard error away from 20%, and from the normal distribution tables it can be determined that, if 20% is the true figure, the number of samples (out of a hundred) which are likely to estimate the percentage to be 21% or more would be about 27 (that is, when $Z = 0.6$, the area under the curve from the mean to this point = 0.2257 and because the area to the right of the mean = 0.5, then the area to the right of $Z = 0.6$ is: $0.5 - 0.2257 = 0.2743$, or 27.43%).

Thus, if the true market share percentage is 20%, due to sampling variations, we could expect 27 out of every hundred similar sized surveys to estimate it to be 21% or more – although this may appear to be a slightly rare event, it is quite possible and so we would probably conclude that the true market share is indeed 20%, and the fact that our sample result is 21% does not suggest a significant difference.

On the other hand, if our sample result were 25% and the sequence above were applied again, but using 25% as a sample result (p) rather than 21%, then: (a) the mean of the sampling distribution that we are testing remains the same, at 20%; (b) its standard error also remains at 1.63; (c) but the position of our sample result of 25% would be different from that of a sample result of 21%, because, according to the 'Z value' formula

$$\frac{p - \pi}{SE} = \frac{25 - 20}{1.63} = 3.07 \tag{6.4}$$

As can be seen from Figure 6.4, a sample result of 25% would be quite a distance from the mean (20%). To be more precise, if 20% is still the true market share figure, the number of samples that would estimate it to be 25% or more would be about 1 in every 10,000 (that is, the area under the

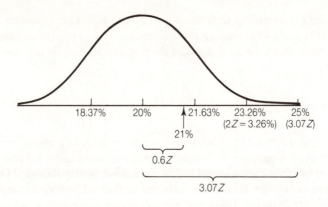

Figure 6.4 Probability of 20% being true if samples estimate it to be (a) 21% and (b) 25%.

curve to the right of the mean is 0.5, and the area from the mean to 3.07 Zs is 0.001).

Here, it might be valid to conclude that because it is such a rare event to obtain a sample result of 25% when the true figure is 20%, our sample result suggests the true figure is significantly different from 20%.

Note that the conclusion is not that the true figure is 25% or 21% or any specific figure at all, just that it is likely to be something other than 20%.

It is tempting to use the significance test as a 'decider' – that is, to allow the test to make a decision, but this would not be valid. All the test provides is additional information on the chances of the figure tested being true, when a sample suggests something else.

In the above example, the levels of chance associated with the different sample results of 21% and 25% were so clear that they could probably have been used to help make the above decisions without further processing. However, where such calculations produce a Z position of the sample result of (say) something around $Z = 2$, what sort of conclusions should then be drawn? Before discussing what to do with such 'grey' areas, it should be pointed out that statistical tests provide a guide for decision makers and should not be used to make decisions *per se*.

To help sort out such grey areas, two levels of significance have traditionally been used. One uses the argument that if a sample result is so rare (if the true figure is the one being tested) that less than 5% of all sample results would produce a similar figure, then the result is significant, and the figure being tested would therefore be rejected. The other significance level is the 1% level and uses the same logic in the case of a sample result in the extreme 1% minority. See Figure 6.5.

Sometimes a sample result concerns just one end, or tail, of the sampling distribution (that is, for one-tailed tests) and sometimes both ends of the dis-

	One-tail test	Two-tail test
0.05 level	+1.64 SE or −1.64 SE	±1.96 SE
0.01 level	+2.33 SE or −2.33 SE	±2.58 SE

Figure 6.5 Significance level.

tribution are relevant (two-tailed tests). Figure 6.5 demonstrates the difference between one- and two-tailed tests. This figure shows these significant levels for both one- and two-tail tests, and their associated Z values which give the beginning of the rejection areas – that is, if the sample result Z is further away from the mean than this, the **null hypothesis** (NH) may be rejected.

To demonstrate how this might operate, referring back to the example testing the 20% market share whichever significance level were chosen, the sample result of 21% would not fall in any 'rejection area', thus providing further justification for our conclusion that the sample result did not challenge the population figure of 20%. With the sample result of 25% whichever significance level were taken, it would fall within the rejection area, thus indicating that the figure being tested (20%) is likely to be wrong.

A relatively formal structure for significance testing sometimes helps, such as the following:

(1) An hypothesis is set up (for example, an assumption about the value of a population parameter). This is the null hypothesis and is the initial assumption – the parameter that the significance test goes on to test. For the first example this was 20% – that is, NH: $\pi = 20$ (where π represents the population percentage).

(2) An alternative hypothesis (AH) is defined – it is important to do this, since it specifies what happens if the null hypothesis is rejected. In the first example, it could have been stated that AH $\pi > 20$ (that is, if the market share is not likely to be 20% then it is likely to be something more than 20%, rather than less than). This means that this particular example is concerned with only the right hand side of the sampling distribution and as such is therefore termed a one-tailed test.

(3) An appropriate significance level is chosen – usually either 5% or 1% – assume a 1% level for the first example and, referring to the above paragraph and to Figures 6.5 and 6.6, it can be seen that for a one-tailed test using the 1% level, the 'rejection' level begins at 2.33 standard errors away from the mean of the distribution. Thus, if the sample result is calculated to be more than 2.33 Zs away from the population ·parameter being tested (and therefore taken to be the

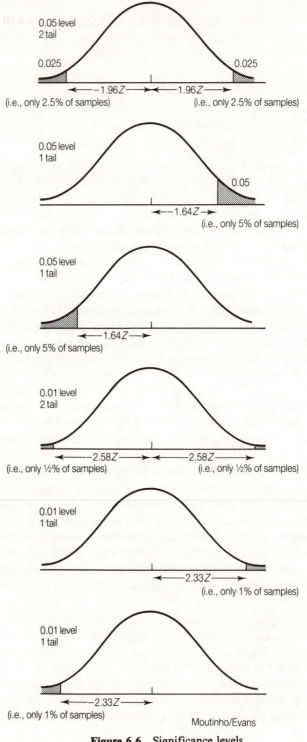

Figure 6.6 Significance levels.

mean of the sampling distribution) then it could indicate that the chances are that the population figure being tested is wrong and, in this instance, is likely to be something greater.

(4) The *standard error* of the sampling distribution (which has a mean equivalent to the population parameter being tested) is calculated according to:

$$SE = \sqrt{\frac{(100 - \pi)}{n}}$$

Types of significance testing other than the one appropriate for this first example require different formulae and these are described later.

(5) The position of the sample result in the sampling distribution under test is found from the following calculation

$$Z = \frac{p - \pi}{SE}$$

This value is compared with the *Z* value for the rejection of the null hypothesis as specified in stage (3) and if it is further away from the mean than this figure, the null hypothesis can be rejected in favour of the 'alternative' hypothesis.

Other significance tests

Comparing two sample percentages

If one survey was conducted in one area and another in another area, there would be two sample results – each is an estimate of the true figure in the respective area. For example, if a randomly sampled survey of 500 consumers in Northumberland produced a 25% awareness figure of a brand and a survey of 600 consumers in South Glamorgan produced an awareness figure of 19%, then there is a significance test which helps determine whether there is likely to be a difference in brand awareness between the *populations* of Northumberland and South Glamorgan.

The starting point for this test is that the null hypothesis assumes no difference between the actual levels of awareness in the two areas. Thus, the population percentage for Northumberland (π_1) is the same as the population percentage for South Glamorgan (π_2).

Working through the five steps:

(1) The null hypothesis is that

$$\pi_1 = \pi_2 \tag{6.5}$$

(2) If (1) is rejected the alternative hypothesis is that

$$\pi_1 \neq \pi_2 \qquad\qquad (6.6)$$

Here the concern is with a difference which could be either side of the mean, therefore it becomes a two-tailed test.

(3) A significance level is selected for example 0.05 which, for a two-tailed test, identifies the beginning of the rejection areas as 1.96 standard errors (Zs) either side of the mean.

(4) If there is no difference between the awareness levels in the two counties and if a large number of (pairs of) surveys were conducted then it is likely that, on average, the difference between the results of these pairs of surveys would be nil.

Thus, where p_1 and p_2 refer to sample percentages for Northumberland and South Glamorgan respectively, the test tests the likelihood of our pair of samples producing a difference of 6% (that is, 25% − 19%) if there is no difference between the population percentages in reality.

$$SE = \sqrt{\frac{p_1(100 - p_1)}{n_1} + \frac{p_2(100 - p_2)}{n_2}} \qquad\qquad (6.7)$$

(Where n_1 and n_2 denote sample sizes for Northumberland and South Glamorgan respectively.) Thus

$$SE = \sqrt{\frac{25 \times 75}{500} + \frac{19 \times 81}{600}} = 2.5 \qquad\qquad (6.8)$$

From this, if there is no actual difference between the two areas in terms of brand awareness, it could be expected that 34 out of every 100 pairs of samples taken might estimate a difference of between nought and 2.5% as shown in Figure 6.7. Our pair of samples produces an estimated difference of 6%, so the Z value of this has to be found from:

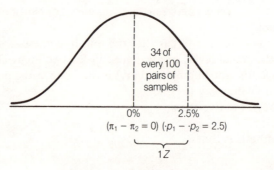

Figure 6.7 Comparing two sample percentages.

$$Z = \frac{(p_1 - p_2) - (\pi_1 - \pi_2)}{SE}$$

$$(6.9)$$

$$= \frac{6 - 0}{SE} = 2.4$$

This shows that the Z value is not merely the difference between p_1 and p_2 but the difference between their difference and a difference of nil (that is, the assumption that there is no difference between the two areas) and this is 'relative to' the spread of the distribution as described by its standard error.

Because our pair of samples produce a difference that is within the rejection area (the Z value for a difference of 6% is further away from the mean (that is, 0%) than the beginning of the rejection area (at 1.96) as defined in stage (3), a conclusion might be that this is such a rare event, if there really is no difference between the counties, that we challenge the validity of our initial (null) hypothesis. Thus, we might accept the alternative hypothesis. In other words, it is likely that there *is* a significant difference between the two populations in terms of brand awareness.

Testing a population mean

In this kind of problem the chances of a population average (mean) are tested when a sample survey suggests an alternative mean.

To take an example, if average spending in a store last year was £10 per customer and a random sample of 100 customers this year suggests it is £12, with a standard deviation of £5, there is a significance test that tests the likelihood of £10 still being the true average spending level.

The test is carried out in a similar way but here it is initially assumed that £10 *is* the true population figure and the test expands on the chances of this being the case when a sample produces a figure of £12. Our null hypothesis is therefore that $\mu = £10$ (where $\mu = $ population mean) and the alternative hypothesis is that $\mu \neq £10$ (therefore a two-tailed test).

Assume a significance level of (say) 0.01 (that is, the rejection area begins at 2.58 Zs away from the mean). The standard error formula is again slightly different, here it is

$$SE = \frac{\sigma}{\sqrt{n}}$$

$$(6.10)$$

where $\sigma = $ the standard deviation in this case it is estimated by the £5 given by the problem. Thus

$$SE = \frac{5}{\sqrt{100}} = 0.5$$

$$(6.11)$$

This means that *if* the actual average expenditure *is* £10, then 34 out of every 100 samples are likely to estimate it to be between £10 and £10.50 and another 34 out of every 100 samples to estimate it between £9.50 and £10.

Our sample estimates it to be £12, so the rarity of this happening (if £10 is the correct figure) is calculated by positioning our sample result along the horizontal axis, by the formula

$$Z = \frac{\bar{x} - \mu}{SE} = \frac{2}{0.5} = 4 \tag{6.12}$$

(where $\bar{x}$ = the sample mean)

Thus, if £10 is correct a sample result of £12 is so rare (4 standard errors away from the mean) that it falls well within the rejection area. The conclusion here could then be that actual average expenditure is probably not £10 – the alternative hypothesis (see Figure 6.8) might be accepted.

Testing two sample means

If a survey was conducted in one branch of a store and another in another branch in order to compare average spending in these two branches, then the following would be the general sequence of events in this type of significance test:

(1) Null hypothesis – there is no difference between spending in the two branches, that is, $\mu_1 = \mu_2$ where μ_1 refers to average spending in the first branch and μ_2 to average spending in the second branch.

(2) Alternative hypothesis – that average spending in the first is greater than in the second, that is, $\mu_1 > \mu_2$.

(3) Select (say) 0.05 significance level which for a one-tail test gives the beginning of the rejection area at 1.64 Zs away from the mean.

(4) Calculate the standard error, in this case from the formula

$$SE = \sqrt{\frac{\sigma_1^2}{n_1} + \frac{\sigma_2^2}{n_2}} \tag{6.13}$$

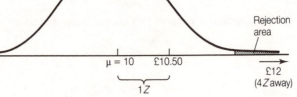

Figure 6.8 Testing a population mean.

where σ represents a standard deviation of a population – we do not possess this information so we have to estimate it by using 's' the standard deviation in our sample results.

(5) The Z value of the 'difference between our two sample averages' is

$$Z = \frac{(\bar{x}_1 - \bar{x}_2) - (\mu_1 - \mu_2)}{\text{SE}} \qquad (6.14)$$

Thus, if 32 customers in branch 1 were interviewed and their average spending was found to be £8 with a standard deviation of £1, and if 40 customers in branch 2 were found to average £7 spending with a standard deviation of £1.50, the standard error of the resulting sampling distribution would be

$$\sqrt{\frac{1}{32} + \frac{1.5}{40}} = £0.30 \qquad (6.15)$$

and the Z value of this pair of samples that produce a 'difference' of £1 would be

$$Z = \frac{(8 - 7) - (0)}{0.3} = 3.33 \qquad (6.16)$$

Figure 6.9 depicts the above and Figures 6.10 and 6.11 summarize these 'other' tests. As can be seen, our sample results are extremely rare if there is really no difference between spending in the two branches. So it is possible to conclude that it is likely that spending in branch 1 is significantly greater than spending in branch 2 (that is, the alternative hypothesis can be accepted).

This chapter has sought to clarify in very practical terms the minimum requirements for handling the data produced through marketing research projects.

The completion of the research process requires that the data should be checked and edited, coded and tabulated, and tested for the significance

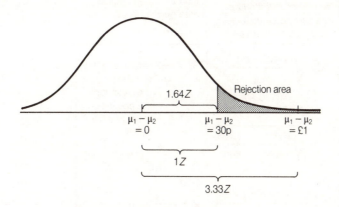

Figure 6.9   Testing two sample means.

Stages	Types of problem		
	(1)	(2)	(3)
	A random sample of 500 consumers in Northumberland produced a 25% awareness figure for a brand, and a survey of 600 in South Glamorgan produced a 19% brand awareness figure. Is there a significant difference in brand awareness between the populations of the two counties?	Average spending in a store last year was £10 and a random sample of 100 this year suggests it is £12 with a standard deviation of £5. Is spending significantly more than £12?	If a survey were carried out in two branches of a retail chain to compare average levels of customer spending, and in the first, average spending was £8 with a standard deviation of £1 (from 32 customers), and in the second, the average was £7 with a standard deviation of £1.50 (from 40 customers), is there a significant difference?
Stage 1 Null Hypothesis:	NH: $\pi_1 = \pi_2$	NH: μ (population mean) $= £10$	NH: $\mu_1 = \mu_2$
Stage 2 Alternative Hypothesis:	(π_1 is population percentage for Northumberland. π_2 is population percentage for South Glamorgan) AH: $\pi_1 \neq \pi_2$	AH: $\mu > £10$	μ_1 and μ_2 are average spending in the two branches respectively AH: $\mu_1 \neq \mu_2$
Stage 3 Significance level:	(say) 0.05 so, for a two-tail test (concern is with *both* sides of the distribution) the rejection area begins at ± 1.96 SE (p_1 represents the sample percentage for Northumberland and p_2 the sample percentage for South Glamorgan)	(say) 0.01 so, for a one-tail test (concern here is with the right-hand tail because we are interested in the possibility of the 'average' being more than £12) the rejection area begins at $+2.33$ SE	(say) 0.05 so, for a two-tail test (because we are concerned with a 'difference' that could be either side of the 'mean' being tested), the rejection area begins at ± 1.96 SE
Stage 4 Standard error calculation	$SE = \sqrt{\dfrac{p_1(100 - p_1)}{n_1} + \dfrac{p_2(100 - p_2)}{n_2}}$ $= \sqrt{\dfrac{25 \times 75}{500} + \dfrac{19 \times 81}{600}}$ $= 2.5$	$SE = \dfrac{\sigma}{\sqrt{n}}$ (where σ is the standard deviation for the population, estimated here by £5) $= \dfrac{5}{\sqrt{100}} = 0.5$	$SE = \sqrt{\dfrac{\sigma_1^2}{n_1} + \dfrac{\sigma_2^2}{n_2}}$ $= \sqrt{\dfrac{1^2}{32} + \dfrac{1.5^2}{40}} = £0.3$
Stage 5 Z value of sample results	$Z = \dfrac{(p_1 - p_2) - (\pi_1 - \pi_2)}{SE}$	$Z = \dfrac{\bar{x} - \mu}{SE} = \dfrac{12 - 10}{0.5}$	$Z = \dfrac{(\bar{x}_1 - \bar{x}_2) - (\mu_1 - \mu_2)}{SE}$

	$= \dfrac{6 - 0}{2.5} = 2.4$	$= 4$ (where $\bar{x} =$ sample mean)	$= \dfrac{(8 - 7) - (0)}{0.3} = 3.33$
INTERPRETATION	Since 2.4 is within the rejection area which starts at 1.96 SE, the NH may be rejected and AH accepted.	Since 4 is further away from the mean than 2.33, the NH may be rejected – there is likely to be an average expenditure in excess of £12.	3.33 is within the rejection area, therefore the NH may be rejected.

Figure 6.10   Other significance tests.

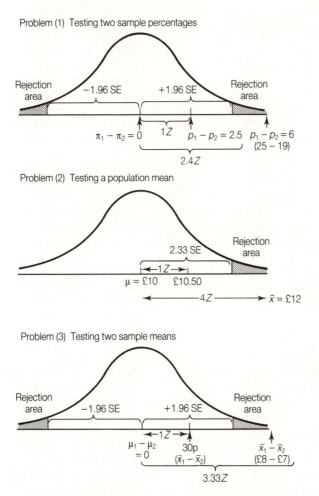

Figure 6.11   Sample distributions for the problems in Figure 6.10.

to be placed on apparent findings, leading to the compilation of a report and presentation.

Part II of the book changes emphasis by working through the marketing mix elements and applying marketing research approaches from that perspective. Before we do this, however, we provide in Chapter 7 a series of short case studies and problems based on Part I. Some relevant and topical 'clippings' from the press follow Chapter 18.

These and other issues are supported by the Instructor's Manual accompanying this text.

APPENDIX 1: DATA SET

```
MTB〉READ C1-C8;〈R〉            DATA〉11112134〈R〉
SUBC〉FORMAT(8f1.0).〈R〉        DATA〉11323124〈R〉
DATA〉31331111〈R〉             DATA〉11212114〈R〉
DATA〉23333221〈R〉             DATA〉31323124〈R〉
DATA〉31333321〈R〉             DATA〉23333124〈R〉
DATA〉13113131〈R〉             DATA〉21231124〈R〉
DATA〉31112131〈R〉             DATA〉21231124〈R〉
DATA〉11311131〈R〉             DATA〉13321214〈R〉
DATA〉11321121〈R〉             DATA〉11221224〈R〉
DATA〉11311331〈R〉             DATA〉11122114〈R〉
DATA〉11321121〈R〉             DATA〉12332124〈R〉
DATA〉11321321〈R〉             DATA〉23132335〈R〉
DATA〉11321211〈R〉             DATA〉33322135〈R〉
DATA〉11311231〈R〉             DATA〉32312135〈R〉
DATA〉13112331〈R〉             DATA〉11323135〈R〉
DATA〉11122231〈R〉             DATA〉11131135〈R〉
DATA〉12323211〈R〉             DATA〉23123335〈R〉
DATA〉11123221〈R〉             DATA〉33322135〈R〉
DATA〉11123221〈R〉             DATA〉11322135〈R〉
DATA〉11122121〈R〉             DATA〉33322135〈R〉
DATA〉11321111〈R〉             DATA〉32121135〈R〉
DATA〉11322311〈R〉             DATA〉23123335〈R〉
DATA〉31311221〈R〉             DATA〉33112225〈R〉
DATA〉31211221〈R〉             DATA〉12113225〈R〉
DATA〉31211321〈R〉             DATA〉11332325〈R〉
DATA〉13111221〈R〉             DATA〉21132235〈R〉
DATA〉11311231〈R〉             DATA〉31311236〈R〉
DATA〉11111231〈R〉             DATA〉31212136〈R〉
DATA〉12113131〈R〉             DATA〉11212236〈R〉
DATA〉11123111〈R〉             DATA〉31311136〈R〉
DATA〉31331112〈R〉             DATA〉32121336〈R〉
DATA〉11331223〈R〉             DATA〉31232126〈R〉
DATA〉11311133〈R〉             DATA〉11112136〈R〉
DATA〉21313133〈R〉             DATA〉31131136〈R〉
DATA〉31233123〈R〉             DATA〉31332335〈R〉
```

```
DATA)32111133(R)          DATA)11312235(R)
DATA)32311133(R)          DATA)11312115(R)
DATA)31312233(R)          DATA)11323135(R)
DATA)11111223(R)          DATA)23312125(R)
DATA)11313123(R)          DATA)12322125(R)
DATA)31321133(R)          DATA)11211325(R)
DATA)31333323(R)          DATA)11222115(R)
DATA)31311223(R)          DATA)13322125(R)
DATA)21231123(R)          DATA)33123125(R)
DATA)23221124(R)          DATA)11321135(R)
DATA)11322124(R)          DATA)23321135(R)
DATA)11321224(R)          DATA)end(R)
DATA)12322224(R)          MTB)WRITE 'FILENAME' C1-C8(R)
DATA)21331124(R)
```

Note C8 codes: 1 = home economics students; 2 = Martin Evans; 3 = fashion students; 4 = MBA p/t students; 5 = MBA f/t students; 6 = engineering students.

REFERENCE

Koerner R. (1980). The design factor – An underutilized concept? *European Research*, **8** (6), 266–72

FURTHER READING

Babbie E. (1973). *Survey Research Methods*. California: Wadsworth
Cass T. (1974). *Statistical Methods in Management*. London: Cassell
Churchill G. A. (1979). *Marketing Research*: *Methodological foundations 2nd edn*. Illinois: Dryden Press
Ehrenberg A. S. C. (1975). *Data Reduction*. New York: Wiley
Green P. E. and Tull D. S. (1975). *Research for Marketing Decisions* 3rd edn. Englewood Cliffs NJ: Prentice-Hall
McDonald C. (1982). Coding open-ended answers with the help of a computer. *Journal of the Market Research Society*, **24** (i), 9–27
Nie N. H., Hull C. H., Jenning J. G., Steinbrenner K., and Bent D. M. (1975). *Statistical Package for the Social Sciences*. New York: McGraw-Hill
Ryan T. A., Joiner B. L. and Ryan B. F. (1981). MINITAB *Student Handbook*. North Scituate, Mass: Dixbury Press

The authors acknowledge the cooperation and help of MINITAB INC, of 3081 Enterprise Drive, State College, PA 16810, USA. Tel: 814/238-3280 Fax: 814/238-4383

7

Problems and Cases

Problem 1: The role of marketing research within a marketing information system

Introductory comments

Marketing managers have a great need for the right kind of information. A well-designed marketing information system (MKIS), or marketing decision support system (MDSS), begins and ends with the user. A MKIS or MDSS must evaluate manager information needs and develop information through the use of internal records, a marketing intelligence system and an analytical marketing system (which includes a model bank and a statistical bank).

A MKIS is a continuing and interfacing structure of people and equipment, and procedures to gather, sort, analyse, evaluate, and distribute pertinent, timely, and accurate information for use by marketing decision makers to improve their marketing planning, execution and control.

A well-designed MKIS reconciles what information managers would like to have, what they really need and what is feasible to offer. The company must decide whether the benefits of having an item of information is worth its costs.

Marketing research involves collecting information that is relevant to a specific marketing problem facing the organization. Marketing research involves defining the problem and setting research objectives, designing the research plan, implementing the plan, and interpreting and reporting findings.

Problem

Clara Frozen Products Limited, a fast-moving consumer goods company, based in Cianella (Milano), has decided to increase its marketing research budget for the next year of operations from 1.2% to 2% in order to measure the effectiveness of its marketing mix strategies. The company is concerned about the different types of research tasks to be implemented which would help its brand managers to make better distribution, product mix, advertising, personal selling and pricing decisions.

Question

Define the appropriate research tasks and techniques that could be used by the company in order to improve the decision-making process in these five marketing mix areas.

Problem 2: Sample size determination – The case of simple random samples and multinomial populations

Introductory comments

We are frequently interested in obtaining estimates from multinomial populations. A multinomial population is one in which each element can be classified into one of more than two categories. All multiple choice questions involve multinomial populations. Estimating the proportion of users of each of three or more brands of a product, or the proportion of viewers of each of the four UK television channels during a given 15-minute period during the day are examples in marketing research.

In such cases, if both the specifications of error that can be allowed (e) and the confidence coefficient are to apply to the estimates of proportions for each of the several categories (rather than to only two of them, as it would if it were a binomial estimation problem), a larger sample will have to be taken than if the population were a binomial one. This is because three or more proportions are being estimated simultaneously and the estimates are such that the error in one of them affects the error in one or more of the others.

The direct determination of sample size for estimates of proportions from multinomial populations involves a somewhat complicated set of calculations. Fortunately, however, a table is available that permits conversion of the sample size that would be used if the estimate were to be treated as if it were to be made from a binomial population to the one that is appropriate for the multinomial population. The method for calculating the sample size directly and the conversion table are given in Tortora (1978). This table (Table 7.1) and a set of procedures for using it are described shortly.

The steps in the procedure to determine the appropriate sample size are:

(1) Specify the allowable error (e) that is applicable to each proportion to be estimated.

(2) Specify the confidence coefficient for the estimates.

(3) Using prior information, estimate the population proportion for each item.

(4) Calculate the sample size that would be required for the estimate of the proportion for each item, if the population were treated as if it were binomial.

Note If the same confidence coefficient is used for the estimate of the population proportion for each of the items, one needs to calculate only the sample size for the item whose estimated population proportion is closest to (or equal to) 0.50. This sample size will always be the largest because the product $\hat{P}_1 (1 - \hat{P}_i)$ in the numerator becomes larger as $\hat{P}_i$ approaches 0.50.

(5) Multiply the largest sample size obtained in step (4) by the appropriate conversion factor from Table 7.1. The result is the proper sample size for the estimates to be made from the multinomial population.

Table 7.1 Factors for converting binomial sample size to multinomial sample size.

Confidence coefficient	Number of proportions to be examined					
	3	4	5	10	15	20
95 per cent	1.53	1.66	1.73	2.05	2.37	2.53
90 per cent	1.71	1.84	2.04	2.44	2.76	2.91

(*Source*: Adapted from Tortora R. D. (August 1978). A note on sample size estimations for multinomial populations. *The American Statistician*, p. 101)

Problem

Viceroy Consumer Products wants to estimate the proportion of all users of air freshener products who use brand A, brand B and brand O (all other brands). Robin Jones, the company's marketing research manager, is assuming that the proportion of users of brand A, brand B and brand O are each to have an allowable error of ±0.05. He is also assuming a 95% level of confidence ($Z = 1.96$). Using prior information, Robin was able to assume the following population proportion estimates for the brands:

Brand A $\hat{P}_A = 0.30$
Brand B $\hat{P}_B = 0.20$
Brand O $\hat{P}_O = 0.50$
_____
1.00

Questions

(1) Calculate the sample size that would be required for the estimate of the proportion for brand A if the population were treated as if it were binomial (ignoring the finite population correction).

(2) Calculate the sample size that would be required for the estimate of the proportion for brand B using the same procedure.

(3) Make the same calculations for brand O.

(4) Calculate the proper sample size for the estimates to be made from the multinomial population.

Problem 3: Interval estimation of $\mu_1 - \mu_2$ – Two normal populations with equal variances

Introductory comments

Let us consider the interval estimation procedure for the difference between the means of two populations when the populations have normal distributions with equal variances, that is, $\sigma_1^2 = \sigma_2^2 = \sigma^2$. We will be assuming that independent random samples are selected from the populations. In this case the sampling distribution of $\bar{x}_1 - \bar{x}_2$ is normal, regardless of the sample sizes involved. The mean of the sampling distribution is $\mu_1 - \mu_2$. Because of the equal variances, the equation . . .

$$\text{Standard deviation: } \sigma_{\bar{x}_1 - \bar{x}_2} = \sqrt{\frac{\sigma_1^2}{n_1} + \frac{\sigma_2^2}{n_2}}$$

where:

σ_1 = Standard deviation of population 1.
σ_2 = Standard deviation of population 2.
n_1 = Sample size for the simple random sample selected from population 1.
n_2 = Sample size for the simple random sample selected from population 2.

Distribution form: Provided that the sample sizes are both large ($n_1 \geqslant 30$ and $n_2 \geqslant 30$), the sampling distribution of $\bar{x}_1 - \bar{x}_2$ can be approximated by a normal probability distribution and can be written:

$$\sigma_{\bar{x}_1 - \bar{x}_2} = \sqrt{\frac{\sigma^2}{n_1} + \frac{\sigma^2}{n_2}} = \sqrt{\sigma^2 \left(\frac{1}{n_1} + \frac{1}{n_2}\right)} \tag{7.1}$$

the sampling distribution of $x_1 - x_2$ is shown in Figure 7.1.

If the variance σ^2 is known, then equation (7.1) can be used to compute $\sigma_{\bar{x}_1 - \bar{x}_2}$.

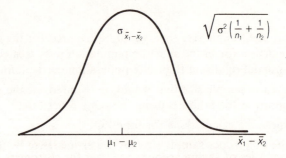

Figure 7.1   Sampling distribution of $x_1 - x_2$ when populations are normal with equal variances of σ^2.

Interval estimate of the difference between the means of two populations (large sample case with $n_1 \geqslant 30$ and $n_2 \geqslant 30$)

$$\bar{x}_1 - \bar{x}_2 \pm Z\alpha/2^\circ \bar{x}_1 - \bar{x}_2 \tag{7.2}$$

where $1 - \alpha$ is the confidence coefficient and Z = normal distribution. Equation (7.2) can be used to develop the interval estimate of the difference between the means of the two populations. However, if σ^2 is unknown, the two sample variances, s_1^2 and s_2^2, can be combined to compute the following estimate of σ^2

$$s^2 = \frac{(n_1 - 1)s_1^2 - (n_2 - 1)s_2^2}{n_1 + n_2 - 2} \tag{7.3}$$

The process of combining the results of the two independent samples to provide one estimate of the population variance is referred to as **pooling**, and s^2 is referred to as the **pooled estimator** of σ^2.

With s^2 as the estimator of σ^2 and with equation (7.1), the following estimate of the standard deviation of $x_1 - x_2$ can be obtained

Estimate of

$$\overline{\sigma_{\bar{x}_1 - \bar{x}_2}}$$

$$S_{\bar{x}_1 - \bar{x}_2} = s^2 \left(\frac{1}{n_1} + \frac{1}{n_2} \right)$$

Recall that whenever a population standard deviation σ is unknown and whenever the population possesses a normal distribution, the T distribution can be used to develop interval estimates of a population mean. When σ is unknown and when normal populations exist for a two-population case, the T distribution can be used to compute a confidence interval for the difference between the two population means. This procedure is as follows.

Interval estimate of the difference between the means of two populations (normal populations with equal variances estimated by s^2)

$$\bar{x}_1 - \bar{x}_2 \pm {}^{T\alpha/2^s}\bar{x}_1 - \bar{x}_2 \qquad\qquad (7.4)$$

where the T value is based on a T distribution with $n_1 + n_2 - 2$ degrees of freedom and where $1 - \alpha$ is the confidence coefficient.

Problem

The Clearlake Savings Bank has conducted a sampling study in which independent random samples of saving account balances for customers at two Clearlake Savings branch banks have shown the following results:

Branch bank	Number of savings accounts	Sample mean balance	Standard deviation
Garden Grove	12	$\bar{x}_1 = £1000$	$s_1 = £150$
Beechtree	10	$\bar{x}_2 = £\ 920$	$s_2 = £120$

Question

Demonstrate the interval estimation procedure for the sampling study conducted by the Clearlake Savings Bank. Use the above data to develop a 90% confidence interval estimate of the difference between the mean saving account balances for the two branch banks.

Case 1 – Temple Nathan

An established entity found itself losing ground in the marketplace as a result of erosion in its traditional customer base and an inability to attract new customers. At the same time, competitors in the area were thriving and even growing. What made this situation unique, however, was that the entity with the marketing problem was not a soap powder or soft drink. It was a synagogue.

To some, it may seem almost sacrilegious to mention marketing and religion in the same sentence. But when you consider that the definition of marketing is to identify the needs of a target group of consumers, to develop a product or service to meet those needs, and to communicate the benefits to that target group, it becomes clear that classic marketing techniques are not only appropriate for religious institutions, they can even be a necessity.

In the case of Temple Nathan, an established synagogue in a major metropolitan area, we have a classic example of an organization that had been coasting along on assumptions – assumptions that it understood the needs of the local Jewish community and was effectively serving those needs.

However, as membership began to decline steadily and a dynamic, high profile 'competitor' began to dominate the 'market', the synagogue's administration realized that the time for assumptions was over. Borrowing a strategy from big business, the administrators turned to marketing research for answers and solutions.

At TRC Marketing Research Company, crisis marketing research was almost routine, but now they had the added element of religion, a sensitive subject under the best of circumstances. To identify the major issues, they began with a series of focus groups involving current members of Temple Nathan's congregation, former members and non-members from the Jewish community at large. Next, they developed a questionnaire for phase two of the research process: a phone survey targetting the same three population groups.

As they had suspected, the key issues ran the gamut from the purely practical to the purely emotional. They ranged from the amount and quality of the religious education offered by the institution to whether the respondents liked the rabbi.

On most of the key issues, Temple Nathan received high ratings from its current members. However, it seriously lagged behind its chief 'competitor' on these same issues in the estimation of non-members. Was this because Temple Nathan had somehow acquired a 'bad' reputation in the community? Not at all. The marketing research company discovered that much of the synagogue's problem stemmed from the Jewish community's overall lack of information about its programmes and practices, even though these same people were much more familiar with the programmes and practices offered by its competition.

One major issue was the importance of available education programmes and activities for children. Although Temple Nathan offered many excellent facilities for children, few respondents outside the congregation were aware of them. The result was a higher number of 'don't know's' and generally lower ratings on this key issue for Temple Nathan.

The same lack of knowledge was also partially responsible for the comparatively low ratings given to Temple Nathan's rabbi by non-members. In the focus groups and phone survey, 'the rabbi' was named as the most important aspect of any synagogue and was considered by many as the one factor that could persuade them to change from one synagogue to another. While the rabbi at the main competitor had a high recognition factor and received high ratings from the general Jewish population, the rabbi at Temple Nathan, while receiving high ratings from members of his own congregation, was not nearly as well-known by non-members.

From the focus groups involving Temple Nathan members, it was also noted that the synagogue's rabbi was much more effective at relating to people on a one-to-one basis than at services. Another logical conclusion was that even non-members who said they were familiar with the rabbi may not have seen him at his 'best'.

To help Temple Nathan solve its recognition and familiarity problems, TRC proposed some fairly simple 'repackaging' and 'repositioning' strategies. (The Temple has begun implementing them, but it is too early to report results.)

First, they suggested that the synagogue initiate a campaign of targeted communications, emphasizing its many family- and youth-orientated programmes and activities to members with children.

They also recommended that Temple Nathan organize and encourage its members to participate in a 'Bring a friend' programme of small, informal gatherings hosted by the rabbi. These gatherings would also present the rabbi in his best environment and allow him to establish a personal rapport with prospective members.

Repackaging and repositioning could, however, solve only one part of the Temple's problems. In at least one basic, and very sensitive, area it became clear that the synagogue would have to undergo some 'reformulation' as well. Because reform synagogues attract members from all types of Jewish upbringing (reform, conservative and orthodox), it is crucial for these institutions to be aware of, and sensitive to, the practices and traditions that are most prevalent in the communities they serve.

In the community served by Temple Nathan, most people had come from orthodox or conservative backgrounds and had been brought up with their more formal traditions. Although a significant portion of the general Jewish population identified itself as 'reform', most of those who were familiar with Temple Nathan perceived it as 'too reform' for them. On the other hand, they perceived the synagogue's leading competitor, also a reform temple, as being much more successful at blending reform liberalism with tradition.

If Temple Nathan hoped to survive in the community, it would have to reformulate its atmosphere and practices to attract the more tradition-orientated prospects. At the same time, reformulation had to be subtle enough to avoid sacrificing the open, relaxed atmosphere that was so important in the less tradition-orientated current congregation.

To accomplish these goals, TRC recommended that the Temple make a concerted communications effort emphasizing its long history in the community and, indirectly, its high regard for, and adherence to, basic traditional values, standards and customs. At the same time, more traditional elements, such as wearing traditional garb, could be introduced as options for congregants, with emphasis on how the synagogue's openness and acceptance of a wide range of customs and traditions make it possible for Jewish people of all backgrounds to worship and socialize together.

Questions

(1) Comment on the use of group discussions as a qualitative research method.

(2) The questionnaire developed by TRC for attitude measurement was based on interval scaling. Comment on the most important characteristics of this type of scaling.

(3) What are the limitations involved with the use of the telephone survey method?

(4) The results of the survey research carried out in this case included a higher proportion of 'don't know's'. How would you handle the uncertainty and ignorance of the respondents?

Case 2 – Llaneaton Hospital

Roger Craven is administrator of Llaneaton Hospital in Frodsby, a medium-sized city. Five years ago he retained the services of a well-known health care management consultancy company to develop long-range plans for the hospital. Since that time new pressures and problems have arisen in the health care industry, not least because of the recent National Health Service legislation and Mr Craven feels that there is now a need to pay greater attention to the marketing aspects of the operation. He feels strongly that a marketing orientation will ensure the successful utilization of expanded facilities and aid other developmental efforts. He has, therefore, been taking steps to accomplish more of a marketing orientation for Llaneaton Hospital.

The hospital is located in a suburban area of Frodsby. In addition to the metropolitan area of the nearby city, the hospital also serves eight predominantly rural communities. Llaneaton Hospital is one of the two major hospitals located in this area of the city. The second hospital, Bessimer, is much larger than Llaneaton and services the same health care market area. Both Llaneaton (LAN) and Bessimer Hospital (BH) are actively pursuing facility expansion and medical staff development programmes. LAN management consider BH a major competitor in this health care market area.

Based on LAN records, over 93% of the patients at the hospital listed as their place of residence one of the eight communities in close proximity to the hospital. According to population growth projections, the number of residents within the service market area of Llaneaton Hospital will increase 35.2% between the years 1990 and 2000. Together, Llaneaton and Bessimer hospitals provide some 873 beds, with an additional 150 beds currently under construction at BH.

As a first step in developing a long-range marketing strategy for the hospital, Mr Craven decided that a comprehensive market research study should be carried out as soon as possible. He felt that the study should examine the attitudes of local residents towards hospital facilities and services, as well as investigate the behaviour of those who would make use of these facilities and services in the local area. To carry out the study, Mr Craven procured the services of a local marketing consultancy company. After various and extensive consultations, the marketing consultants submitted a research proposal to Mr Craven for his approval. Some extracts from the major parts of this proposal are shown below.

A study of the demand for medical services in the LAN Service Area

Objectives and scope of the study

The major purpose of the proposed research study is to delineate the 'image' profile of LAN among the general public and doctors in the LAN health care market service area. Concurrently the research study will identify related patient and doctor 'choice criteria' when making decisions relative to choosing a medical centre in the service area. More specifically the study will be concerned with investigating the following research issues:

(1) What factors are considered important to the public and to the doctors when selecting a medical centre?

(2) Considering the various important factors, how do the public and doctors evaluate LAN and BH? This data will enable the researchers to develop the image profile of not only LAN but also the other major medical centre in the health care market service area.

(3) Develop a comparative analysis between LAN and BH so that LAN's strengths and weaknesses can be compared and contrasted with those pertaining to BH.

(4) Investigate the various dimensions of patient and doctor decision making processes in relation to their choice of a medical centre.

(5) The data will be analysed not only for the groups of households and doctors, but also for subgroups on the basis of demographics for households and some other appropriate basis, such as medical specialization for doctors.

The consulting company also wants to analyse the respondent assessment of the 'influentials' in hospital selection. A segmentation analysis would also be performed. The major purposes of this segmentation analysis were to see whether there were any significant differences among the various segments with regard to the behaviours investigated.

The study

Four months after contracting with the local research company, Mr Craven received a copy of the results of the study. Out of 159 questionnaires mailed to doctors, 48 were returned. This represents a 30.2% response rate of the total

Table 7.2 Frequency of transfer of patients to alternative hospitals in the area.

Hospital	Frequency of transfer (%)	
	Several times daily	*Infrequently*
Llaneaton	10.6	42.6
Bessimer	43.8	14.6

Table 7.2(a) Extent of doctor usage of area hospital.

Hospital	Extent of usage (%)	
	Extensive	*Infrequent*
Llaneaton	32.6	34.8
Bessimer	42.9	30.9

Table 7.3 Doctor choice criteria in selecting a hospital.

Factors of importance	%
Bed availability	74.9
Quality of emergency room	75.6
Friendliness of staff	71.0
Quality of nursing	93.4
Availability of consultants	76.0
Quality and type of equipment	91.2
Overall hospital reputation	56.8
Patients' choice of hospital	65.0
Competent management of hospital	79.9
Quality of medical records	60.8
Geographical proximity to office	64.6

and was judged to be above average for these types of surveys. Some results from this phase of the study were as shown in Tables 7.2, 7.2(a) and 7.3.

According to doctors' evaluation of the two hospitals, it transpired that BH offered a superior service in the following respects:

- Contact with suppliers
- Nursing staff
- Physiotherapy
- Radiology
- Laboratory facilities
- Proximity of office space to hospital
- Anaesthesiology
- Operating facilities

- ITU facilities
- Medical records

LAN could only offer a superior service in respect of its housekeeping.

The consumer opinion survey questionnaires were mailed to about 1000 randomly selected households in the Llaneaton service market area. An additional 200 questionnaires were mailed to past patients of the hosptial. Through the consumer mail questionnaire survey, 308 responses were generated. After adjusting for undelivered questionnaires, the 308 responses accounted for approximately 33% of the mailings. This response rate in a consumer mail questionnaire survey was judged to be highly satisfactory. Some results from this phase of the study, that is, consumer use of hospitals, were as follows.

(1) Did the household use any hospital within the past two years?
    (a) Yes – 73.1%
    (b) No – 26.9%

(2) Name of area hospital utilized?
    (a) LAN – 48.5%
    (b) BH – 39.0%
    (c) Other – 12.5%

(3) Frequency of hospital use over the last two years?
    (a) Once – 42.7%
    (b) Twice – 16.7%
    (c) Three times – 16.4%

The consumer choice pattern of area hospitals was as shown in Tables 7.4 and 7.5.

Table 7.4 Consumer choice pattern.

Hospital	1st choice	2nd choice
Llaneaton	60.9	33.0
Bessimer	33.7	54.6
Other	5.4	12.4

Table 7.5 Consumer choice criteria in selecting a hospital.

Hospital facility	Very important (%)
Good doctors	95.7
Good nursing care	88.2
Good emergency room	86.5
Latest medical equipment	81.3
Keeps patients informed about their care	71.4
Good reputation	68.7
Price of service	59.1
Overall hospital management	56.3

Questions

(1) If you were the LAN administrator, how would you evaluate the proposed research study?

(2) What modifications, if any, do you suggest before approving the research proposal?

(3) Discuss how the information that may be generated from implementing the research study methods proposed would help the LAN management to develop long-term strategies and to import greater marketing orientation to LAN operations.

(4) What conclusions can you draw from the results of both phases of this study?

Case 3 – Prohealth UK

Prohealth UK's major quest is better service. The organization wants to make sure all of its customers are satisfied – the patients, the doctors and the employess. To achieve such service, this health care company recently launched QUEST (Quality Utilizing Excellence, Service, and Teamwork). The programme is designed to establish and maintain clinical and service standards.

'We will measure our quality improvement in important areas such as clinical outcomes, appropriateness of care and access to services', said managing director Peter Clarke.

Quest teams have worked throughout the system to develop standardized questionnaires that will provide comparative data for determining clinical and service improvement. These questionnaires were sent by mail to three groups: employees, doctors and patients. 'The data will be used to establish a benchmark for the programme', said John Fletcher, spokesperson for Prohealth UK. Prohealth UK also plans to use the information to identify trends among its nine hospitals. According to Fletcher, 'It's often difficult to measure quality in health care because it reaches such broad and varied audiences, each of which defines quality differently. For example, a patient defines quality service by "hospitality factors" such as whether the food was good. A doctor, however, will look at factors such as the number of operating theatres available.'

Until the results are available, John Fletcher says Prohealth UK is focusing on 'informing all of our employees of QUEST, on what such a quality programme is trying to establish and the role they play in making it successful'.

QUEST teams are being set up at every operating entity and have been given the power to make constructive changes. 'We're not just talking about quality', said Ken Potter, who heads the QUEST task force, 'we're doing something concrete'.

Questions

(1) The problem related to quality assessment by means of marketing research raises the issue of attitude scaling. Provide examples of several measurable responses which can offer clues about people's attitudes.

(2) In order to measure customer (patients, doctors and employees) satisfaction, Prohealth UK is planning to use comparative rating scales. Discuss the advantages and disadvantages attached to the application of these scales.

(3) Prohealth UK is well aware that the stage of 'questionnaire design' is a critical factor within the company's marketing research planning process. Comment on the key questionnaire design tasks and the relationships among them.

(4) The company was concerned about finding ways to minimize non-response errors in the three mail surveys. Comment on specific approaches and techniques that could be utilized in order to reduce non-response errors.

(5) In order to assess the impact of specific market trends and critical variables on the success of its QUEST programme, Prohealth UK is planning to use regression analysis. Comment on all of the most important features associated with this measure of association and statistical technique.

REFERENCE

Tortora R.D. (1978). A note on sample size estimations for multinomial populations. *The American Statistician*, August, 101.

Part II

Marketing Research: Applications and Industry

8

Market Research

The approach in this chapter is to illustrate the application of marketing research data and techniques to analyse markets.

The main components of market analysis can be summarized as investigating:

(1) a market's requirements;
(2) the actions taken by other firms;
(3) market size.
(Cravens *et al.*, 1980)

In reality, however, it is reasonable to evaluate a study of the characteristics of both customers and potential customers, along with their requirements, as an analysis of market potential. Therefore, we consider as a framework for market analysis, first market size and second market characteristics and segmentation.

Market size and share

A starting point is to identify the size of the market as a base for marketing planning, new product development and sales forecasting.

Market size dimensions include numbers of customers, the volume of product consumed and the financial value of this consumption, although there may also be a reservoir of *potential* customers to be tapped by greater and/or more effective marketing effort. There are, therefore, two sides to the market size question: first, what is happening in terms of total current industry sales, and second what could happen if current non-customers were converted.

Reference to various sources of secondary data often yields basic information on industry sales, as the earlier coverage of secondary data shows. At local level, market size in terms of potential volume can be calculated with reference to the Family Expenditure Survey, which provides information on the amounts that families of different types spend per week on products and services in different geographic regions.

A recent approach has been suggested by CACI (1981), the operators of ACORN, whereby the catchment area is defined by street, and then analysed by ACORN to give a profile to be compared with indices of product use by ACORN classes. For example, if it is known that the national average propensity of adults to take foreign holidays is 16% of the population, then a local travel agent could use ACORN analysis of his or her catchment area (of, say, 7000 adults) to determine whether a potential of anything other than 1120 people can be expected.

The profile of the catchment area, analysed in terms of the percentage of the population who are in each ACORN group to take foreign holidays, is provided by CACI (from their ACORN analysis of the TGI). The resulting catchment area profile provides an overall 'weight' for the entire catchment area's propensity to take foreign holidays, as shown in Figure 8.1. This 'weight' gives a more localized market potential estimation than one for a whole geographical region – which is all the Family Expenditure Survey can manage.

Acorn profile of catchment area	% of area	×	Index for taking foreign holidays	=	Area sales potential
A	1.4	×	61	=	0.85
B	–		108		–
C	9.7		84		8.15
D	7.9		39		3.08
E	–		41		–
F	11.4		53		6.04
G	–		34		–
H	13.9		124		17.24
I	29.1		230		66.93
J	22.5		217		48.82
K	3.1		84		2.60

Area sales potential index = 153.71

If 16% of national population buy this model and catchment area here is 7000, one would expect sales potential of 7000 × 16% = 1120 but, index here is 153.71 so for this catchment area, potential is 7000 × 1.5371 = 10760

Figure 8.1 Catchment area profile.

ACORN is but one geodemographic system – others include MOSAIC by CCN, Superprofiles and so on, but it demonstrates the greater depth of analysis now available in this report.

Additional dimensions of markets are also frequently provided by secondary sources, such as demographic, psychographic and geodemographic profiles of product users.

Primary methods can also yield this sort of information. An indication of brand share, for instance, may come quickly and inexpensively from a question on an omnibus survey, such as 'Which brand was your last purchase'?

Market characteristics, needs and wants

A fundamental market characteristic involves analysing consumer needs and wants – that is, what motivates customers. Several models of motivation may be adopted in order to structure research design. For example, Maslow (1954) has put forward a hierarchy of needs that suggests that individuals progress from one level to the next when each level is satisfied to a reasonable degree. Maslow's approach is open to debate but it does show how individuals can be motivated by 'non-necessities' such as social, psychological and even spiritual or aesthetic needs, and may continuously strive for more. The point here is not to ask merely about the 'functional' motivators of products – there may also be higher level motivators.

Another approach has been summarized by Kotler (1964), in a Freudian psycho-analytic model which introduced the concept of 'good' and 'real' reasons for behaviour. The research implications of this are that indirect questioning methods may be needed and that the subconscious may be analysed through subtle and specialized techniques. The research implications of these points were discussed earlier with respect to the Mason Haire coffee study where indirect questions revealed 'real' reasons for not buying instant coffee.

Segmentation analysis

This section examines segmentation approaches and associated research implications.

Kotler suggests that 'the term market is often used in conjunction with some qualifying term that describes a human need or product type or demographic group or geographic location' (Kotler, 1976). If marketing offerings cannot generally hope to be all things to all people, differences between groups, and similarities within groups, may be analysed for marketing planning purposes.

Segmentation involves homogeneous buying behaviour within a segment, but heterogeneous buying behaviour between segments. For a potential segment to be considered as a target for a distinct marketing mix (which does not necessarily involve a different product but may be a variation in one or more mix elements, such as a differing pricing approach, different retail outlets or differences in promotional methods), it should satisfy three criteria. These are defined by Kotler as follows:

(1) *measurability*, allowing identification of members;

(2) *substantiality*, being large enough to provide a worthwhile target;

(3) *accessibility*, to allow the segment to be isolated with marketing weapons.

This model is of great significance in researching potential segments: the measurability criterion gives research direction in identifying primary segmentation characteristics; the substantiality criterion indicates market size, potential and share as dimensions to research; and accessibility suggests the importance of secondary or profile characteristics. This said, a cautionary guide for research is what Davidson (1975) has referred to as 'market fragmentation' or 'over-segmenting' – perhaps British Rail's plethora of price segments, or the baffling array of shampoos on the market are examples.

Another practical point is that, conversely, research methods may determine segmentation since if some dimensions of market behaviour are difficult, time consuming, or costly to research, then sometimes the market will be segmented (perhaps artificially) according to those dimensions that are more conveniently analysed – such as, demographics (age, sex, socio-economics and family influence) rather than more complicated segmentation bases to research, like personality or lifestyle.

Demographic segmentation

This is the most widely used method in the UK and generally involves no more than age, sex and socio-economic analysis which, coupled with geographic location, provides market profiling data for such uses as media selection. The approach appears to work – a working party (Market Research Society 1981) set up to evaluate the discriminatory ability of socio-economics, concluded that no decline in such powers had occurred over the previous decade, although whether demographics actually explain *why* there are differences in customer behaviour is, perhaps, more debatable.

The demographic and geographic characteristics of credit card owners could be used in targetting, for example for off-the-page selling that involves mail ordering via credit cards. Those publications read predominantly by the sort of people who possess a credit card can easily be identified and selected from the National Readership Survey. This demonstrates the research ease of segmenting by demographics, and in part this explains the predominance of this segmentation base.

There are some more complex issues with respect to demographics, for example, because of changes in sex roles in society over time, there is evidence to suggest that although women still do most of the buying in the country (though much of it is for the household), the way that marketing treats them through female stereotyping in advertising (traditionally 'mother' and 'mistress' images) is becoming less and less realistic (Scott, 1978; Women in Media, 1981; Hamilton *et al.*, 1982).

One research implication of this has been identified by the US Celanese Fibres Marketing Company which has found it necessary to segment the female market further into working women and career women.

Another framework for segmentation research to some extent combines age and sex dimensions. The family life cycle concept shows that the family unit's interests and buying behaviour change over time due to the progression from the single bachelor stage, through newly married, married with children, married with children who no longer live in the parental home, to the solitary survivor stage. It has been found that some product categories like life assurance are predominantly chosen by the husband, while others like food and children's clothing are 'wife dominated', and yet others such as choice of holiday and housing, are rather more based on joint decision making (Davis and Rigaux, 1974).

Yet another 'combination' approach has been developed by Research Services Ltd in their SAGACITY Systems. Here, market analysis of consumers is based on three variables, occupation (ABC, vs C2DE, family life cycle (dependent on parents, pre-family household, household with children, post-children households) and income (whether both partners are working or not). Overall, this produces categories of analysis – or potential market segments as shown in Figure 8.2.

A very different research design would be required for a segmentation programme based on *psychographics* rather than demographics. Figure 8.3

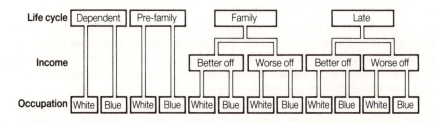

Sex
SAGACITY will often be applied to the male and female populations separately as in the published tables.

Figure 8.2 SAGACITY groupings.

Results from using the following:

Respondents asked to agree/disagree with:

'I like the outdoor life . . . .'
'I like to meet new people . . .'
'I aim to be promoted in my work as soon as possible . . .'
'I would rather read a good book than go to a party . . .'
'I am cautious about trying new products . . .'

Might reveal segments in terms of descriptive, stereotyped profiles like:

- The introverted traditionalists
  who keep themselves to themselves, do not go out much and rarely vary their daily routine.
- The go-getters
  who want to be seen to be trendy and using the latest products, go to the 'right' social events to meet the 'right' people for their own advancement.

Figure 8.3 Psychographic research (lifestyle statements).

demonstrates typical psychographic questioning, which often involves the use of Likert scales, where such statements are presented and respondents invited to state their degree of agreement with each.

This approach emerged as a compromise between some very in-depth, but extremely subjective research based on small samples and Freudian psychology that was conducted during the 1950s, and larger scaled quantitative research of the 1960s that was perhaps lacking in useful insight due to its superficiality. Psychographics allow attitudes, opinions and interests to be profiled from quite large samples, and the resulting 'profiles' can create a very useful mental picture of target customers for copywriters. However, in order to *reach* such segments the psychographics may have to be supplemented with a demographic profile, for media selection and so on.

The psychographic approach is employed in the US rather more than in the UK. For example, Levi Strauss have used a lifestyle profile of America to select their prime segments, namely 'the traditionalists', 'the new conformists', and 'the forerunners'. Other examples of psychographic research are to be found in Richards and Rachman (1978).

A variation on the personality theme in psychographic segmentation is based not on what sort of personality traits customers possess (as identified through administering standardized personality inventory tests) but on how customers perceive themselves. Indeed, it has been suggested that 'of all the personality concepts which have been applied to marketing, this one (self-concept) has probably provided the most consistent results and the greatest promise of application to the needs of business firms' (Foxall, 1980). The usual methodology involves semantic differential scales and the positioning of respondents by how they perceive themselves (or appropriate variations such as how they would like others to perceive them), and how they position different brands on the same dimensions, as shown in Figure 8.4.

The lower the distance score, the greater the degree of congruence between brand- and self-images, and brand preferences can be predicted on the basis of such congruence.

Although self-concept theory has been well-established in the behavioural sciences, it is only since the late 1960s that it has been employed to explain buyer behaviour. Birdwell (1968) used the semantic differential methodology to compare self- with car-images and found general congruence, though not at the lower end of the socio-economic scale due to financial constraints. Kassarjian (1971) found the matching of self- with car-image even greater after purchase, perhaps as a way of reinforcing the purchase choice. As an expression of self-perception, this approach could be of further significance because there is evidence to suggest that people are becoming more orientated to self-expression and 'inner direction' as opposed to following mass social movements. There appears to be greater *pluralism* in the market today, as has been pointed out by the Henley Centre for Forecasting (1978), Shay (1978), MINTEL (1981) and Evans (1981), in that a greater variety of attitudes and behaviour (for example, as reflected in fashion styles) is now evident, as compared with some ten or twenty years ago.

PLAIN	A S B	SOPHISTICATED
PRACTICAL	BSA	UNPRACTICAL
* SENSUAL	AS B	INNOCENT
* ADVENTUROUS	A S B	CAUTIOUS
TRADITIONAL	B A S	FASHIONABLE
* VIBRANT	A S B	LETHARGIC
SENSITIVE	B S A	UNEMOTIONAL
STANDOFFISH	B S A	SOCIABLE *
CALCULATING	B S A	IMPULSIVE *

Congruence between brand and self-image can be determined from the 'Distance score' formula:

$$\sqrt{\Sigma d^2} \text{ (e.g., } S_A = \sqrt{1^2 + 0 + 0 + 1^2 + 2^2 + 1^2 + 1^2 + 1^2 + 1^2} = 3.16$$
$$S_B = \sqrt{2^2 + 0 + 3^2 + 2^2 + 3^2 + 1^2 + 1^2 + 2^2 + 2^2} = 6)$$

The approach would not only suggest that image 'A' is more congruent with self-image in this instance, but that the image dimensions marked '*' would be the strongest and most relevant to promote to this market segment.

An alternative method could be to *start* with a measurement of self-image (or ideal self-image) dimensions in order to *create* a brand image.

Figure 8.4 Brand and self-image research. (*Source*: Evans (1981))

Another market model that demonstrates the research implications of primary (needs/interests) versus secondary (profile characteristics) segmentation dimensions comes from *diffusion–adoption* theory. Under this, a continuum of innovativeness of customers is loosely correlated with the product life cycle, thus providing for a segmentation of the market over time, as is shown in Figure 8.5.

In order to reach these segments, a demographic profile is generally assumed (especially in terms of age and status) as is suggested in Figure 8.6.

An important dimension of this approach, is *opinion leadership*. Aiming marketing effort at opinion leaders will speed up the diffusion process because these often influence others so a two- or even multi-step flow of communications results, and it is the research task to identify opinion leadership. It is possible, but not very practical (due to time and expense), to identify those specific individuals who are real opinion leaders in a product-market. For example, psychographic-type research might reveal those who are considered 'leaders' as opposed to 'followers', and other techniques like socio-metrics can be used in a similar manner. Socio-metrics, for example, entails asking each member of a group which other members he or she considers knowledgeable or good at giving advice, and a pattern of perceptions within the group emerges showing those who are higher in opinion leadership than most.

An alternative method might be to use guarantee cards for new products, by asking the new buyer of a new product to return such a card, but additionally requesting details on the consumer's demographic profile. When the next new

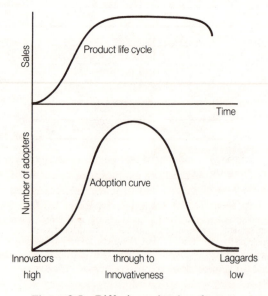

Figure 8.5   Diffusion–adoption theory.

Innovators – are eager to try new ideas, they do not need much persuasion. They are fairly well off and are willing to take risks. Tend to be younger and to have higher status and education. Their reading goes beyond 'local' and mass media communications. They have the closest contact with scientific and specialist sources of information and in general rely on impersonal sources. They seek social relationships outside their local peer circle, they are extrovert in a jet set sense. They have a broad range of interests and are socially mobile.

Early adopters – tend to have the greatest contact with salespeople and local people and are often leaders in local clubs and organizations. They exhibit the greatest *opinion leadership* and are highly 'localite'. Have high status and are fairly well off. They are highly respected in local society and are often asked for their opinions and advice.

Early majority – have contact with mass media and salespeople, but also with early adopters. They do not exhibit so much opinion leadership and deliberate over adoption decisions.

Late majority – tend to be sceptical and need much pressure from peers before they adopt. Are below average in terms of income, status and education, etc. They adopt when they perceive little risk – perhaps when they see others like themselves using a given product.

Laggards – are bound in tradition and often use other laggards as sources of information. The past is their frame of reference. Some are semi-isolates. Do not use the mass media or salespeople as information sources. Tend to be older and from lower socio-economic groups and are less wealthy. Become adopters when innovators are adopting next innovation.

As can be deduced from the above a major factor in speeding up the diffusion process is the use of *opinion leaders* – *real* opinion leaders or *simulated* opinion leaders.

Figure 8.6 Characteristics of 'adopter' categories.

product is launched some direct mail shots could be sent to these people, who, because they were early adopters of the last new product, may contain a fairly high proportion of early adopters and opinion leaders for this next one. Thus, as can be seen, there is a variety of research implications to be drawn from these segmentation and market analysis approaches.

International market segmentation

This is a more specialized case where examples of cultural differences between countries abound. For example, cultural differences often revolve around the role of women in different societies. In some Middle Eastern countries female interviewers would not be tolerated because of their position in society – further demonstrated by the need to promote (say) sewing machines, not to women, but to their husbands on the grounds that their women will become more useful and efficient!

More will be said on international markets and marketing research in Chapter 14.

Organizational markets

Organizational markets may require different research. Many models of organizational buying exist, for example, the Robinson, Faris and Wind 'Buygrid' model (Figure 8.7). (See Robinson and Faris 1967; Robinson *et al.*, 1968.)

This can be of assistance in researching the type of buying that is appropriate to an organization at a particular point in time. The level of problem-solving for a particular purchase can indicate those buying phases that are likely to be the most relevant, which in turn might suggest the sort of information the buying organization might be searching for – and perhaps even the individual in the organization responsible for those stages.

As with some consumer markets, there may be a geographic concentration of organizational markets, thus a kind of geographic segmentation approach would be called for. Traditionally, the UK has had a concentration of certain industries in particular areas, such as textiles, shoe manufacturing and car manufacturing, but as a result of government regional policy over the years some of these are changing due to the financial assistance given to firms to move to Enterprize Zones and so on. Volume segmentation also applies in organizational markets where sometimes an extremely high proportion of consumption is accounted for by a very low number of buyers. Because of such concentration (geographically, as well as in terms of volume) research could employ a census as opposed to sampling. Other aspects of industrial marketing research are examined in Chapter 14.

Since 'the market' provides the starting point for marketing activities, we have also started our coverage of marketing research 'applications' with

Buy phases	Buy classes		
	New task	Modified rebuy	Straight rebuy
Need	*		
Specs	*		
Sources	*	*	
Evaluate and select	*	*	
Purchase	*		*
Evaluate	*		*

More than one type of selling may be required – perhaps on a sort of division of labour according to these stages

Segmentation base for industrial selling?

Missionary ⎫
Technical ⎪
Order getter ⎬ Different types of salespeople may be required along the buy phases
Order taker ⎭

Figure 8.7 Robinson, Faris and Wind 'Buygrid' model.

'the market'. We now continue to work our way through the marketing mix elements of product, price, distribution and promotion, and devote chapters to each in terms of marketing research applications.

REFERENCES

Birdwell A. E. (1968). Influence of image congruence on consumer choice. *Journal of Business*, (1)

CACI (1981). *ACORN – A New Approach to Market Analysis*.

Cocks D. (1981). Children and young people: Marketing and social research. *European Research*, January, 19–21

Cravens D. W., Hills G. E. and Woodruff R. B. (1980). *Marketing Decision Making: Concepts and strategy*. Illinois: Irwin

Davidson J. H. (1975). *Offensive Marketing*. Harmondsworth: Penguin

Davis H. and Rigaux B. P. (1974). Perceptions of marital roles in decision processes. *Journal of Consumer Research*, **1**

Evans M. J. (1981). Who's a dedicated follower of fashion? SSRC/MEG, Seminar on buyer behaviour, University of Strathclyde

Foxall G. (1980). *Consumer Behaviour: A practical guide*. London: Croom Helm

Hamilton R. A., Haworth B. and Sadar N. (1982). *Adman and Eve*. Department of Marketing, University of Lancaster

Henley Centre for Forecasting (1978). *Planning Consumer Markets*

Kassarjian H. H. (1971). Personality and consumer behaviour – A review. *Journal of Marketing Research*, **8**

Kotler P. (1964). Behavioural models for analysing buyers. *Journal of Marketing*, **29**(4), 37–45

Kotler P. (1976). *Marketing Management: Analysis, planning and control* 3rd edn. London: Prentice-Hall

Maslow A. H. (1954). *Motivation and Personality*. New York: Harper and Row

MINTEL (1981). Teenage markets. *Special Mintel Market Report*

Richards E. and Rachman D. (1978). *Market Information and Research in Fashion Management*. Chicago: American Marketing Association

Robinson P. and Faris C. W. (1967). *Industrial Buying and Creative Marketing*. Boston: Allyn and Bacon

Robinson P. J., Faris C. W. and Wind Y. (1968). Generalised simulation of the industrial buying process. Marketing Science Institute Working Paper, June, 46–52

Scott R. (1978). *The Female Consumer*. London: Associated Business Programmes

Shay P. (1978). A consumer revolution is coming. *Marketing*, September

Women in Media (1981). *Women in Advertising*. A video produced by WIM, London

FURTHER READING

Boyd H. W., Westfall, R. and Stasch S. F. (1977). *Marketing Research: Text and cases* 4th edn. Illinois: Irwin

Bradley U. (1982). *Applied Marketing and Social Research*. Wokingham: Van Nostrand Reinhold

Day R. L. and Ness T. E. (1970). *Marketing Models: Behavioural science applications*. Scranton: Intext

Engel J. F., Blackwell R. D. and Kollat D. R. (1978). *Consumer Behaviour* 3rd edn. Illinois: Dryde

Hill R. W. and Hillier T. J. (1977). *Organisational Buying Behaviour*. London: Macmillan

Hughes G. D. (1973). *Demand Analysis for Marketing Decisions*. Illinois: Irwin

Market Research Society (1981). *An Evaluation of Social Grade Validity*. MRS, London

McCarthy E. J. (1981). *Basic Marketing*. Illinois: Irwin

Naert P. and Leefland P. (1978). *Building Implementable Models in Marketing*. Boston: Martinus Nijhoff

National Readership Survey (1976). Joint Industry Committee for National Readership Surveys

Parfitt J. H. and Collins B. J. K. (1968). The use of consumer panels in brand share prediction. *Journal of Marketing Research*, **5** (5)

Piercy N. (1982). *Export Strategy: Markets and competition*. London: Allen and Unwin

9

Product Research:
New Product Development

This chapter and Chapter 10 focus on aspects of applying marketing research within the product element of the mix. Specifically they cover new product development, packaging and brand name testing. This chapter starts by analysing the contribution of marketing research within programmes to develop new products.

New product development

While there is probably no universal model of the new product development programme, Figure 9.1 suggests the general framework from which appropriate stages may be extracted and adapted, according to the type of product involved.

Research methods for generating ideas for new products, or for modifications to existing ones, are outlined in Figure 9.1, as are the subsequent stages of the process which are intended to screen ideas to identify those which are most likely to be successful. Typically, many ideas will have emerged from Stage 1, perhaps in excess of 100 (Booz, Allen and Hamilton, 1968). Before any such ideas are converted into product form various tests can be conducted to determine whether such a conversion appears to be wise. These tests are referred to as concept tests.

If a product idea survives concept testing, it might be made up into prototype form and its various components tested – for example, if applicable, its package, colour, smell, shape and so on. Finally, before a full-scale launch, the proposed product could be evaluated in some scaled down version of the intended market, perhaps in an ITV region. If the results of the test market are favourable, then a national launch might follow.

Stages in new product development programme

Stage 1 Idea generation	Stage 2 Screening	Stage 3 Business analysis	Stage 4 Development	Stage 5 Test marketing
Gather ideas for new products, or for modifications to existing products.	Is the idea compatible with both the *aims* and *resources* of the organization?	Project *cost, sales* and *profit* estimates.	Develop technically and also commercially, e.g. brand personality and other aspects of marketing.	Launch in some scaled-down version of the intended market to test the marketing plan.

Research approaches

Stage 1 Idea generation	Stage 2 / 3 Concept testing	Stage 4 Development	Stage 5 Test marketing
Idea generation Identify gaps in market • new wants, etc. • can use multi-dimensional scaling. Observation of product use or misuse – for new uses or refinements to existing product. Can use group discussions or feedback from panels. Customer complaints can be another source of ideas, as can feedback through salesforce. Secondary data sources may provide ideas, for example, changes in technology.	*Concept testing* Concepts (ideas) can be presented (a) verbally, perhaps using a standardized tape recording, (b) written statements, perhaps on cards, (c) drawings, on cards, (d) dummy packs (where a picture of the product would convey less than its pack, which includes descriptions, instructions, etc.), (e) mock advertisements, perhaps dummy press ads., or perhaps using video to demonstrate in a 'simulation'. Concepts may be communicated 'in home', 'in hall' or perhaps using a mobile van. Sometimes a concept that is easy to understand can be described in questions on an omnibus survey. Aim is to determine levels of customer acceptance, and possible levels of sales. Often, existing products can be used as points of reference.	*Product testing* To 'evaluate' proposed product features – style, design, package, colours, etc. Such evaluation may not necessarily lead to rejection if unfavourable, but to modifications and adjustments. Respondents may be asked to evaluate product in *placement tests* – *monadically or paired.* Paired tests can be *simultaneous, staggered or non-directive.* Can also be *blind or open.* Dilemma: Holistic versus Atomistic tests.	*Test marketing* Monitor, as well as *sales* levels, awareness, interest, intentions, trial, preference, repeat purchase rates, etc. Consumer panels can be used to monitor brand trial, loyalty and brand switching behaviour of individual households. Retail audits provide brand share and distribution outlet information.

Figure 9.1 Model of market research in new product development.

Considering the major elements shown in Figure 9.1, the first stage of the process is to gather ideas.

Idea generation

Many ideas appear as a result of the application of intuitive processes. Some ideas are the result of technological or Research and Development (R & D) breakthroughs, so a continuous monitoring of changes in technology, together with more proactive efforts with respect to technology, can be sources of ideas for new or modified products. Some important approaches to the generation of ideas are summarized below:

(1) *Group discussions* When conducted properly, they provide a relaxed, supportive and idea-stimulating atmosphere that often produces worthwhile suggestions for new products.

(2) *Brainstorming within the organization* Brainstorming is designed to elicit suggested solutions by a group that is presented with a problem (in this case to suggest potential new products).

(3) *Examining customer complaints* Problem inventory analysis is a method of unearthing problems that consumers have with existing products which can be used to suggest new products/product variations that are needed.

(4) *Attribute-based customer surveys* A similar technique to problem-inventory analysis is attribute listing, which involves listing the attributes of a product and then systematically attempting to modify one or more of the attributes to see what would improve the product.

(5) *Secondary data sources – for example, for exploring changes in new technology* This activity can be an important source of competitive intelligence, as well as a contributor of new product ideas. The typical marketing research department has as one of its responsibilities the active monitoring of such secondary sources as patent disclosures, products offered for licence by other companies and so on.

These points are generally self-explanatory, but it is worth discussing a specific form of attribute-based surveying, namely multi-dimensional scaling.

There are several methodologies for multi-dimensional scaling and one involves identifying the two main criteria that consumers use to evaluate brands in a market and converting these to scales. Respondents can then use these scales to position their perceptions of the various brands. Presenting these results by turning the two scales at right angles to each other will produce a perceptual mapping of the brands so positioned – relative to all the other brands in that product market. Figure 9.2 demonstrates this approach.

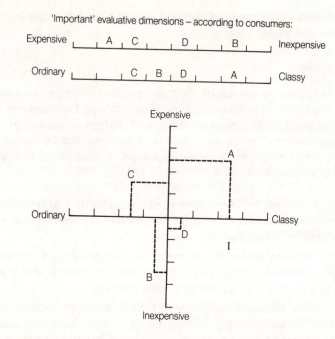

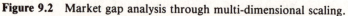

Figure 9.2　Market gap analysis through multi-dimensional scaling.

A way of identifying gaps in the market is to ask respondents where their 'ideal' brand would be, relative to their perceptions of the existing brands ('I' in Figure 9.2). An alternative method involves asking respondents to rank pairs of brands in terms of similarity, on a specified basis, and then converting

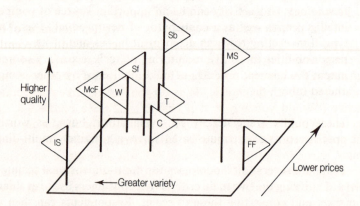

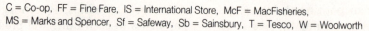

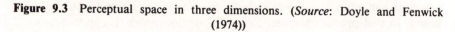

C = Co-op, FF = Fine Fare, IS = International Store, McF = MacFisheries,
MS = Marks and Spencer, Sf = Safeway, Sb = Sainsbury, T = Tesco, W = Woolworth

Figure 9.3　Perceptual space in three dimensions. (*Source*: Doyle and Fenwick (1974))

these rankings to perceptual space. Axes can then be superimposed from the single dimension to produce the familiar two-dimensional graphic and labelled after the positioning. This is feasible manually only when there is a small number of brands. Three-dimensional positioning is also possible, as described by Doyle and Fenwick (1974) and shown in Figure 9.3.

Holistic versus atomistic testing

Once ideas have been generated, the dilemma to be confronted in testing both ideas and resulting products is whether to test the 'whole' (product features, probable price, brand name, packaging, promotion and so on), or whether to attempt to evaluate each component. This is the holistic versus atomistic debate – customers buy the 'whole' but an overall evaluation may not identify specific problem areas.

Concept tests

Concept tests are initial screens of consumer reactions to new product concepts. The purposes of a concept test are to:

(1) Choose the most promising from a set of alternatives
(2) Gain an initial notion of the commercial prospects of a concept
(3) Find out who is most interested in the concept
(4) Indicate what direction further development work should take.

Samples are often convenience-orientated. Common sample sources could include central locations such as shopping centres. The most common approach is to present consumers with a verbal/written statement of the product idea (called a folder test) and then record their reactions. Recently, many researchers have chosen to also include physical mock-ups and advertising statements in the concept test. These are really prototype/concept tests. The data gathered is both diagnostic ('Why do you like/not like the product?') and predictive ('Would you buy it if it cost £____?') See Figure 9.4. Including a concrete 'Would you buy?' question is crucial if the results are to be at all useful predictively. Concept testing has proven effective for most kinds of products, excepting products that are radically innovative and that require significant changes in existing consumption patterns. Because such new products diffuse slowly through the population and require substantial commitment and behavioural change, a consumer's stated intentions with regard to them are likely to be somewhat unreliable. The data collection procedures fall into the following three major categories.

Plain verbal description of the product or service and its major benefits

A major soft drink manufacturer would like to get your reaction to an idea for a new exotic fruit soft drink. Please read the description below before answering the questions

New exotic fruit soft drink

Here is a tasty, somewhat sparkling beverage that quenches thirst, refreshes and makes the mouth tingle with a delightful flavour blend of passion fruit, lime and mango. It is a totally natural fruit drink and it contains absolutely no calories. It comes in tetrapack-type packages and costs 55p per drink.

(1) How different, if at all, do you think this new exotic fruit soft drink would be from other available products now on the market that might be compared with it?

Very different ☐

Somewhat different ☐

Slightly different ☐

Not at all different ☐

(2) Assuming you tried the product described above and liked it, about how often do you think you would buy it?

More than once a week ☐

About once a week ☐

About twice a month ☐

About once a month ☐

Less often ☐

Would never buy it ☐

(3) What, if anything, do you particularly like about the product described above?

(4) What, if anything, do you particularly dislike about the product described above?

Figure 9.4 Concept test format.

Surveys

Surveys are useful for obtaining large samples for projection purposes. On the other hand, it is often difficult to properly convey a concept in a survey, thus, to be successful, concept testing must capture and effectively communicate the spark of an idea. Concept testing should provide a system for reshaping, redefining and coalescing ideas to arrive at a basic concept for a product with greater vitality and potential for market acceptance.

Group discussions

The strength of group discussions lies in their diagnostic power, in that they can be used to obtain detailed discussion of various aspects of the concept. As predictors of actual sales, they are fairly inaccurate due to their small sample sizes.

Demonstrations

A popular way to present a concept is to gather a group of consumers, present them with a 'story' about the new product and record their reaction. Questions asked are typically related to:

(1) Do they understand the concept?

(2) Do they believe in the concept?

(3) Is the concept different from other products in an important way?

(4) Is the difference beneficial?

(5) Do they like or dislike the concept and why?

(6) What could be done to make the product more acceptable?

(7) How would they like to see the product (colour, size, etc.)?

(8) Would they buy it?

(9) What price would they expect to pay for it?

(10) What would their usage be in terms of volume, purpose, source of purchase and so forth?

Some years ago Unilever was considering ideas for new household cleaning products. One such product was a combined floor cleaner–polisher. At this stage the company had not succeeded in physically developing the product so a way had to be found to present the concept not the product. They eventually used the film technique – by making a film of a dirty floor being cleaned by a fluid in washing-up liquid type packaging. The film cut from 'before' to 'after' scenes of the effect on the floor of the product idea. In fact the liquid in the film was merely milk and water but respondents were not informed of this and the film was very successful in conveying what the company had in mind for this product concept. Incidentally, this project was later subjected to product tests (including a sniff test for the perfume used and package tests) and went into a test market. It was launched nationally with the brand name 'Dual'.

Overall, then, concept tests themselves vary and Figure 9.1 summarized some of the approaches that can be employed. The most basic concept test is a concept screening test where many concepts are described briefly and subjects are asked for an overall evaluation (for example, intention to buy). These tests are used to reduce the concepts under consideration to a manageable number. Next, concept generation tests (often involving group discussions) are used to refine the concept statements. This is typically followed by concept-evaluation tests. These tests are based on larger samples and attempt to quantitatively assess demand for the concept based on samples of 200 to 300. These tests are typically carried out competitively, in the sense that other new concepts and/or existing products are also evaluated at the same time. This introduces another testing dilemma – whether to present ideas monadically (in isolation from other ideas) or comparatively, thus providing respondents with a point of reference to be able to compare ideas.

Product use tests

This type of research consists of physically producing the product and then getting consumers to use it. The purpose of a product test is to

(1)   uncover product shortcomings

(2)   evaluate commercial prospects

(3)   evaluate alternative formulations

(4)   uncover the appeal of the product to various market segments

(5)   gain ideas for other elements of the marketing programme.

It is worth repeating the 'holistic–atomistic' dilemma here – whether to replicate reality by asking respondents to evaluate products one at a time (monadically) as they would normally use them, or to allow for some reference point by presenting products in comparison tests. It is common to adopt the latter because it produces far more responses, but when respondents are aware that they are required to compare products they perceive many more differences between them than in a non-directive comparison test, where a product is given to a respondent to use with no mention of follow-up questioning at the end of the use period (see Figure 9.5).

This is the difference, then, between a paired comparison test and the staggered comparison. The former involves respondents in the evaluation of

	Paired comparison	Staggered comparison	Non-directive
Awareness of difference	79%	78%	7%

Figure 9.5   Comparison tests. (*Source*: Boyd, Westfall and Stasch (1977))

two products at the same time, whereas the latter allows respondents to evaluate one product first, and then to go on to the second.

These tests are what are called 'placement tests' because the product is placed in those homes sampled for an extended period. For packaged goods, this is usually a period of about two months, the advantage of this extended period is that the results allow for both the wear-out of initial expectations and the development of problems which only manifest themselves over time. Subjects are required to complete before and after questionnaires, as well as maintain a diary of actual use of the new and competitive products over the period of the test. Here again, the inclusion at the end of the test of an actual choice situation helps to give the results a bottom-line orientation.

Blind tests are where brand names are removed, as is typical in the car industry where 'clinics' are run with several competing models being lined up with prototype versions of the car being tested. It is usual here for all 'badges' to be removed, and for all the cars to be the same colour to avoid colour perceptions distorting results, as described by Hill (1982) with reference to Ford and Talbot.

Apart from the usual 'in hall' testing (that is, some local hall is hired for tests, which is a widespread way of interviewing respondents in busy shopping areas because it allows for more time to be taken, in more conducive surroundings than the street itself, to conduct taste, packaging and advertising tests, for example), new technology is now providing greater potential for 'in home' tests. As Bushman and Robinson (1981) propose, with the development of cable technology and Viewdata product pictures can be sent to wired homes for instant feedback. Indeed, it would be possible to send different versions to different households – as 'split run' tests (which test alternative approaches such as those decided here).

Preference tests

The best known preference tests are the taste tests conducted for food and drink products. Here, the purpose is to experiment with alternative formulations which are supposed to (a) taste better or (b) cut costs. The problem is greatly complicated by carry-over effects (does the second beer ever taste as good as the first?) and the lack of discriminatory power for most consumers (try to tell Heineken from Kestrel in a blind test). Taste tests also fall into the following categories, as described earlier:

- *Monadic* The respondent uses once product one and then evaluates it.
- *Paired comparison* Respondents use two products at the same occasion and then indicate which they prefer.
- *Staggered comparative test* (sometimes also called a successive monadic test) The respondent uses several products sequentially and rates each one.

Table 9.1 Actual reported preference.

First preference (%)		Second preference
A	*B*	
48	15	A
13	24	B

Table 9.2 Probability of expressed preference, given true preference.

'True' consumer preference	*AA*	*BB*	*AB,BA (Neither)*
A	1	0	0
B	0	1	0
Neither	$\frac{1}{4}$	$\frac{1}{4}$	$\frac{1}{2}$

To discover more clearly consumers' ability to discriminate, it is common to replicate the paired test. It is also possible to use groups of three products – called *triangles* or *triads*, where two of the products are identical – to better estimate the ability of consumers to discriminate. To see why a replicated test is useful, consider the following situation.

A set of subjects is presented with a pair of products (A and B) on two different occasions. We will assume there are three kinds of consumers:

(1) Those who can tell the difference and prefer A.

(2) Those who can tell the difference and prefer B.

(3) Those who cannot distinguish between A and B and who randomly indicate preference.

The key is to estimate these three fractions. First we must look at the actual reported preference table (Table 9.1). The naïve interpretation is that 48% prefer A (since they consistently chose it) and 24% prefer B. As we will see, however, this is a bad estimate. Returning to the three kinds of consumers, we have the conditional probabilities of the test result giving true consumer preference as shown in Table 9.2. Hence, the expressed per cent is a function of true preference as follows:

$$\% \ AA_e \ = \% \ A_T + \tfrac{1}{4} \ (\% \ \text{Neither}_T)$$
$$\% \ BB_e \ = \% \ B_T + \tfrac{1}{4} \ (\% \ \text{Neither}_T)$$
$$\% \ \text{Neither}_e = \tfrac{1}{2} \ (\% \ \text{Neither}_T)$$

where:

% AA_e = the expressed per cent who chose A both times.

% A_T = true per cent who prefer A.

Solving this for the true fractions gives:

% $Neither_T$ = 2 (% $Neither_e$)

% A_T = % $AA_e - \frac{1}{4}$ (% $Neither_T$)

% B_T = % $BB_2 - \frac{1}{4}$ (% $Neither_T$)

For our example, we get:

% $Neither_T$ = 2 (13% + 15%) = 56%

% A_T = 48% $- \frac{1}{4}$ (56%) = 34%

% B_T = 24% $- \frac{1}{4}$ (56%) = 10%

The correct interpretation of the results is thus (a) most people do not perceive a difference and (b) B is in trouble.

Factor tests

Factor tests involve separately testing for the effect of varying elements of the marketing programme, such as price, advertising copy and so forth. These tests are conducted in essentially the same way for new products as they are for existing products. Most such tests are conducted in central locations or labs (simulated stores) and involve exposing consumers to different treatments and seeing how they respond.

One of the most interesting ways to do this is through a controlled store test. This entails testing a product in an actual store, in which complete control over price, point-of-purchase displays and so forth is maintained. As such, this procedure falls somewhere between a lab and field experiment in both realism and cost. This method is especially useful in testing packaging, pricing and point-of-purchase displays.

Test markets

The ultimate in realism is a test market. The purpose of such a test is (a) to predict sales and profits from a major product launch and (b) to 'practise up' so marketing, distribution, and production skills are developed before entering full-scale operations. Often, ITV regions can be used for test marketing purposes.

Also using TV technology it is now possible for a new product to be available only through mail order via TV advertising, rather than setting up channels of distribution. If successful, the product could later be put into stores. Strictly speaking though, a test market should be selected on the basis of being representative of the intended market, and in practice IBA television regions have traditionally been used. The expense involved, however, has more recently led to a relative decline in the use of this approach in favour of more product testing – for example, using simulated store tests and the like.

Some test marketing exercises are necessarily extremely short lived – for example, where fashion is a factor. In this case a test market of, say, six months (which might be appropriate for some fast-moving consumer goods) could be counter-productive because the garments tested would be for the imminent season – which would probably only last six months in total.

Marks and Spencer plc, for example, put test ranges into selected branches (that have high turnover, so a more rapid reading of the market can be taken) for sometimes no more than a weekend.

At the other extreme, some products either have to be launched or dropped, without scope for test marketing. For example, cars take years to develop and, apart from minor cosmetic refinements, cannot easily be changed fundamentally after launch. The 1989 relaunch of the Ford Fiesta, however, did follow a period when the model was on restricted sale before the main launch and this represents a form of test market even for this product category.

Another consideration when deciding whether or not to test market, is how competitors are thought likely to react. There is, perhaps, a thin line between marketing research and industrial espionage – a competitor could monitor a firm's test market and refine its own new product on this basis. The competitor could then launch nationally before the original firm's test market has even been completed (Davis, 1970).

In spite of potential hazards of test marketing, and indeed their high cost, the technique is of great importance because, as Cadbury (1975) has stated, no other research method can replicate market circumstances as well as the real thing.

Projections are typically made for both market share and actual sales, appropriately adjusted to national levels. The major sources of concern are as follows:

(1)   Trial rate.
(2)   Repeat rate (for frequently purchased goods).
(3)   Usage rate (number bought per customer).

In addition, awareness, attitudes and distribution are usually monitored. Given these measures a projected sales estimate can be made. In designing a market test, it is important to delineate clearly what information is to be gathered, and why, before proceeding. Several decisions must be made.

Action standards

Standards for evaluating the results should be set up in advance. These standards should specify when the various possible decisions (for example, stop the test, continue the test, revamp the product, go national) will be implemented.

Where

The choice of where to test market is a serious problem. Most market tests are done in two or three cities. This further emphasizes that the 'test' is not designed to try out numerous strategies – at most two to three alternatives can be used. Cities are chosen on the basis of representativeness of the population, the ability of the company to gain distribution and media exposure in the area, and availability of good research suppliers in the area. Also, areas which are self-contained in terms of media (especially TV) are preferred. The result is that certain medium-sized cities are often chosen, such as Newcastle upon Tyne, Aberdeen and Cardiff.

What to do?

The best test market designers are careful to make the effort in the area proportional to what would reasonably be expected in a national launch. Notice here that we mean effort and not budget. If a city has particularly expensive (the usual case, when buying spot TV ads) or inexpensive media costs, allocating budget on a population basis would result in a media schedule which had either too few or too many exposures. The goal is to make distribution and price to consumers (price deals to retailers and wholesalers are needed to gain distribution) as representative as possible. What typically happens, however, is that the effort afforded the product is somewhat greater than the comparable national effort.

How long?

The question of how long to run a test is not easily answered. Obviously, a longer run gives more information, but it also costs more and gives competitors more time to formulate a counter-attack. Consumer packaged goods typically stay in test markets for between six and twelve months. The reason for the length of the test market is to include several purchase cycles, so repeat usage as well as the trial can be accurately assessed. It is not uncommon for a product to gain a large initial share, due to trial, and then lose market share as repeat business fails to live up to trial.

How much?

For a consumer packaged good, test marketing costs run close to £0.5 million. Advertising and promotion typically account for 65–70% of the budget, with the rest of the budget divided between information gathering and analysis and miscellaneous administrative and other expenses.

Information gathering

During a test market, a variety of information is gathered, most of it related to actual sales. In monitoring sales, it is important to recognize that a large percentage of first-year factory sales (for example, 30%) represent a one-time stocking up by the channels of distribution and not sales to final consumers. The three major data sources are:

(1) actual sales (typically at least 40 stores per area) plus distribution, promotion and so forth

(2) surveys which measure awareness, attitude and so forth

(3) consumer panels which report actual purchase and allow monitoring of trial and repeat rates.

A useful breakthrough in the researching conducted during test markets was made by Parfitt and Collins, when they formulated and validated a model for predicting brand share in the main market, but from test market results only.

The Parfitt–Collins model

For this model, consumer panel data provide the consumption patterns of each household that reports, so it is possible to identify when an individual household buys a product for the first time and when it buys the product again.

The Parfitt–Collins (1968) model utilizes such data to calculate the *penetration* of the market and the *repeat purchasing rate* in order to estimate eventual brand share (thus, this is a *predictive* model).

Figure 9.6 shows how panel households bought different brands (T, R and S) in the same product category, from the time (week 1) that new brand (T) was launched. In week 1, two households purchased this brand for the first time, so this is the cumulative number of new buyers for week 1. In the second week, household numbers 3 and 4 bought T for the first time, bringing the cumulative number of new buyers to 4 in week 2 and so on. When expressed as a percentage of those buying in the product category, this provides the market penetration rate. In Figure 9.6 the cumulative number of buyers for the first few weeks was projected forward as an estimate of what the eventual

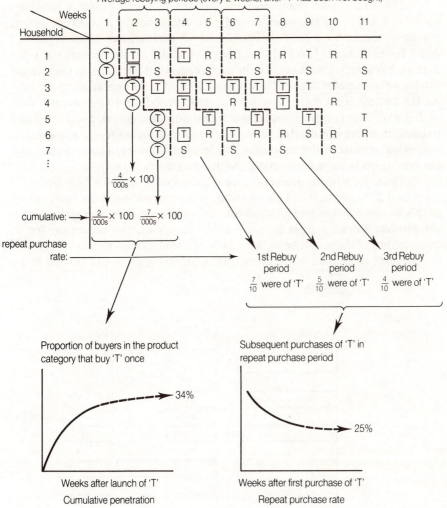

Figure 9.6 The Parfitt–Collins model of brand share prediction. 34% of buyers in product category will buy 'T' once and 25% of those will repeat buy 'T' (buy it, on average, once per fortnight). Therefore 25% of 34% of market equals 8.5% (brand share prediction).

penetration percentage would be. In this case, it was estimated that 34% of those buying in the product category would have tried T once. From the entire panel (Figure 9.6 shows only seven households from a panel that might have comprised several thousand), an average period for repurchase is calculated – that is, some buyers in this category will buy every week, some every 2 weeks, and others less frequently. The average repurchasing period in this case was estimated to be a fortnight.

The first repeat purchase period is not in weeks 2 and 3 for every household, but in the two-week period immediately following the time of first purchase by each household – weeks 3 and 4 for households 3 and 4, weeks 4 and 5 for households 5, 6 and 7, and weeks 2 and 3 for the households 1 and 2. In each repeat purchase period, the percentage of all purchases in the product category that were of brand T is calculated – this is the repeat purchase rate. As can be seen from the first repeat purchase period, of 10 purchases 7 were of T and of 10 purchases in the second repeat purchase period, 5 were of T and so on. This figure is projected forward after calculating it for just a few weeks, to give an estimate of the eventual stable level of repeat purchase – in this case the prediction is for a 25% repeat purchase rate.

Thus, 34% of the market will (it is estimated) eventually have bought T once, and 25% of these will go on to buy it on a repeat purchase basis (which in this instance means every fortnight). If T is consumed at average levels for the product category (that is, once every fortnight), the prediction for its eventual brand share will be 25% of 34% of the market (which is 8.5%). If T is consumed more than other brands, then obviously more will be sold and it

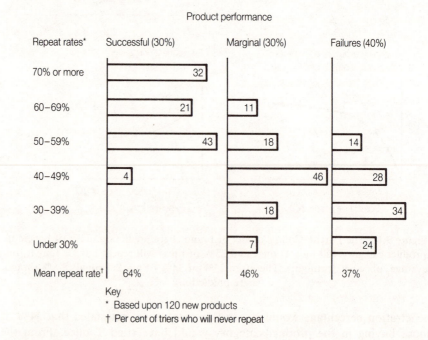

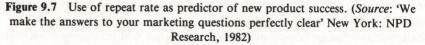

Figure 9.7 Use of repeat rate as predictor of new product success. (*Source*: 'We make the answers to your marketing questions perfectly clear' New York: NPD Research, 1982)

will have a higher market share. A buying level index can be calculated – again from the panel data – for the level of usage of T. If it is purchased more than every fortnight, on average, then a corresponding 'weight' of something more than 1 will increase the estimated 8.5% to an appropriate level. Likewise, if T is bought only (say) half as frequently as other brands, then a buying level index of 0.5 will weight the 8.5% down to the appropriate level (4.25%). In fact, the repeat rate alone is often a good predictor of success, as Figure 9.7, based on 120 products studied by 'NPD Research', demonstrates.

A large number of other models exist which attempt to project these three factors early in the introduction of the new product.

The Fourt–Woodlock model

The earliest of the new product models which attained widespread interest was that of Fourt and Woodlock (1960). This model was intended to predict the market success of grocery products. The first stage in the model attempts to predict penetration (eventual level of trial). It assumes that (a) there is an eventual penetration level (P) and that (b) in each period some percentage of the non-buyers who eventually will buy the product do buy it. The second stage in this model focuses on the repeat ratios, the proportion of initial buyers who repeat purchase once (N_1/N_F), the proportion of first repeat purchasers who purchase a second time (N_2/N_1) and so forth. This stage is used for forecasting sales in the next period, as the sum of new buyers plus first repeaters plus second repeaters, and so on.

This model has proved to be somewhat cumbersome in application. It also assumes that the market is constant in terms of advertising, distribution, pricing, and so on – a very troublesome, albeit useful, assumption.

The Ayer model

Both the Fourt–Woodlock and Parfitt–Collins approaches are based on observing repeat purchasing from panel data. The Ayer model, on the other hand, is based on the notion that the adoption of a product follows a series of stages. More specifically, three main stages are used:

- awareness
- initial/trial purchase
- repeat purchase/loyalty

Using data from several product introductions, this model estimated the relationship between marketing variables and these three variables. This was done by means of three regressions:

Awareness $= a + b_{11}$ (product positioning)
$\quad + b_{12} \sqrt{ \{ \text{(media impressions)(copy execution)} \} }$
$\quad + b_{13}$ (advertising message containing consumer
$\qquad$ promotions)
$\quad + b_{14}$ (category interest) $+ e_1$

Initial
purchase $= + a_2 + b_{21}$ (estimated awareness)
$\quad + b_{22} \{ \text{(distribution) (packaging)} \}$
$\quad + b_{23}$ (if a family brand)
$\quad + b_{24}$ (consumer promotion)
$\quad + b_{25}$ (satisfaction with product samples)
$\quad + b_{26}$ (category usage) $+ e_2$

Repeat
purchase $= f$ (initial purchase, relative price, product satisfaction,
$\qquad$ purchase frequency)

By inputting data to the estimated model, sales projections can be derived. Notice that many of the variables are marketing variables, which is, in some sense, an improvement over the previous models. Notice also, however, that many of these variables (for example, copy execution) must be subjectively estimated thus making the results potentially more subject to researcher bias (Claycamp and Liddy, 1969).

Extensions of Parfitt–Collins

The News model (Pringle, Wilson and Brody, 1982) is advertising agency BBD & O's model for predicting sales of a new consumer product. As such, it competes with Blattberg and Golanty's (1978) Tracker model (used by the Leo Burnett advertising agency). These models use consumer survey data and explicitly include the impact of controllable marketing variables, mainly focusing on advertising as it impacts on awareness and trial. As such, they are extensions of the Parfitt–Collins approach.

The awareness and trial stages of the Tracker model are:

Awareness

$$\ln \left(\frac{1 - A_T}{1 - A_{T-1}} \right) = a - bG_T$$

where:

A_T = cumulative awareness in period T
G_T = gross rating points in period T

Trial

$$T_T - T_{T-1} = \alpha(A_T - A_{T-1}) + \beta(A_{T-1} - T_{T-1})$$

where:

T_T = cumulative trial in period T

The News model awareness stage breaks apart awareness due to advertising and promotion. Similarly, the trial model is also different from Tracker. Experience with the model has been quite good, with predicted share within 1% of actual share when test market data is used as input, and within 2% when only pretest market data is used (Pringle, Wilson and Brody, 1982).

Laboratory experiment based models

Silk and Urban's (1978) ASSESSOR, Burke's BASES, and Blackburn and Clancy's (1980) LITMUS models, use pretest market data to estimate sales. Specifically, ASSESSOR uses a simulated shopping trip following advertising exposure and an in-home use period. In most cases the market share estimates are within one share point of the share observed in the market. With LITMUS, movement from awareness to trial, and trial to repeat, is estimated based on laboratory experiments. These are, not surprisingly, both less expensive and somewhat less reliable than models based on actual market experience. They have grown substantially in popularity during the 1980s.

Other models

A variety of other models exist for forecasting new product sales, including Sprinter (Urban, 1970) and Eskin (1973). A summary of many of these models is available in Kotler (1971), Urban and Hauser (1980), Wind and Mahajan (1981), Narasimhan and Sen (1983) and Shocker and Hall (1986).

In summary, test marketing is a major undertaking, which entails both time and money expenses, as well as a loss of surprise. Given notice of a test market, a competitor will often react by (a) trying to protect sales in the test market area by advertising or promotional programmes, which also serve to confuse the interpretation of the test market; (b) doing whatever possible to mess up the results of the test; and (c) planning a counter-offensive for a possible national launch. Also, there are many cases where test marketing is not practical. For example, any major durable which requires extensive tooling is not suitable for test marketing. For these and other reasons, many researchers and companies use less costly and more controlled alternatives to test marketing.

Component parts of developing new products – or indeed of ongoing developments for existing products – include name and package testing and these are addressed specifically in the next chapter.

REFERENCES

Blackburn J.D. and Clancy K.J. (1980). LITMUS: A new product planning model. In *Proceedings: Market Measurement and Analysis* (Leone R.P., ed.) Providence: Institute of Management Sciences, 182–93

Blattberg R. and Golanty J. (1978). Tracker: An early test market forecasting and diagnostic model for new product planning. *Journal of Marketing Research*, **15**, 192–202

Booz, Allen and Hamilton (1968). *Management of New Products* 4th edn. New York: Booz, Allen and Hamilton

Boyd H., Westfall R. and Stasch S. (1985). *Marketing Research: Text and cases* 6th edn. Illinois: Irwin, p. 723

Bushman F. A. and Robinson R. (1981). Two way TV for new product research. *Business Horizons*, **24** (4), 69–75

Cadbury N. D. (1975). When, where and how to test market. *Harvard Business Review*, May–June, 96–105

Claycamp H. and Liddy L. (1969). Prediction of new product performance: An analytical approach. *Journal of Marketing Research*, **4**, 416

Davis E. J. (1970). *Experimental Marketing*. London: Nelson

Doyle P. and Fenwick I. (1974). How store image affects shopping habits in grocery chains. *Journal of Retailing*, **50** (4), 39–52

Eskin G. J. (1973). Dynamic forecasts of new product demand using a depth of repeat model. *Journal of Marketing Research*, **10**, 115–19

Fourt L. A. and Woodlock J. W. (1960). Early prediction of market success for new grocery products. *Journal of Marketing*, **25**, 31–8

Hill M. (1982). The going gets tough but Ford's still the one to beat. *Marketing Week*, **4** (34), 41–4

Kotler P. (1971). *Marketing Decision Making: A model building approach*. New York: Holt, Rinehart and Winston

Narasimhan C. and Sen S. K. (1983). New product models for test market data. *Journal of Marketing*, **47**, 1124

Parfitt J. H. and Collins B. J. K. (1968). Use of consumer panels for brand-share prediction. *Journal of Marketing Research*, **5**, 131–45

Pringle L. G., Wilson R. D. and Brody E. I. (1982). News: A decision-oriented model for new product analysis and forecasting. *Marketing Science*, **1**, 1–29

Shocker A. D. and Hall W. G. (1986). Pretest market models: A critical evaluation. *Journal of Product Innovation Management*, **3**, 86–107

Silk A. J. and Urban G. L. (1978). Pre-test market evaluation of new packaged goods: A model and measurement methodology. *Journal of Marketing Research*, **15**, 171–91

Urban G. L. (1970). Sprinter Mod. III: A model for the analysis of new frequently purchased consumer products. *Operations Research*, **18**, 805–54

Urban G. L. and Hauser J. R. (1980). *Design and Marketing of New Products*. Englewood Cliffs NJ: Prentice-Hall

Wind Y. and Mahajan V. (1981). A reexamination of new product forecasting models. In *The Changing Marketing Environment: New theories and applications* (Bernhardt *et al.*, eds.), pp. 358–68. Illinois: American Marketing Association

FURTHER READING

Dillon W. R., Madden T. J. and Firtle N. H. (1990). *Marketing Research in a Marketing Environment* 2nd edn. Illinois: Irwin

Ehrenberg A. S. C. (1972). *Repeat-buying: Theory and application*. New York: North-Holland

Lehmann D. R. (1989). *Market Research and Analysis* 3rd edn. Illinois: Irwin

Lin L. and Parkalleskog Y. S. (1984). A state-of-the-art eye movement research. Burke diagnostic package test and print ad test. Paper presented at the ESOMAR Congress, Copenhagen, 17–19 October

Manis R. A. (1984). Name-Calling. *Inc. Magazine*, July, 67–74

Massy W. F. (1969). Forecasting the demand for new convenience products. *Journal of Marketing Research*, **6**, 405–12

Pope J. (1981). *Practical Marketing Research*. New York: AMACOM, 157–58

Young E. C. (1985). Judging a product by its wrapper. *Progressive Grocer*, July

Young E. C. (1987). Packing research – Evaluating consumer reaction. *Strategic Packaging 1987 International Seminar*, September: Toronto, Canada

10

Brand Name and Package Testing Research

The name of a new product and its package design are two integral components which influence ultimate market acceptance. With the advent of self-service retail environments during the last two decades, name and package testing have become more important. Consumer recognition and product visibility are necessarily vital considerations in marketing any product.

Brand name tests

Brand names are important because of the information they convey; the name of a product communicates both denotative and connotative meaning. Denotative meaning refers to the literal, explicit meaning of a name. Connotative meaning refers to the associations that the name provokes or implies beyond its literal, explicit meaning – in other words, the imagery that is associated with a brand name. Specifically, a brand name (a) identifies the product to consumer, retailer, distributor and manufacturer and (b) differentiates the product from competitive products and conveys physical and emotional benefits.

In the current climate of product 'me-too-ism', a dull or otherwise inappropriate name can be a severe handicap, even to a superior product. Recognizing the value of a good name, many companies now make use of commercial names experts.

Philosophy and objectives

Obviously, a brand name should be legible, pronounceable, memorable and distinctive. However, the denotative and connotative meanings associated with a name should be consistent, and should support the overall brand strategy plan and corporate direction. Once a brand name has been decided upon, all of the advertising, packaging and promotional efforts are directed towards implanting the name in the minds and vocabulary of consumers. Thus, probably the last thing manufacturers want to do is change the names of their products, although there have been exceptions, such as Datsun to Nissan and TAP to Air Portugal.

Name testing research is conducted for one or more of the following reasons:

(1) To generate new name ideas.
(2) To measure legibility and pronounceability.
(3) To measure association with product category.
(4) To measure distinctiveness.
(5) To measure relative ability to project strategy – supporting promises of product use and end benefits.

There are many different strategies in developing brand names for products. For example, some companies choose to give meaning to a meaningless name like 'Radion', whereas others choose names like 'Rice Krispies', which literally describe the physical product. Only recently have car names become rational benefit-orientated. For Nissan Motors, the message suggested by 'Sentra' is safety. The public accepts the coined term to be a quality of the product. But good names are not always names at all, for example, '320i' works symbolically well for BMW, denoting cool efficiency.

Another example relates to the genesis of microcomputing. Apple was the first. The marketing challenge back then demanded a symbol of friendliness, trustworthiness and simplicity – concepts of 'non-specific affect'. Thus, an innocuous fruit, irrelevant to technology, was appropriate.

Approaches to naming a product include the following (Pope, 1981).

Company names

Scott Paper and Kraft are examples of companies that attach their corporate names to the products they market. In contrast, other companies, such as Procter and Gamble, follow a strategy of using individual brand names for their products.

Explicit descriptive names

Shake 'N' Vac and Vanish are examples of names meant to describe the physical product.

Line names

These names are assigned to a variety of specific products that the company markets. Persil and Kattomeat are examples of line names.

Implicit imagery names

A common strategy is to use a name that does not literally describe the product, but implicitly and indirectly conveys characteristics about the product. Examples include Domestos and Mr Sheen.

Created names

These names do not have a literal meaning with respect to the characteristics of a product. However, through advertising they may acquire indirect meaning that can reflect favourably on the product. Examples of created names include Flake, KIT KAT and Marlboro.

Designer names

These names are associated with individuals who are leading figures of fashion design. They lend their names to mass-marketed fashionable clothing and accessories, and in some cases even to unrelated products. Examples include Yves St Laurent and Pierre Cardin.

Procedures

There is no one 'right' way to choose a name. Only general guidelines can be offered. To gain some perspective on how names are given to products, consider the story of COMPAQ, Namelab's (a US consulting company) biggest success. The client had ordered up a word that would be memorable and at the same time 'take command of the idea of portableness', something that would distinguish itself from all the other IBM Personal Computer compatibles. Namelab developed a table of basic word parts called 'morphemes', of which 6200 exist in the English language. 'Compaq' was fashioned from two 'messages', one of which indicated computer and communications and the other a small, integral object. The 'com' part came easily. The 'pac' followed with more difficulty, since its phonetic notation included endings in 'k', 'c', 'ch', and, possibly, 'q'. Namelab considered all four of them. When they used 'q' 'paq' was also considered affectively scientific. As a significant benefit, the 'paq' suffix fitted neatly into what could become a product family name: Printpaq, Datapaq, Wordpaq, and the like. Combining a corporate name with a product name results, by mere repetition, in consumer acceptance of substance and reliability. By naming subsequent products 'paq', the company could get added free exposure. It does not cost the company a pound in advertising. Namelab reckoned that the Compaq name would become the dominant symbol for portable computers, like Xerox is the symbolic identity for copiers (Manis, 1984).

A very general procedure for creating a list of new names is to:

(1) list objectives and benefits of the brand strategy and corporate direction statement;

(2) list appropriate synonyms and antonyms;

(3) combine appropriate objectives and benefits with appropriate synonyms and antonyms to produce a list of 'promising' words, prefixes and suffixes.

It is good practice never to test a new name in isolation. At least two alternatives should be tested for comparison. Note that reactions to a given name may be affected by the other names in the test, therefore, you should exercise extreme caution when comparing the results of one name test with that of another name test.

Interviewing practices

The format for presenting names to respondents is quite simple. Each new name is placed on a separate card and the respondent is exposed to either the entire set of names (cards) or a limited set. Actually, the respondent is shown a concept statement containing one of the test names and a brief description of the product. If a brand strategy has been agreed upon, the product statement should be strategically orientated. The order of the names is rotated from respondent to respondent in order to dampen position-bias (sometimes referred to as order effects). After exposure to each name, the respondent is typically asked to read and pronounce the name and answer other questions.

Questions asked

Typically name tests collect information on:

(1) *Legibility and pronounceability* Respondents are asked to read and pronounce one new name at a time, for example, 'How *do you* pronounce ECOVER?'

(2) *Association* Respondents are asked to associate the name with a product category. For example, typical questions are: 'What type of product do you think this is?' 'Which one of the products on this

card do you most associate with (name)?' 'Which others do you associate with it?'

(3) *Distinctiveness* Respondents may be asked to indicate the level of distinctiveness of the new name by asking such questions as: 'What brand(s) does this (name) most remind you of and why?' 'Who do you think manufactured it, and why?'

(4) *Imagery and end benefits* Respondents are asked to use semantic differential scales to describe the new name/product. In such cases the respondent will be shown a concept statement containing one of the test names and a brief description of the product. Note that product descriptors should:
    (a) adequately cover all of the important end benefits.
    (b) focus on product-orientated issues, such as 'smooth', as opposed to name-orientated issues, such as 'sounds good'.
    (c) be consistent with brand strategy and corporate direction statements.
    The set of scales can also be used for a competitive product or for a respondent's ideal brand.

Frequently the name given to a product is that of a celebrity (for example, *'Paloma'* perfume). In so-called designer or celebrity name studies, interest is focused on:

(1) *Familiarity* How familiar is the celebrity to the target segment?

(2) *Appropriateness* Respondents are asked to indicate the appropriateness of the celebrity and the product category.

(3) *Imagery* Respondents are asked to use semantic differentials to describe the imagery of the celebrity.

As an example, consider these issues with regard to Brut's (by Fabergé) use of Gazza (the footballer, Paul Gascoigne) in selling their aftershave and cologne. The use of Gazza is clearly consistent with all three criteria.

Sampling practices

Standard practice is to use a minimum of 100 product category users per name variation and no less than 50 respondents for a subgroup analysis. Specific age and gender (sex) quotas may also be imposed, based on total category volume contribution or national census estimates.

Action standards

Various criteria for name evaluation can be used. Performance criteria include:

(1) The relative importance of the various measurements.

(2) The relative importance of the various descriptors and associations.

(3) The resources available to develop a creative name, that is, to render a 'meaningless' name 'meaningful' (Dillon, Madden and Firtle, 1990).

Although the specific criteria for name evaluation will vary, it is important to explain them clearly.

Approach to analysis

Typically, the approach to analysing the information collected in name tests is straightforward. First, new names are screened for their legibility and pronounceability. Names that respondents have difficulty reading or pronouncing are generally not candidates for further consideration. With respect to the association, distinctiveness, imagery and end benefits data, the typical approach is to use one- or two-tailed tests of proportions and means. A one-sample proportion test is a test of the hypothesis that a proportion is equal to some prespecified value. When using a one-sample test of means we want to test if a sample mean is equal to, greater than, or less than some hypothesized mean value of a particular population.

By way of summary, Figure 10.1 presents an example of a marketing research proposal for a new name test.

Package tests

The package design is one of the most important marketing components for a product. A package serves several basic functions, it:

(1) Contains, protects and dispenses the product.

(2) Provides point-of-purchase advertising.

(3) Serves as an attention-getting device.

(4) Provides a reminder to current users.

(5) Is a source of information about directions, ingredients and potential cautions.

(6) Provides a vehicle for announcing promotions and special deals.

(7) Promises physical and emotional end benefits.

(8) Encourages purchase.

There are some very good reasons for focusing on the efficiency of a package. The package is the one piece of information that every consumer sees. In fact, it has been estimated that an average package in the supermarket

Name Test

Brand: SLIMBAR diet chocolate
Project: SLIMBAR sugarless chocolate

Background and objectives:
The product group has available five objective alternative brand names for the SLIMBAR diet chocolate product. The objective of this test is to determine if any of the alternatives offer greater potential than the SLIMBAR name in terms of communicating the appropriate product category and conveying a favourable brand image.

Research design:
A total of 300 respondents will be interviewed in a central location. All respondents will be past 30-day users of diet foods or confectionery. Age and sex specifications will be as follows:

Males   45%   Aged 18–24   20%
Females   55%   Aged 25–34   30%
                          Aged 35–49   30%
                          Aged 50+   20%

Each respondent will be exposed to three of the six names (five test names and the SLIMBAR name), and will evaluate each brand name in terms of product associations. The respondent will be exposed to the remaining three names and will evaluate each in terms of brand image. Thus, each name will be evaluated by a total of 150 respondents. The purpose of exposing different names in the two phases of the interview is to separate the brand image ratings from the respondent's preconceptions about the names occurring in the initial product association section. The order of the names will be rotated from respondent to respondent in order to dampen position bias.

Information to be obtained:
This project will provide information on the degree of association with the product category on both aided and unaided bases, and an image profile on each brand name tested on the semantic differential scales.

Action standard:
The research group will recommend the brand name that generates the highest ratings on the critical attributes of (in order of importance):

For me/Not for me
Tastes good/Does not taste good
Natural taste/Artificial medicinal taste
Sugarless/Contains sugar
and which shows adequate association (50% very/somewhat appropriate) with the product category.

Cost and timing:
The cost for this research project will be £28,000 (+10% contingency), and we will adhere to the following schedule:

Fieldwork   – 2 weeks
Data analysis – 2 weeks
Final report   – 2 weeks

Selected supplier:
TESTMAR Marketing Research.

Figure 10.1   Marketing research project proposal: Brand name test.

generates approximately 15 billion exposures per year (Young, 1987). A number of facts about today's shoppers and the shopping environment also point to the importance of packaging and other point-of-purchase displays. For example:

- Estimates indicate that the average supermarket contains over 17,000 items; of that amount, 2300 new products are introduced each year.
- The average shopper is spending approximately 30 minutes on his or her normal shopping trip, which translates as 1800 seconds in which to consider the 17,000 items (Young, 1987).

Can packaging and point-of-purchase displays make a difference? Surely one simply has to look at the influence that packaging and point-of-purchase displays have had on the success of such brands as Kodak, Ariel Liquid, Andrex toilet rolls and kitchen towels, Cadbury's Cream Eggs, Mars Milk, Kellogg's Variety Pack and Bird's Eye children's products to realize that there is more to the product than its physical contents. Table 10.1 presents some comparative data on the relevance of packaging for a new product.

The importance of package design is exemplified by the North American Philips Lighting Corporation's strategy. Studies of consumer buying habits and eye-tracking studies of prototype package designs preceded the selection of the new package design, which brings a unified, colour-coded, family appearance to the product line. The studies also found that consumers view the new packaging graphics as attractive, contemporary and aesthetically pleasing. Consumers also perceive the packaging as representing a high-quality product and a brand they can trust. Philips has converted to a four-bulb pack to appeal to its primary customers – women, most of whom work and who prefer larger packages.

Revamped packaging is not the only tool in NAPLC's arsenal to capture consumers' attention. The company is extending use of its unique 'shape of quality' in the line. The high-quality soft white bulbs are being converted to this distinctive T-shape. Philips is confident that consumers will come to recognize

Table 10.1 The relevance of packaging for a new product.

	A poor package	A good package (%)	Difference
Visibility on the shelf	39	59	−20
Interest in trial	13	48	−35
Negative comments	81	31	−50
Looks appealing	28	82	−54
Good value for money	40	55	−15
Attractive	3	30	−27

(*Source*: Young E. C. (1985). Judging a product by its wrapper. *Progressive Grocer* (July)

these distinctively shaped bulbs as a symbol of their quality. (*Source*: *Marketing News*, 22 November, 1985, p. 26.)

Put simply, an effective package:

- Is simple.
- Quickly communicates what the product is.
- Makes use of focal points.
- Stands out from the competition.
- Makes selection within a product line easy.
- Has the right quality impression.
- Reflects the image of the product.

Philosophy and objectives

Obviously, the package design must work; however, other aspects of the package must be tested as well. Most consumer goods package tests are conducted for the following purposes:

(1) To assess the visibility of package alternatives, relative to one another and usually relative to a competitive brand.

(2) To assess the ability of package alternatives to convey perceptions of physical and emotional end benefits.

(3) To assess the believability of claims.

(4) To assess the effectiveness of the package in stimulating trial.

(5) To assess how functional the package is and whether there is any confusion concerning either the label or instructions.

Procedures

The procedures related to package-testing research are somewhat more involved than those used in name tests. Exposure to the package and measurement of its visibility and image must be carefully controlled. A package design should never be tested in isolation because a package alternative that may have high visibility scores when tested alone can lose its impact when placed among competitive products. In addition, when testing packages designed for established products, the product's current package design should be included in the test as a control.

Control over exposure to package alternatives is sometimes accomplished by using slides and a tachistoscope (T-Scope). Slides allow greater control over exposure to the shelf space than if an actual display was used. The use of the T-Scope allows the researcher to control light intensity and exposure duration. Although package alternatives could be tested in actual store environments, either in test markets or in simulated test markets, this is rarely done. The substantial practical and cost considerations involved in producing the product in several different packages generally preclude this approach. There are also some problems with using the T-Scope procedure. In the context of testing packaging and other point-of-purchase displays, the T-Scope has three primary deficiencies:

(1) The time the researcher chooses to show each package is largely arbitrary – it is unimportant in package testing that package A communicates better than package B in one-fifth of a second.

(2) Familiar brands are generally identified faster. If the T-Scope procedure is used, new brands are therefore at a severe disadvantage.

(3) For a product to win the T-Scope 'contest', the designer must simply put the product logo in big, bold letters in the centre of the package.

For these reasons some researchers have moved from the T-Scope procedure to what is called the *find test* (Findability Tests) when evaluating packaging. Findability tests are aimed at:

(1) Measuring the length of time a respondent searches for a product name to assess ease and time of find.

(2) Providing initial exposures to measure the 'impression retention' of a package.

(3) Acquiring diagnostic information to assess what image the package conveys.

The rationale behind such a procedure is that a strong package should be easy to find and should elicit an appropriate image. If a findability test is used, the shopper is asked to look at a cluttered in-store shelf scene and find specific products. Again, the assumption behind the test is that the package that can be found fastest is the most effective.

Eye-tracking methods do overcome some of the problems of using the T-Scope procedure. Technological advances in fibre optics, digital processing and advanced electronics have moved the eye movement research field away from the old days of 'eye cameras' and heavy equipment with bite bars and forehead restraints. Today, lightweight equipment is used, and, typically, a minicomputer paces the stimulus material for the respondent and records and displays eye movement automatically through a dual disk-drive system.

A description of the eye-tracking procedure is as follows. The individual views a screen onto which 35 mm slides are projected. Each person is provided with a remote control switch, the switch permits him or her to control viewing time. The eye-tracker device records each participant's visual experience. The tracker simultaneously pinpoints where the respondent is looking and superimposes that point directly onto the material being viewed. The tracker device is able to determine not only where the respondent looks, but how long he or she stays on a particular point.

Eye-tracking information is recorded directly onto computer tape for data processing. This allows for a continuous record of the visual response as it takes place. Some tracking devices have the capability of recording sixty eye movements per second. It can also be placed on videotape for client viewing.

For analytical purposes, a software program depicts the test item in terms of individual components. These components can be modified at any time for additional analysis. For shelf display work, each package on a shelf may become a component.

The movement of the eye is charted from the time the test item is first viewed until the time the viewing is terminated. Accordingly, there is a record of the viewing sequence, the time given to each item and, most importantly, those areas that are quickly bypassed or totally overlooked. Eye-tracking shows stopping power.

As indicated in Table 10.2, eye-tracking measurement methods have considerable advantages over early electronic measurement devices such as the tachistoscope, which varied the amount of time (for example, $\frac{1}{10}$ of a second, $\frac{3}{10}$ of a second and so on) a visual image was exposed to the subject, thereby attempting to simulate split-second duration of a consumer's attention in much the same way that a package might in part of a mass display.

In this eye-tracking measurement context, respondents would see close-up pictures of packages, including the test design, for a time period controlled by the respondent. Eye movements are recorded on the extent to which each element on the package (for example, brand name, product type illustration, list of ingredients and so on) is noted, the speed of noting, the sequence of viewing, the clarity of the copy and the time spent. In the case of eye-tracking procedures, elements of a package that are quickly bypassed or totally overlooked can be easily identified.

Table 10.2   Advantages of eye-tracking technology.

T-Scope	*Eye tracking*
Sensitivity subject to selected exposure duration	No requirement to select exposure duration
	Continuous measurement
Discrete measurement	Stable across greater range of lighting conditions
Highly sensitive to lighting conditions	
No ability to determine scan path	Ability to determine scan path

(*Source*: Lin L. and Parkalleskog Y. S. (1984). A state-of-the-art eye movement research Burke diagnostic package test and print ad test. Paper presented at the ESOMAR Congress, Copenhagen, 17–19 October)

Because slides are used to project pictures of the various package alternatives, the location must allow for total darkness (with the exception of a safety light), and it should include a partitioned-off interviewing area where respondents cannot overhear one another. The projector is usually placed 3 metres (and respondent, 2.4 metres) from the viewing screen. Before exposure to a test slide, each respondent is shown a 'dummy' slide so that they fully understand the procedure.

When the test begins, the respondent is exposed to one test variant that shows a picture of an alternative package among those of other products that appear in its normal environment; in other words, the test is monadic and no respondent is exposed to more than one test variant. The pictures of the test variants are projected from standard 35 mm slides. The slides are constructed so that their longest dimension is on the horizontal, to depict an actual store environment. Pictures are taken against light-grey backgrounds to control colour effects. Typically, there are about 8 to 12 evenly distributed products per slide and to minimize bias three random layouts of each test variant are used. Respondents are exposed to each slide at four different intervals: $\frac{1}{8}$ second, $\frac{1}{4}$ second, $\frac{1}{2}$ second and 1 second. After each exposure, the respondent indicates to the interviewer which brand he or she has seen. When imagery and end benefits data are needed, the respondent is escorted to a separate area and shown the product. The product can be displayed in a number of different formats; for example, the respondent can be shown a story board, the actual product or a 35 mm slide.

Questions asked

Package tests typically focus on the following areas:

(1) *Brand imagery* Respondents are asked to describe with, say, semantic differential scales, their impressions of the product.

(2) *Aesthetic appeal* Does the respondent like the package? Is it pleasant to look at? Is it the kind of package that generates interest?

(3) *Functional characteristics* Respondents are asked to evaluate the functional aspects of the package. Does it prevent contamination or damage? Does it provide a convenient means of storing and dispensing the product?

(4) *Likes and dislikes* Generally open-ended questions that allow the respondent to express spontaneous reactions to the package and product.

(5) *Purchase interest* Questions designed to demonstrate degrees of commitment or resistance to trial.

(6) *Product usage and demographics* Respondents are asked to provide category usage data along with standard demographic information.

Package Test

Brand: Carlton Crackers
Project: Carlton melba toast test

Background and objectives:
The brand group has three possible package designs for a new melba toast product that Carlton plans to roll out nationally. The objective of this test is to determine which package design is superior with regard to registering the Carlton brand name, conveying end benefits that are associated with freshness and quality, and initiating trial.

Research design:
A total of 450 respondents (150 per package alternative) category users will be recruited and interviewed at a central testing location. All respondents will have purchased melba toast or French toast in a supermarket for themselves or a member of their family within the past 30 days. Respondents will be seated at an eye-tracking recorder and will take a visual walk through a supermarket. Slides will include a series of in-store displays with one display showing the test package. Respondents will be asked to pick one of the packages. The respondent can take as much or as little time as needed with each slide.

Information to be obtained:
Eye-tracking will determine precisely which brands a shopper looks at in a display and in what order. It will record how quickly each brand draws attention, the number of times a respondent looks at a particular package and the total time the respondent spends with facings on the shelf. After exposure to the store slides, recall questions will be asked to determine how the package helps to register the brand name. Additional questions will be asked, focusing on:

(1) Beliefs about product freshness and quality.

(2) Brand image.

(3) Aesthetic appeal.

(4) Purchase intent.

Action standard:
The brand group will recommend the package that:

(1) Registers the highest brand name recognition.

(2) Generates the highest top-box scores on freshness and quality.

(3) Generates the highest top-box intention scores.

Cost and timing:
The cost for this research project will be £34,000 (+10% contingency), and we will adhere to the following schedule:

Fieldwork   – 2 weeks
Data analysis – 2 weeks
Final report   – 2 weeks

Selected supplier:
MECHCON Research Services.

Figure 10.2   Marketing research project proposal: Package test.

Sampling practices

Standard practice is to use a minimum of 100 category users per test variant and no fewer than 50 respondents for a subgroup analysis. As in name testing, specific age and gender requirements may be established.

Action standards

Various standards for package test evaluation can be used. Performance standards include:

(1) Whether the package must be equal to, or have greater visibility than, the current package designs or competitive packages.

(2) Whether the package must equal or achieve better ratings on key attribute/end benefit scale.

(3) Whether visibility or image is to receive the greater weight in making the analysis (Dillon, Madden and Firtle, 1990).

Approach to analysis

The analysis focuses on the visibility and image measures. As in name testing, visibility and image scores are usually tested across alternative package designs with a test of proportions and means.

By way of summary, Figure 10.2 presents a prototypical marketing research proposal for a package test study.

We now turn to other elements of the marketing mix. In the next chapter the application of marketing research to studies in pricing research is investigated.

REFERENCES

Dillon W. R. Madden T. J. and Firtle N. H. (1990). *Marketing Research in a Marketing Environment* 2nd edn. Illinois: Irwin

Manis R. A. (1984). Name-calling. *Inc. Magazine*, July, 67–74

Pope, J. (1981). *Practical Marketing Research*. New York: AMACOM, 157–8

Young E. C. (1985). Judging a product by its wrapper. *Progressive Grocer*, July

Young E. C. (1987). Packing research – Evaluating consumer reaction. *Strategic Packaging 1987 International Seminar*, September. Toronto, Canada.

11

Price Research

Pricing research

Price, as an element of the marketing mix, communicates various meanings to the market. Research may evaluate alternative price approaches for new products before launch, or any proposed changes once on the market (Gabor, 1977). For example, multiple retailers are in a good position to evaluate different price levels, by conducting before–after experiments, perhaps using other branches as controls. The argument of 'reality', as applied to test marketing, also applies here and has been further supported by Stout (1969), who found that trying products at different prices in actual stores produced far more discriminating results than trying them in an artificial store (a form of 'hall' test). It was also better than showing respondents pictures of the products at different prices and asking for probable purchase intentions.

According to Krauser (1982), there are two general approaches to pricing research. The first is the well-established Gabor and Granger method (1966). Here, different prices for a product are presented to respondents (often by using test-priced packs) who are then asked if they would buy. A 'buy–response' curve of different prices with the corresponding number of affirmative purchase intentions is produced.

Krauser describes a second approach in which respondents are shown different sets of brands in the same product category, at different prices, and are asked which they would buy. This multi-brand choice method allows competitors' brands to be taken into account by respondents – as they normally would outside such a test. As such, this represents a form of simulation of the point of sale.

Monroe and Bitta (1978) have provided a comprehensive listing of price decision models for researchers.

Decisions concerning the price range for a new product have to be made early in the development stage. A product concept cannot be tested fully, for example, without providing an indication of the price of the product. When the product is ready for introduction, a decision has to be made about the specific price of the product. Decisions concerning changing prices – Should we change price and if so, in what direction and by how much? – will then need to be made over the life of the product.

There are two general pricing strategies that can be followed. The first is a profit-orientated strategy, in which the objective is to generate as much profit as possible in the present period. The other is a share-orientated strategy, which has as its objective the capturing of an increasingly larger share of the market. This is accomplished, in so far as pricing is concerned, by entering the market at a low price and continuing to reduce price as increasing volume results in lowered production costs. Some potential profits in the early stages of the product life cycle are forgone in the expectation that higher volumes in later periods will generate sufficiently greater profits, so that over the life of the product the highest overall profits will result.

There is a substantial difference in the information required for pricing under the two strategies. It follows that pricing research for the two different approaches differs substantially in terms of information sought.

Profit-orientated pricing

The manager using a profit-orientated pricing strategy is attempting to price the product at the point at which profits will be the greatest until changes in market conditions or supply costs dictate a price change. The optimal price using this strategy is the one that results in the greatest positive difference in total revenues and total costs. This means that the researcher's major tasks are the forecasting of these two variables over the relevant range of alternative prices.

Research for cost forecasting is described in the section on share-orientated pricing. In this section we concentrate on describing methods of predicting quantities that will be sold according to prices set.

There are eight general methods of demand estimation: judgement (the Delphi technique), statistical analyses of sales data, surveys, value analyses, laboratory experiments, simulated test markets, sales tests and simulations.

The Delphi technique

A formalized way of obtaining the expressed judgements of a number of persons involved in the pricing process is to use the Delphi technique. It consists of a series of rounds of predictions made by the participants, each prediction being made anonymously and turned over to an administrator. The method consists of:

(1) Having the participants make separate forecasts (point, interval, probability distribution, or some combination of the three).

(2) Returning forecasts to the analyst, who combines them using a weighting system.

(3) Returning the combined forecast to the forecasters.

(4) The forecasters make a new round of forecasts with this information.

This process is continued until it appears that further rounds will not result in an added degree of consensus.

The underlying premises on which the Delphi method is based are (a) that successive estimates will tend to show less dispersion and (b) that the median of the group response will tend to move towards the true answer. Convergence of the group estimates is almost invariably observed. The critical issue is whether the movement is towards the true value.

It is desirable to obtain interval estimates from the participants of the quantities that will be sold at each price. This serves two purposes:

(1) It identifies the probable upper and lower limits of the quantities that will be sold at each price.

(2) It serves as an indication of whether additional information is needed before the decision is made.

If optimistic, pessimistic, and most likely estimates are obtained and these estimates, both for each participant and between participants, show only limited differences, the implication is that additional information would have little value – that is, no additional research may be needed. If, conversely, there is wide dispersion in the individual and/or combined estimates, the need for additional research is indicated. For this reason, it is appropriate to use the Delphi technique before carrying out other research for a specific pricing decision.

Statistical analysis of sales data

Price changes over time and price differentials between sales territories result in natural experiments. The level of one important variable affecting sales is changed (usually) without meeting all of the conditions of a true experimental design. The result is sales data that reflects the effect of price changes as well as that of changes in other causal variables.

Statistical analysis of sales data is useful for helping to sort out the effects of price versus that of other variables on quantities sold. The principal technique employed is regression analysis. It is inexpensive and can be carried out in a relatively short time. Consumer panel data lend themselves particularly well to regression analysis to determine the sales effects of price changes, because both prices paid (at retail) and quantities bought are reported. This eliminates the problems imposed by the time required for the effects of price changes made by the marketer to work their way back through the distribution channel to the point where they affect the manufacturer's sales.

Two actions can be taken by marketers to improve the quality of the inferences that can be drawn about price effects on past sales. The first is that, whenever it is reasonable to do so, price changes can be made between territories such that the changes conform to the requirements of an experimental design. Changes can be made in a few territories that are randomly chosen, for example, and the rest of the territories will serve as a control group. If this makes sense from a business standpoint, that is, it is believed necessary to make a change in a marketing programme in response to a change in market demand and/or a competitor's programme, such action comes at essentially no cost and has all the advantages of a field experiment.

The second thing that can – and should – be done to obtain better information from past sales data on price effects is to keep a log of significant marketing events that occur in each territory. If competitors raise prices, lower prices, run special promotions, introduce new products, add sales offices, or increase advertising, their actions may well affect your sales. Similarly, an extraneous event, such as a factory in the area closing down, a strike affecting the availability of products in the area or the like, will also affect sales. In order to interpret historical sales data more accurately, a record of the time and nature of all events likely to affect sales is essential.

Surveys

A commonly used method for research on pricing decisions is the conduction of a survey. Questions such as, 'By how much would your sales increase (or decrease) if prices were lowered (or increased) to . . .?' are asked of both sales representatives and distributors. Consumers are queried on the perceived effects of relative price changes on their brand preferences and intentions to buy. Price surveys are subject to all the sampling and non-sampling errors associated with surveys in general. The measurement error inherent in most price surveys is a particularly acute one, however. In addition to the estimation errors present in the responses of salespersons and middlemen when asked, 'How much would your sales change if . . .?', there is a substantial potential for bias. Sales commissions and distributor profits are affected by price levels, and the respondents from both groups are well aware that this is the case. Responses may be shaded in a favourable direction as a result.

Consumers are typically unable to give reliable responses to direct questions about how prices affect their brand preferences and purchases. A purchase decision is made up of many considerations, of which price is only one. In general, to ask consumers to assess the effect of the price variable alone is to be highly optimistic about their abilities both to evaluate and to verbalize the role that price plays in their decisions.

Conjoint analysis avoids this problem. Price is usually included as one of the characteristics used to describe the concept in concept tests in which conjoint analysis is employed. Conjoint analysis to test for the effects of price changes on sales of existing products can be made as well. Conjoint analysis, like multi-dimensional scaling (MDS), is concerned with the measurement of psychological judgements, such as consumer preferences. However, one of the main distinctions between the two sets of methods is that in conjoint analysis the stimuli are designed beforehand, according to some type of factorial structure. Typically, conjoint analysis deals with preference (and other dominance type) judgements rather than similarities. However, more recent research has extended the methodology to similarities judgements.

In conjoint analysis the objective is to decompose a set of overall responses to factorially designed stimuli, so that the utility of each stimulus component can be inferred from the respondent's overall evaluations of the stimuli.

The solution technique involves a type of analysis of variance, in which the respondent's overall preferences serve as a criterion variable and the predictor variables are represented by the various factorial levels making up each stimulus. The major difference is that in the non-metric version of conjoint analysis, the criterion variable is only ordinally scaled. A second difference is that in problems of realistic size the researcher often employs fractional (rather than full) factorials in conjoint analysis. Two principal methods for collecting conjoint analysis data are in use.

Two-factor evaluations Perhaps the simplest way to obtain trade-off information for conjoint analysis involves a two-at-a-time procedure. The respondent is asked to rank all the combinations of stimuli (product/service attributes) from most to least preferred. The problem, then, is to find a set of utility numbers within all pairs of trade-offs. These utility numbers are often called part-worths.

Having found the part-worths, we could then construct a predicted set of utilities for all the possible two-way tables, by adding the separate part-worths to find the total utility of any two-factor combination. The entries in each of the prediction tables could then be ranked so as to provide a counterpart set of tables. The objective is to find the separate utility numbers so that the correspondence between actual and predicted ranking is highest, when considered across all pairs (actual versus predicted) of tables.

Multiple-factor evaluations Eighteen cards, in all, are made up according to a special type of factorial design. Highly fractionated factorial designs are pretty much a necessity if the researcher wishes to keep the stimulus set down to some reasonable number. Orthogonal arrays represent a special type of fractional design that allows for orthogonal estimation of all main effects (the type of model assumed in additive utility formulation) with the smallest possible number of combinations. The respondent is then asked to group the

18 cards into three piles (with no need to place an equal number in each pile) that are described as:

- definitely like
- neither definitely like nor dislike
- definitely dislike.

Following this, the respondent takes the first pile and ranks the cards in it from most to least liked, and similarly so for the second and third piles. By means of this two-step procedure, the full set of 18 cards is eventually ranked from most liked to least liked. Again, the analytical objective is to find a set of part-worths for the separate factor levels so that, when these are appropriately added, one can find a total utility for each combination. The part-worths are chosen so as to produce the highest possible correspondence between the derived ranking and the original ranking of the 18 cards.

The multiple-factor evaluative approach makes greater cognitive demands on the respondent since the full set of factors appears each time. In practice, if more than six or seven factors are involved, this approach is modified to handle specific subsets of interlinked factors across two or more evaluation tasks.

Analysing the data

Since both the two-factor and multiple-factor approaches utilize similar computational procedures, let us illustrate the solution technique with the multiple-factor version. You should note the following features of this approach:

(1) The respondent is presented with a set of stimulus profiles, constructed along factorial design principles.

(2) The respondent ranks the stimuli according to some overall criterion, such as preference.

(3) The problem is to find a set of part-worths for the factor levels such that the sum of each specific combination of part-worths equals the total utility of any given profile.

(4) The goodness-of-fit criterion relates to how closely the derived ranking of stimulus profiles matches the original ranking.

The main analysis also yields a useful by-product, namely, the relative importance of each of the factors used in the experimental design. The dependence of utility on factor levels underscores the need to choose realistic ranges for each of the factors under study.

Wherever possible, visual props can help in transmitting complex information more easily and uniformly than verbal description. Visual props work particularly well for the multiple-factor approach, since a relatively large amount of information can be communicated realistically and quickly by this means.

The output of conjoint analysis is frequently employed in additional analyses. Since most studies collect full sets of data at the individual respondent level, individual utility functions and importance weights can be computed. This fosters two additional types of analyses: (1) market segmentation and (2) strategic simulation of new factor-level combinations. Frequently, both kinds of analyses are carried out in the same study. A specific type of conjoint analysis – categorical conjoint measurement – is specially tailored and appropriate for market segmentation purposes.

In segmentation studies, the respondents are usually clustered in terms of either their commonality of utility functions or their commonality of importance weights. Having formed the segments in one of these ways, the analyst can then determine how the segments differ with regard to other background data – product-class usage, brand-selection behaviour, demographics and so on.

In addition to single, *ad hoc* studies, conjoint measurement can be used in the ongoing monitoring (via simulation) of consumer imagery and evaluation over time.

An example of a question displayed on a microcomputer in a conjoint analysis pricing study of an existing product is shown in Figure 11.1.

Value analysis

Value analysis for pricing involves assigning a monetary value to quality differences, feature differences, and differences in service provided, so that a net differential relative to competitor prices can be established.

An example is an auxiliary computer-processing unit recently developed by a company that had not previously been in the computer field. Connected to the central processing unit of most large computers, it permits up to twice

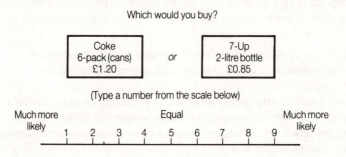

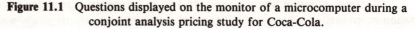

Figure 11.1 Questions displayed on the monitor of a microcomputer during a conjoint analysis pricing study for Coca-Cola.

the amount of computing to be carried out with it as without it. Before setting the price on the unit, information was developed by the marketing research department on how many of the host computers were being used in (a) quantities of two or more by the same company, and (b) in single machine installations that are supplemented by one or more additional smaller computers, or that have time-sharing arrangements on another computer. By estimating the costs to the users of each of these arrangements, a price-potential market schedule was developed. The price was then set at a level which matched the estimated quantities to be sold with the company's production and marketing capabilities.

Laboratory experiments/simulated market tests

Laboratory experiments on pricing generally involve a simulated 'store' in which prices are changed experimentally and the level of purchases of the products participating in the experiment is measured.

Some marketing research firms that conduct such experiments for clients have trailers fitted out as supermarkets. Some simulated test market services also use a laboratory type store to test for the effects of price and other variables on the purchase rates of prospective new products. Some researchers have experimented with simulated 'shopping trips', in which subjects are given a certain amount of money and allowed to purchase well-known products from assortment sheets on which prices were experimentally varied.

Laboratory experimentation is a relatively inexpensive and quick method for estimating demand for a product at various prices. Its use is largely limited to existing products, however, as it is difficult to simulate both introductory promotional campaigns and buying conditions in a psychologically realistic manner.

The question of psychological realism (which is impaired by reactive error) is critical in evaluating laboratory pricing experiments. That is, will participants make buying decisions on the same basis in a laboratory store as they would in an actual purchasing situation? If not, the results of a laboratory experiment are not likely to be a valid predictor of operating results.

Sales tests

A standard market test is one in which a sample of market areas – usually cities – is selected and the product is then sold through regular distribution channels, using one or more combinations of product, price and promotional levels. A number of techniques, particularly cluster analysis, can be used to assist the researcher in selecting both representative and equivalent test areas.

A disadvantage of standard test marketing is its cost. A primary goal for most test marketing programmes is to project market response, typically sales, from the test area to the entire market. This normally requires that the test area potential market be a minimum of 2% of the total market potential. Because trial rates and repeat purchases are the keys to projecting test-market sales, the test must be long enough to ensure that both of these elements are measured. If the purchase cycle lasts more than a few weeks, several months is a minimum length of time for the test, and a year or more may be required to provide reasonably reliable data. The cost of market tests of adequate size and time often exceeds £500,000 and sometimes is as much as £5 million.

Standard test markets will continue to be widely used, though less frequently and for shorter time periods than in the past. The primary reason for their continued use is the high cost of new product failure coupled with the difficulty of projecting new product success (or other marketing mix changes) without standard test markets.

To overcome some of the problems associated with standard market tests, controlled-store and minimarket tests are being used with increasing frequency. In controlled-store and minimarket tests, a market research firm handles all the warehousing, distribution, pricing, shelving and stocking. The research firm typically pays a limited number of outlets to let it place the product in their stores.

In a controlled-store test a few outlets in several areas are utilized. A minimarket test involves enough outlets to represent a high percentage (usually 70%) of the all-commodity sales volume in a relatively small community. In a controlled-store test, media advertising typically cannot be used because of the limited distribution of the product. The minimarket test partially overcomes this problem but increases the cost and visibility of the test.

These methods offer several important advantages over standard test markets. First, it is virtually impossible for competitors to 'read' the test results since the research company is the only source of sales data. Second, the tests are somewhat less visible to competitors, though most controlled stores and minimarkets are actively observed. Third, they are substantially faster since there is no need to move the product through a distribution channel. Finally, they are much less expensive than standard test markets.

Controlled-store tests and minimarkets are often used as a final check prior to standard test markets. The essentials of these descriptions apply to the testing of the sales response to different prices. One aspect of sales tests, as they apply to pricing, is that often competitors 'jam' sales tests of prices by not reacting at all. They recognize that a sales test of prices is taking place and do not react. If it is a market test that is being conducted and data from a syndicated consumer panel service is being used to measure the results, the competitors will generally be receiving the same data as the testing company. Thus, it is to the competitors' advantage not to react, as the information will be useful to them in helping to decide what action to take should the sponsoring company decide to change prices after the test is run.

Either the deliberate jamming of sales tests involving prices by competitors who run 'deals' or special promotions during the test, or jamming by not taking any action at all, are shortcomings of sales tests of prices. They should be kept in mind, both in deciding to run the test and in projecting test results to the actual marketing situation.

Simulation

As distinct from testing price in a simulated test market, a price simulation uses only a model of the purchase situation rather than data from an experimental procedure. The use of simulation for researching administered pricing decisions has been limited.

By contrast, price simulations are routinely run by many companies for competitive bid pricing. Competitive bidding models have been developed that use data on winning past bids of important competitors as a ratio of the estimated cost for the same project of the company using the model. This allows a probability distribution to be developed, and a determination of the bid price can be made that will give the maximum expected profit.

Competitive bidding is used for pricing a surprisingly large proportion of non-consumer product items such as fleets of cars, oil and gas well drilling, custom machining, food service contracts, construction projects, and virtually all government purchase contracts are awarded on the basis of competitive bids. Simulation of competitive bid prices is, therefore, an important part of pricing research.

Share-orientated pricing

A requisite for the successful use of share-orientated pricing is that average unit production costs continue to go down as cumulative output increases. For some products, this reduction takes the form of an experience curve. An experience curve is a cost curve such that each time the accumulated output doubles, the total cost per unit goes down by a fixed percentage. An example is provided by the cost history of video cassette recorders. Each time the output for the industry has been doubled, unit costs have declined on average by about 20%.

Experience curves are commonly referred to by the complement of the unit cost reduction percentage. The formula for determining unit cost for a point on the experience curve is:

$$UC_i = UC_1 \times i - b = \frac{UC_1}{i^b}$$

where:

UC_i = unit cost of the nth unit
UC_1 = unit cost of the first unit
$\quad i$ = number of cumulative units produced
$\quad b$ = a constant determined by the level of experience

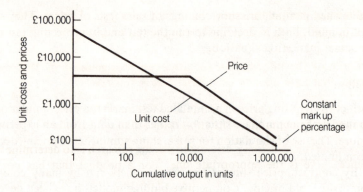

Figure 11.2   Share-orientated pricing.

All costs are included in the applicable cost data; marketing, engineering, production and overhead costs are all included. The only variable in the formula that varies with the level of experience curve is *b*. For example, for an 80% curve, b is 0.322, whereas for a 90% curve it is 0.152.

When plotted with cumulative output on log paper, unit production costs that follow an experience curve fall on a straight line (as shown in Figure 11.2).

The pattern of pricing that is followed for the purpose of increasing market share is to:

(1)   Enter the market at a price that is substantially below cost.

(2)   Hold the entering price constant until unit costs have fallen to the point that a desired percentage mark-up on cost is being obtained.

(3)   Reduce price as costs fall to maintain mark-up at the same desired percentage of costs.

The pricing pattern is illustrated in Figure 11.2.

Research for share-orientated pricing

Share-orientated pricing decisions require information that is either not required or is different in nature from the information required for more traditional pricing. In this section we describe the types of information required to:

(1)   Determine the nature of the experience curve.

(2)   Estimate break-even points.

(3)   Determine cost of units sold to additional market segments.

(4)   Estimate competitor costs.

(5)   Forecast the 'decline' stage of the product life cycle.

Some of the information required can be generated by the research techniques that have already been described in this text.

Determination of the level of the experience curve

The first requirement in share-orientated pricing research is to determine which experience curve is the appropriate one. For a product that has not been manufactured by the company before, it is necessary to rely on experience with a similar product or on the experiences of other companies.

For a product which has a cost history, the applicable experience curve can be calculated from the appropriate accounting data. It is often useful to consider first the unit costs of each of the discrete activities that collectively comprise the overall unit costs of the product, and to calculate an experience curve for each of them. This procedure will tend to disclose the sources of the cost savings. This information allows an analysis of the likelihood of the present rate of savings continuing. In short, the aggregated costs per unit at the various cumulated output levels can then be used in the determination of the overall experience curve level.

Estimating break-even points

In business analyses for potential new products, it is almost always desirable to estimate the output at which break-even will occur. A common procedure in making such an estimate is to assume that average variable costs are constant over the range of output and to calculate the break-even volume by the formula:

$$V_{BE} = \frac{FC}{P - AVC}$$

where:

V_{BE} = break-even volume
FC = fixed costs
P = price
AVC = average variable cost

By definition, for products for which an experience curve is applicable, the assumption of constant costs per unit is not valid. It is therefore necessary to use a different mathematical relationship to estimate the break-even volume. This point can be determined by setting the price equal to UC^i and solving for *i*. For example, if the price of a new product is set at £5.00, the first unit cost is estimated at £65.00 and the applicable experience curve is 80%, how many units must be sold before the unit cost will be equal to price?

Unit value   The formula for determining unit cost for a point on the experience curve is:

$$UC_i = UC_1 \times i - b = \frac{UC_1}{i^b}$$

where:

UC_i = unit cost of the $n$ith unit
UC_1 = unit cost of the first unit
   i = number of cumulative units produced
  b = a constant determined by the level of experience

   Applicable cost data should contain all costs; marketing, engineering, production and overhead costs are all included.

   UC_1 = £65.00, $b_{80\%}$ = 0.322 (from experience curve table-unit values)
   UC_i = £5.00

Substituting into formula:

$$£5.00 = \frac{£65.00}{i^{0.322}}$$

Rearranging:

$$i^{0.322} = \frac{£65.00}{£5.00} = 13.0$$

Raising both sides to the $\frac{1}{0.322}$ power gives:

$$(i^{0.322})\frac{1}{0.322} = 13.0\frac{1}{0.322}$$

$$i = 2883$$

Determination of cost of units solds to an additional market segment

Managers frequently need to determine the incremental costs of serving a new market segment in order to establish a price for that segment. Examples are sales for private branding, a bid on a government contract, or selling abroad. Estimates of the incremental costs can be made using the average cost formula given below.

Average values   The formula for determining average cost between points on the experience curve is:

$$AUC_h^i = \frac{UC_1}{1-b} \frac{[(i+0.5)^{1-b} - (h+0.5)^{1-b}]}{i-h}$$

where:

AUC_h^i = average unit costs over the range of output from h units to i units
UC_1 = unit cost for the first unit
b = constant for the learning curve being used

Estimating competitor costs

If market share data is available, the cumulated level of output of the major competitors can be estimated. This in turn allows an estimate of unit and average unit costs for each competitor to be made, given as assumed experience curve level and first unit costs.

Reasonable assumptions can be made about competitors' experience curves from knowing the level of one's own curve and general information about the relative level of automation, marketing effort and wage rates. Reliable estimates of competitor costs are particularly useful in competitive bid pricing. They are also useful in administrative pricing situations in gauging the likelihood of each competitor following suit when a price reduction is being contemplated. The formulae necessary for calculating competitor costs are the same as for one's own company.

Forecasting the declining stage of the product life cycle

An integral part of market share price strategy is the 'cashing in' or 'harvesting' of share in the form of higher prices shortly before and during the decline stage of the product life cycle. There is no purpose in continuing to build share when it would be more profitable for the remainder of the life of the product to sacrifice share in return for increased profits resulting from higher prices.

Forecasting the timing of the downturn of the market for a specific product is, in most cases, a difficult task for managers to do with the requisite accuracy. The decline may come as a result of technological developments that result in better and/or less expensive products that replace those presently on the market. CDs replacing LP records, and HDTV (high-definition television) technology replacing the majority of currently-owned television sets, are two examples of technological developments resulting in the obsolescence of existing products. The decline may also come about through changes in market demand; for example, there is now limited demand for lead additives for gasoline.

The general methods of making technological forecasts are the same as those for sales forecasting: judgemental, time series analysis and projection, and causal. Judgemental methods include: (1) monitoring; (2) the Delphi technique; and (3) historical analogy. Time series analysis and projection methods include: (1) dynamic modelling and (2) morphological analysis.

Using judgement in applying the experience curve to pricing

The experience curve is only a mathematical relationship that has been found to describe the association between unit costs and cumulated outputs of many, but by no means all, companies. There is no necessary assurance that because costs have gone down in the past by a fixed percentage each time cumulative output has doubled they will continue to do so in the future.

Judgement must be used in applying the experience curve to pricing before present prices are set at a low level relative to costs, with the expectation of setting in motion the 'increasing share – lowering unit costs – making higher profits later' chain of events. Sometimes the expected cost reductions do not materialize. For example, the Douglas Aircraft Company established the price of the DC-9 on the assumption that unit costs of the aircraft would follow an 85% experience curve. Costs did not go down that fast and the resulting losses were so severe as to become a major reason for the later merger with McDonnell Aircraft.

Outside factors can also affect the market in such a way as to negate low prices as a means of gaining share.

Having examined pricing research, we now move on to a discussion of marketing research within the sales and distribution area of marketing.

REFERENCES

Gabor A. (1977). *Pricing: Principles and Practices*. London: Heinemann
Gabor A. and Grainger C. (1966). Price as an indicator of quality. *Economics*, **33**, 43–70
Krauser P. (1982). How to research prices. *Management Today*, January, 50–3
Monroe K. and Bitta A. (1978). Models for pricing decisions. *Journal of Marketing Research*, August, 413–28
Stout R. G. (1969). Developing data to estimate price–quality relationships. *Journal of Marketing*, 33, 34–6

FURTHER READING

Blair E. (1983). Sampling issues in trade area maps drawn from shopper surveys. *Journal of Marketing*, **14**, 98–106
Breheny M. J. (1988). Practical methods of retail location analysis: a review. In *Store Choice, Store Location and Market Analysis* Neil Wrigley N. (ed.). London: Routledge
Craig C. S., Ghosh A. and McLafferty S. (1984). Models of the retail location process: a review. *Journal of Retailing*, **60**, 22
Goodchild M. F. (1984). ILACS: A location-allocation model for retail site selection. *Journal of Retailing* **60**, 84–100
Martell D. (1987). Marketing information and new technology. In Piercy N. *Management Information Systems: the technology challenge*. London: Croom Helm, pp. 161–84

12

Sales and Distribution Research

Many companies undertake distribution channel and plant and warehouse location studies. In addition, chain and franchise operations devote considerable efforts to retail outlet location research. Still, the decision made most frequently with respect to distribution channels concerns the number and location of sales representatives. In this chapter we will discuss research in these areas.

Number and location of sales representatives

How many sales representatives should there be in a given market area? There are three general research methods for answering this question. The first, the sales effort approach, is applicable when the product line is first introduced and there is no operating history to provide sales data. The second involves the statistical analysis of sales data and can be used after the sales programme is under way. The third involves a field experiment and is also applicable only after the sales programme has begun.

Sales effort approach

A logical, straightforward approach to estimating the number of sales representatives required for a given market area is to:

(1) Estimate the number of sales calls required to sell to and to service prospective customers in an area for a year. This will be the sum of the number of visits required per year 'Vi', to each prospect/customer 'Pi', in the territory, or

$\Sigma_{i=1}^{n} Vi\,Pi$, where n is the number of prospects/customers

(2) Estimate the average number of sales calls per representative that can be made in that territory in a year, $\bar{c}$.

(3) Divide the estimate in statement (1) by the estimate in statement (2) to obtain the number of sales representatives required, R. That is:

$$R = \frac{\Sigma_{i=1}^{n} Vi\,Pi}{\bar{c}}$$

Statistical analysis of sales data

Once a sales history is available from each territory, an analysis can be made to determine if the appropriate number of sales representatives are being used in each territory. An analysis of actual sales versus market potential for each sales representative may yield a relationship of the kind shown in Figure 12.1.

If so, further analysis will very likely indicate that areas in which the average market is less than X_1 per sales representative have too many representatives, and those with average market potential of more than X_2 have too few sales representatives.

The statistical analysis of sales data to determine how many sales representatives to use in each territory is closely analogous to the analysis of sales data for setting advertising budgets by market area. In general, the same advantages and limitations apply in both applications.

Field experiments

Experimentation concerning the number of calls made is usually desirable. This may only involve more frequent calls on some prospects/customers and less frequent calls on others with a net balancing that leaves the total number

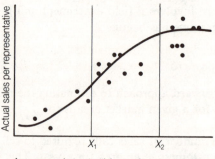

Figure 12.1   Actual sales versus market potential per sales representative.

of calls per year – and the number of sales representatives – in the territory unchanged. Or it may be desirable experimentally to increase the numbers of representatives in some territories and to decrease them in others to determine sales effects.

Again, the design of the experiment(s), and the advantages and limitations of conducting them for determining the appropriate number of sales representatives for each territory, are very similar to those for conducting experiments to help determine the appropriate advertising budget per market area.

Computerized models of salesforce size and allocation by market and by product line

There are a number of computerized models, spreadsheet and others, for determining salesforce size, and for allocating the salesforce by market and by product line. When management is considering using a formal model to assist in making salesforce-related decisions, marketing research often becomes involved in one or more of three ways:

(1) determining what models are available and in recommending which one, if any, should be adopted;

(2) in developing the data needed to operate the model selected (market potential by product and by market, desirable call frequencies by class of customer, and so on;

(3) operating the model.

The model selected should be valid and require data that can be obtained at a reasonable cost. A workable approach to testing the validity of a model is to do run analyses with it under different conditions and see how it performs. A first step is to run the model with actual salesforce data from the past two or three years and to see if it replicates the actual sales overall (and, depending upon the model, by sales territory and product as well) reasonably accurately. After making any necessary calibrating adjustments, the model's 'predictions' and the actual results ought to be reasonably close. Following that, one should set up and run a range of cases that might actually occur. An examination of the model's output for each of them, and a determination of whether or not they seem reasonable, will give a further check on the model's probable validity. Finally, one should try extreme cases. What happens if the salesforce in total is made redundant? Do orders, revenues and expenses all fall to zero (or near zero) over an appropriate time period? What happens if the salesforce is suddenly doubled? Does the increase in predicted orders and expenses over the next few periods appear reasonable?

Data requirements are also an important consideration in the choice of a model. For example, one model requires estimates of sales response functions for each sub-area of each sales territory. If there were currently 100 territories each with 10 sub-areas, estimates of 1000 response functions would be required. If these were to be arrived at empirically, a formidable amount of data collection and analysis would be required.

Warehouse location research

Warehouse location decisions are important because they have substantial effects on both the costs and the time required for delivery of products to customers. The essential questions to be answered before a location decision is made are, 'What costs and delivery times would result if we chose location A? Location B?' and so on through the list of potential locations being considered.

In answering these questions on anything other than a judgement basis some form of simulation is required. It can be a relatively simple, paper-and-pencil simulation for the location of a single warehouse in a limited geographic area, or it can be a complex, computerized simulation of a warehousing system for a regional or national market.

Centre-of-gravity simulation

The centre-of-gravity method of simulation is frequently used for locating a single warehousing site. It is a method for finding the approximate location that will minimize the distance to customers, weighted by the quantities purchased.

To illustrate the method, assume that (1) five retail stores are located as shown in Figure 12.2; (2) stores 1 and 5 each buy, on the average, one ton of

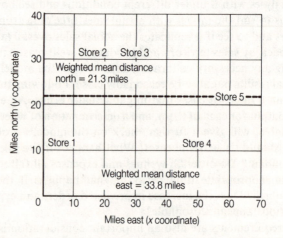

Figure 12.2 Centre of gravity warehouse location to serve five retail stores.

merchandise per year, and stores 2, 3 and 4 each buy an average of two tons per year; and (3) straight-line distances (measured on the grid lines) are the appropriate ones for estimating transportation costs and delivery times.

The procedure for determining the location that will give the minimum weighted average distance from the warehouse to the customers is as follows:

(1) Compute the weighted mean distance north* (y coordinate) from the zero point for the stores:

Distance × weight = weighted distance
Store 1   10 miles × 1 ton = 10 ton-miles
Store 2   30 miles × 2 tons = 60 ton-miles
Store 3   30 miles × 2 tons = 60 ton-miles
Store 4   10 miles × 2 tons = 20 ton-miles
Store 5   20 miles × $\frac{1}{8}$ ton = $\frac{20}{170}$ ton-miles

*weighted mean distance north = $\frac{170}{8}$ = 21.3 miles

(2) Compute the weight mean distance east* (x coordinate) from the zero point for the stores:

Distance × weight = weighted distance
Store 1   10 miles × 1 ton = 10 ton-miles
Store 2   20 miles × 2 tons = 40 ton-miles
Store 3   30 miles × 2 tons = 60 ton-miles
Store 4   50 miles × 2 tons = 100 ton-miles
Store 5   60 miles × $\frac{1}{8}$ ton = $\frac{60}{270}$ ton-miles

*weighted mean distance east = $\frac{270}{8}$ = 33.8 miles

(3) The location giving the minimum weighted average distance from the customers is the point for which the two weighted means are the coordinates. For the example, the location indicated is 33.8 miles east (x) and 21.3 miles north (y) of the zero point.

A single centre-of-gravity calculation provides an approximate location of the least cost and least delivery time location for a single warehouse. The greater the symmetry of customer locations and weights, the more nearly the initial calculation approximates the optimal location. The location indicated by the first calculation can be checked to determine if it is optimal (or near optimal) by using a 'confirming' procedure. If it is not, successive calculations can be made as necessary to 'home in' on the optimal location (Van Auken, 1974).

The confirmation procedure is as follows:

(1) Calculate confirming coordinates x, y using the formulae:

$$x = \frac{\sum\limits_{j=1}^{n} \frac{x_j W_j}{V_j}}{\sum\limits_{j=1}^{n} \frac{W_j}{V_j}} \qquad y = \frac{\sum\limits_{j=1}^{n} \frac{y_j W_j}{V_j}}{\sum\limits_{j=1}^{n} \frac{W_j}{V_j}} \qquad \text{(12.1)}$$

Where x_j and y_j are the coordinates of the jth customer, W_j the weight for that customer and V_j, the distance of the customer from the point defined by the coordinates obtained from the centre-of-gravity calculation is calculated using the equation:

$$V_j = [(x_j - x_g)^2 = (y_j - y_g)^2]^{\frac{1}{2}}$$

(2) If the centre-of-gravity coordinates and the confirmation model coordinates are the same (or nearly the same) no further calculations need be made. If they are not reasonably similar, replace the centre-of-gravity coordinates with the initial confirmation model coordinates and calculate a second set of confirmation coordinates.

(3) Repeat step (2) as necessary until the new confirmation coordinates match the coordinates being confirmed.

The location of a new warehouse is constrained by the sites that are available near the desired location. Once the desired location has been determined through centre-of-gravity and confirmation procedure calculations, the weighted delivery costs should be calculated for each alternative site. In these calculations allowances can be made for such factors as taxes, wage rates, cost and quality of transportation services, reduction in unit costs for volume shipments and the tapering of transportation rates with distances shipped.

Computerized simulation models

Although the centre-of-gravity method is an adequate method in most situations for locating a single warehouse, it is not designed to cope with the complexities involved in determining how many warehouses should be used and where they should be located in an overall regional or national distribution system. A computer is required to work on multiple warehouse location problems because of the large amounts of data that have to be processed for each of the many possible configurations of numbers and locations of warehouses.

The central concept involved in computer simulations for this purpose is very simple. Data that describes the customer characteristics (location of plants, potential warehouse sites) and distribution costs (costs per mile by volume shipped, fixed and variable costs of operating each warehouse, the effect of shipping delays on customer demand) are developed and read into the computer. The computer is then programmed to simulate various combinations of numbers and locations of warehouses and to indicate which one(s) gives the lowest total operating cost. Some very effective results have been achieved by using computer simulations for designing distribution systems.

The role of marketing research in such simulations is typically to validate the simulation model and to develop the data needed to operate it. As in the case of validating salesforce decision models, the first step in the validation procedure should be to compare historical data with the model's predictions for some previous year. Warehouse locations, warehousing costs, transportation rates and demand data for the year can be entered and the model's predicted costs can be compared with the actual costs. A second step is to run sensitivity analyses by making changes in the historical data (adding/substracting a warehouse, moving the location of a warehouse, increasing the fixed cost of operating warehouses), such that the model outcomes are at last qualitatively predictable. For example, increasing the fixed costs of warehouses should result in reducing the optimal number of warehouses in the computer solution. A third step is to run extreme cases (large changes in the overall level of demand, sizeable shifts in the geographic pattern of demand, substantial increases/decreases in transportation rates) to see if the model solutions seem reasonable.

The data that must be developed to operate the model includes customer location (usually given by latitude and longitude), forecast sales volumes by customer, forecasts of the effects of shipping delays on demand, freight rates and in-transit times. Surveys and/or judgements are normally required to evaluate the probable effects of delays in shipping on demand. Freight rates and delivery times are available from secondary sources.

Retail outlet research

Most of the research conducted by retailers on product assortments, prices and advertising is similar to that conducted by manufacturers. However, two aspects of research related to retail distribution require separate treatment: (1) research for catchment area analysis and (2) research for outlet location decisions.

Catchment area analysis

Suppose you manage a chemist store located in a regional shopping centre. You are considering a direct mail advertising campaign. How would you decide where to send the advertisements?

This is just one of several uses for trading area data. Others include its use to evaluate a store's or shopping centre's market positioning, measure competitive customer bases, determine potential of new locations and evaluate regional retail chains and acquisition plans (Paris and Crabtree, 1985).

Formal models have been developed which can be used to predict the trading area of a given shopping centre or retail outlet based on relative size, travel time and image (Huff and Batsell, 1977; Stanley and Sewell, 1976). A variety of other techniques can also be used to establish trading areas. An analysis of the addresses of credit card customers can provide a useful estimate of the trading area. This method assumes that credit customers and non-credit customers live in the same general areas. Cheque clearance data can be used to supplement this information.

The best, but also the most expensive, way of establishing trading area boundaries is to conduct surveys to determine them. Shopping centre intercept surveys are commonly conducted for this purpose. When information on market potential and market penetration is desired, the shopping centre intercept survey needs to be supplemented by a survey of non-shoppers at the shopping centre or store. The non-shopper surveys are often conducted by telephone, with screening to eliminate shoppers. To avoid selection bias when merging the two samples, appropriate weightings based on shopping frequencies must be used (Rothenberg and Blankenship, 1980; Blair, 1983).

Outlet location research

Individual companies and, more commonly, chains, financial institutions with multiple outlets, and franchise operations, must decide on the physical location of their outlet(s). The cost and inflexible nature of the decision makes it one of critical importance.

Three general methods are in use in selecting specific store sites. The first is the analogous location method. This method involves plotting the area surrounding the potential site in terms of residential neighbourhoods, income levels and competitive stores. Regression models have been used for location studies for a variety of retail outlets including banks, grocery stores, liquor stores, chain stores and hotels (Craig, Ghosh and McLafferty, 1984). Data for building the model and for evaluating new potential locations is obtained through secondary data analysis and surveys.

Multiple regression models can be used to generate a relationship between store turnover and a range of store, population and competitor characteristics. The advantage of multiple regression analysis is that the relationship between turnover, as the dependent variable, and a range of independent variables can be assessed more systematically. Multiple regression analysis allows more complex relationships to be investigated. Numerous variables, and even forms of model, can be adopted and tested very quickly.

The multiple regression equation will take the following form:

$$Y = a + bx_1 + bx_2 \ldots bx_m + bx_{m+1} \ldots bx_m \qquad (12.2)$$

store	catchment area
characteristics	characteristics

where *Y* is store turnover, or only flowing to a store outlet from a zone and the *x*s are independent variables, split in this case into those concerned with the characteristics of each store (typically store size, car parking facilities and so on) in the analogue group and those concerned with the characteristics of the catchment area (population and competition). This approach can then be used in forecasting turnover for a proposed store.

A typology of multiple regression models for store-turnover forecasting is put forward here. Breheny (1988) suggested that three basic types of *store viability model* can be developed from multiple regression analysis.

(1) Model I, with store turnover as the dependent variable, regressed against the aggregate characteristics of the defined catchment area of each store in the analogue group.

(2) Model II, with expenditure flowing from each defined area to the store as the dependent variable. This model will produce a single equation to be applied to each area within the catchment area at a proposed store.

(3) Model III, again with expenditure flowing from each area as the dependent variable, but an equation developed for each of a number of typologies of areas. Typologies will reflect distinct differences in customer behaviour towards the stores in question. There will be as many equations as there are typologies.

Figure 12.3 attempts to illustrate the differences between the three models.

Model I: Each observation is an outlet trade area. The single regression equation estimates turnover for a new trade area.

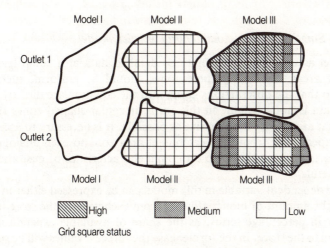

Figure 12.3 Three forms of multiple regression model.

Model II: Each observation is a grid square. The single regression equation estimates turnover for grid squares within a new trade area.

Model III: Each observation is a grid square, but grid squares are grouped into different types. A regression equation is calculated for each type of grid square, and turnover is estimated for each grid square using the appropriate regression equation.

Model I: Single equation catchment area and model

The obvious disadvantage of Model I is that it fails to make use of the detailed variation in the relationship between consumer spending and population/competition characteristics shown up at the zonal level.

In Model I, the values of the independent variables will usually be averages for the whole of the catchment area (for example, percentage of population of certain age group, percentage in specific social group). For each variable there will be one measure for each analogue store, and hence as many values as there are analogue stores. If, as is likely, population data is available at a zonal level when other data is not, a slight variation on the model is possible. Population by a number of distance bands around each store might be included as independent variables. The model can be assessed by forecasting the turnover of an established store which is similar to those used in the analogue group and for which data is available.

One possible variation on Model I is to develop equations not for the whole catchment area of stores but for graded catchment areas, or 'primary, secondary or tertiary markets' (Applebaum, 1968). Summation of the results of forecasts for each area would give store turnover. This approach does, however, imply availability of more detailed information on the geographical origin of store turnover and on catchment area characteristics.

Model II: Single equation, zonal characteristics model

This model assumes the availability of detailed data at a zonal level within catchment areas. Preferably these zones should be uniform, such as grid squares, so that the observations going into the equation are directly comparable. If data is not available in this form, irregular shaped zones should be defined that are as near equal in size as possible. It is necessary to ascertain the flow of expenditure from each catchment area zone to each analogue group store. Information on the socio-economic characteristics of customers might also be useful.

The dependent variable in this model can be expressed either in absolute terms, as the amount of money flowing from each zone to the store in a given period, or in percentage terms, as the share of available expenditure in the zone drawn to the store. In the former case the forecast values will be summated to give store turnover. In the latter case the summation will take place after the percentage figures have been multiplied by an estimated zonal retail expenditure figure.

The assumption behind Model II, and one that should be rigorously tested, is that the spending and socio-economic characteristics of the customers reflect the consistent behaviour of all residents of that zone with regard to the store in question. This is important because information gathered on flows of expenditure will be related back to the total population; for example, the money spent by socio-economic group X from a particular zone might be calculated as a proportion of the estimated total available retail expenditure of that socio-economic group in that zone. In using the model for forecasting we would then need estimates of available retail expenditure by socio-economic group by zones around the proposed store.

In addition to data on customer and zonal characteristics, details of competitors in the area of each analogue store are required. Simple measures, such as the total number of competitors within so many miles, may be used, or more sophisticated measures devised. Model II improves considerably from Model I in offering the possibility of much more sensitive measures of competition. Model II differs from Model I in that it develops an equation based on the detailed zonal variation in the relationship between money spent in the store and zonal characteristics, rather than an aggregate relationship. A single equation will be produced for the analogue grouping. Clearly, a major independent variable in Model II will be the distance of a zone from the store.

An important variant on Model II, which in fact takes it towards Model III, removes distance from the equation. This variant, which we might call Model IIA, takes a number of distance- or time-bands around the store (say five or ten minutes) and develops a regression equation for each. The advantage of this version of Model II is that in the basic form distance is so dominant as a variable that it tends to disguise the possibly important role of other independent variables. Model IIA treats distance explicitly by using time-bands, but outside the equations.

Model III: Typology equations, zonal characteristics model

This model is in principle the most sophisticated of the three, in that it aims to make the best use of the variability in the data available. The approach is similar to Model IIA described above, except that the grouping of zones is done more systematically according to their socio-economic characteristics. The idea behind the model is that certain groups in the population can be identified, each of which has distinct patterns of shopping behaviour in relation to the store in question. Regression equations developed for such groupings/typologies should then be more informative than general equations.

There are various ways in which such typologies of zones could be produced. Standard area classifications could be used. For example, the

ACORN system of classification (CACI, 1981) gives, at the most detailed level, 39 socio-economic classifications into which any small area (grid square) can be allocated. If such classifications are considered relevant, then each zone in the catchment area of each store in the analogue group can be allocated to a typology. CACI, for instance, can provide an ACORN profile of a catchment area ('SITE' analysis) together with the 'index of usage' (based on TGI data) for each ACORN group in the catchment – in terms of their usage of the products or services sold by the retailer concerned. This overall index can be the weighting factor for the more generalized regional statistic of product/service usage (perhaps based on Family Expenditure Survey data). See Figure 12.4. Regression equations can then also be developed, as in Model II but for each typology.

A further alternative approach might be to develop a classification more directly related to knowledge of the socio-economic characteristics of customers of a particular type of store, using surveys.

Having defined typologies in one of these ways, the development of Model III would be the same as that for Model IIA. There will be as many equations as typologies. The dependent variable could be absolute flows of expenditure to a store type, or proportion of available expenditure in each zone. The independent variables representing store characteristics will again be identical for each zone and for each typology. In using the model for forecasting, each zone around the proposed store will be allocated to a typology and will then have the appropriate equation applied to it. Again, zonal values will be summed to give forecast store turnover. It is the information gathered for the stores in the analogue groups that will determine the quality of the resultant

ACORN type in catchment area	% Population	×	ACORN index for taking foreign holidays	=	TOTAL
5 (Modern private housing, medium status)	20.6	×	98	=	20.2
16 (Peripheral low income local authority estates)	7.4	×	34	=	2.5
31 (Medium status inter war private housing)	26.1	×	124	=	32.4
32 (Established high status suburbia)	30.1	×	128	=	38.5
34 (Very high status areas)	15.8	×	202	=	31.9
	100%				125.5

Market potential = 1120 × 1.255 = 1406

Suppose 14% of the national population take foreign holidays and the catchment area of the travel agency is 8000 people. The assumed market potential on this basis would be 8000 × 14% = 1120.

Figure 12.4 Market potential measured by ACORN. (*Source*: Adapted by the authors from CACI (1981))

model. The larger the number of stores in an analogue group the better for statistical reasons.

The third type of model, the so-called location allocation model, encompasses a number of associated techniques that are used to allocate demand to each potential site/store design combination (Goodchild, 1984).

'Location–allocation' models are concerned with the location of facilities and the allocation of consumers, population or trips to those facilities. Other models are based on notions of spatial interaction and gravitation in which allocations of consumers will be on a probability basis, reflecting the distance-decay effect away from centres and the preferences of shoppers.

The gravity model has existed for a long time and it has proved its worth in helping to explain certain types of human spatial behaviour. Gravity theory holds that more people will travel from a particular origin to a given destination than will travel to a more distant destination of the same type and size. Distance, according to gravity theory is a deterrent to travel and empirical evidence supports such a relationship in urban settings. The so-called retail gravitation models use two variables, distance and mass (for example, store size), to explain consumer spatial behaviour (Mayo *et al.*, 1988). Several studies confirm that the effect of distance will in fact vary by product class (Papadopolous 1980; Williams 1981).

Breheny (1988) has identified two main types of location techniques:

Research focus	Research methodology
Customers	Identify catchment area; geographic definition of boundaries. Run competition to get addresses of customers for this purpose. Observation and interview to discover 'profile' of customers. Perhaps image study using semantic differential to make comparisons with competitors. Possibly research customer self-image versus store image for degree of congruence.
Market size and market potential	Based on catchment area, use electoral registers to calculate number of potential customers, then consult Family Expenditure Survey to estimate potential revenue in that region for products stocked, or use ACORN analysis of catchment area.
Competitors	Observation of competitors' merchandising, pricing, service policies, etc.
Advertising and pricing	See promotion and pricing research in chapters 11 and 13.
Merchandising	Observation of competitors' merchandise, plus feedback from customers. Also, see experimental design and stock control systems (such as laser scanners) for identifying sales of different lines.
Locating new branches	In addition to the above: approach local authorities for possible development plans. Gravitation models (for example Reilly's Law). A location will draw residents who are between shopping centres in direct proportion to the populations of the two centres, and in inverse proportion to the square of the distances they are from each centre.

Figure 12.5 Distribution research.

(1) Store-turnover forecasting techniques which are most useful where retail performance is a function of the location of outlets and where the market is outlet-dominated. They may also be useful in a relatively specialized sector of retailing where there is a large number of outlets, as in the case of building societies.

(2) Spatial marketing techniques which are most useful where the performance of an outlet is more dependent on being in the right general location, with the right socio-economic structure, than on local catchment area characteristics.

A sales forecasting model must be sufficiently flexible to allow the consideration of various development options (that is, alternative store sizes, product ranges, store formats and so on) at particular sites and to facilitate an assessment of the vulnerability of the location/investment decision. Nevertheless, there is a distinction between simply collecting information and applying that knowledge strategically.

By way of conclusion, Figure 12.5 summarizes some of the aspects of distribution research focus and methodology.

REFERENCES

Applebaum W. (1968). *Store Location Strategy*. Reading Mass: Addison-Wesley

Blair E. (1983). Sampling issues in trade area maps drawn from shopper surveys. *Journal of Marketing*, **14**, 98–106

Breheny M. J. (1988). Practical methods of retail location analysis: a review. In *Store Choice, Store Location and Market Analysis* Wrigley N. (ed.). London: Routledge

CACI (1981). *ACORN: A New Approach to Market Analysis*. London: CACI Ltd

Craig C. S., Ghosh A. and McLafferty S. (1984). Models of the retail location process: a review. *Journal of Retailing*, **60**, 22

Goodchild M. F. (1984). ILACS: A location–allocation model for retail site selection. *Journal of Retailing*, **60**, 84–100

Huff D. L. and Batsell R. R. (1977). Delimiting the areal extent of a market area. *Journal of Marketing Research*, **14**, 581–5

Mayo E. J., Jarvis L. P. and Xander J. A. (1988). Beyond the gravity model. *Journal of the Academy of Marketing Science*, **16**, (3 and 4), 23–9

Papadopolous N. (1980). Consumer outshopping research, review and extension. *Journal of Retailing*, **56**, 41–58

Paris J. A. and Crabtree L. D. (1985). Survey license plates to define retail trade area. *Marketing News*, **19**, 12

Rothenberg M. J. and Blankenship A. B. (1980). How to survey trading areas. *Journal of Advertising Research*, **20**, 41–50

Stanley T. J. and Sewell M. A. (1976). Image inputs to a probabilistic model: Predicting retail potential. *Journal of Marketing*, **40**, 48–53

Van Auken S. (1974). The centroid locational model: a study in situational dependency. *The Logistics and Transportation Review*, **2**, 149–63

Williams R. (1981). Outshopping: Problem or opportunity?. *Arizona Business and Economic Review*, **7**, 8–11

FURTHER READING

Beswick C. A. and Cravens D. (1977). A multi-stage decision model for sales force management. *Journal of Marketing Research*, May, 135–44

Boyd H. W. Jr., and Massy W. F. (1972). *Marketing Management*. New York: Harcourt Brace Jovanovich, Inc.

Lodish L. M. (1980). A user-oriented model for sales force size, product, and market allocation decisions. *Journal of Marketing*, **44**, 70–8

Stanger W. M. (1985). How to test sales model validity. *Business Marketing*, **70**, 90, 94, 96

Tull D. S. and Hawkins D. I. (1987). *Marketing Research – Measurement and Method* 4th edn. New York: Macmillan

13

Promotion Research

This chapter continues our coverage of 'applications' of marketing research techniques and approaches within the marketing mix. Specifically, we are concerned here with the 'promotion' element and because this is fundamentally based on the nature and processes of marketing communications, this is where we will start.

The communication process involves the following:

- The source or sender of the message.
- The message.
- The communication channels used to convey the message to the receiver(s) (not to be confused with distribution channels).
- The receiver(s) or audience at whom the message is directed.

This communication process can be seen more clearly in Figure 13.1.

The source has to decide what to say (encoding) and then try to convey the message in the right way so that receivers (the single most important element in the communication process) properly decode it. The success of the communication is measured in terms of the feedback to the source and the extent to which the receiver decodes or interprets the message in the manner intended. Research implications of this approach involve the following:

(1) Number, location and type of receiver(s).
(2) Levels of awareness possessed by them.
(3) Influences upon the receiver which affect the acceptance of the message.

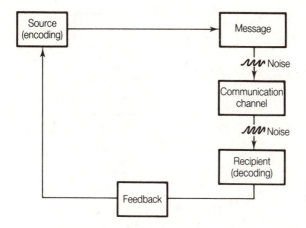

Figure 13.1 A communication process.

This suggests that the range of focus of promotion research is indeed quite wide. Perhaps a helpful framework is to consider promotion research as being concerned with the following: promotional objectives, message decisions and media decisions.

Promotion objectives

Researching existing levels of 'awareness', 'cognitions', 'emotions' and 'intentions' or 'image' dimensions for the advertiser's product or service may form the basis of the objectives of the campaign. For example, misconceptions might be identified and considered desirable to correct. Then, the same dimensions can be remeasured after the campaign to assess its effectiveness.

Taking this even further, integrating factors such as the ones just mentioned into a 'sequential model' of the marketing communications process might also be a useful framework for both strategic and tactical promotional decisions. One of the most basic of these sequential approaches is the AIDA (attention – interest – desire – action) framework. A similar, but more detailed version refers to the stages leading through the adoption process (awareness – interest – trial – evaluation – adoption) for which the innovators and early adopters progress more quickly than the late majority and laggards. Indeed, these approaches were considered important by such writers as Colley (1961) who discussed hierarchies of advertising effects in the context of defining advertising goals for measured advertising results (the Dagmar model).

The AIDA framework (Figure 13.2) consists of four fundamental and inter-related promotion tasks which have been recognized for many years:

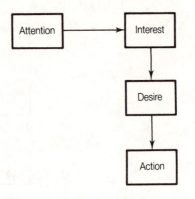

Figure 13.2   AIDA model.

(1)   To gain attention. Obtaining attention is obviously necessary if the potential customer is to become aware of the company's offering.

(2)   To hold interest. Holding interest gives the communication a chance to really build the prospect's interest.

(3)   To arouse desire. Arousing desire favourably affects the evaluation process.

(4)   To obtain action. Obtaining action includes encouraging trial and subsequent adoption. Continuing promotion is needed to confirm the adoption and assure continuing action.

The hierarchy of effects model

This model (Figure 13.3) is slightly more sophisticated in that it recognizes the existence of two additional steps in the process before the recipient becomes a purchaser.

In this model, the recipient is seen to move from an awareness of the product's existence to a knowledge of the product's attributes. From there, recipients progress to a liking for the product, a preference for that product above the others available, a conviction as to the value of that product for them, to the eventual stage of purchasing the product.

We can see from Figure 13.4 that:

- *PR/publicity* is generally more effective at the awareness stage.
- *Advertising* becomes less effective in the later stage of the buyer response process.
- *Personal selling* becomes more effective as the consumer needs dictate a more personal relationship.
- *Sales promotion* can be effective in providing added incentives for buyer 'action'.

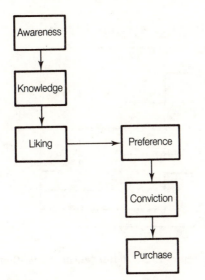

Figure 13.3 Lavidge and Steiner's hierarchy of effects model.

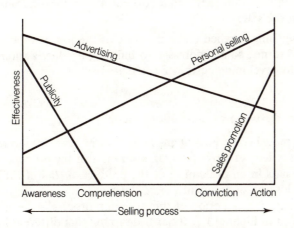

Figure 13.4 Communication methods.

For industrial communication, Figure 13.5 shows that advertising and publicity play the most important roles in the awareness stage. Customer comprehension is primarily affected by education, with advertising and personal selling playing secondary roles. Customer conviction is influenced most by personal selling, followed closely by advertising. Finally, closing the sale is primarily the function of the salesperson.

These findings have the following implications:

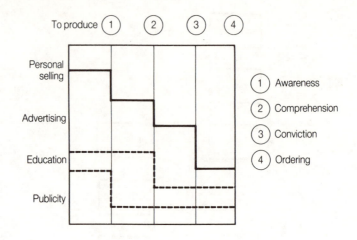

Figure 13.5 Industrial communication.

- The company could effect promotional or communication economies by cutting back on the involvement of salespeople in the early stages of the job, so that they could concentrate on the vital phase of closing the sale.
- If advertising is relied on to do more of the job, it should take several forms, some addressed to building product awareness and some to developing customer conviction.

The adoption–diffusion of innovations model

Parts of this model (Figure 13.6) are similar to the first two models discussed. The recipient is seen to move from an awareness of the product to an interest in it. This results in an evaluation of the product, a trial of the product and finally the adoption or frequent use of the product.

An interesting extension of this adoption process is the *adoption curve concept*, shown in Figure 13.7. It has been found that different individuals go through the stages of awareness–adoption at varying speeds. This means that the more innovative buyers become adopters much more quickly than the more laggardly buyers.

The adoption curve shows how and when different groups accept ideas, and points out the need for varying the promotional effort as time passes. It also emphasizes the inter-relations among groups, showing that some groups act as leaders in accepting new ideas. The adoption curve is related to the product life cycle concept, because it shows when, over time, different adopter categories come in to the market as regular, committed buyers. Indeed, it could even be described as a kind of market segmentation 'over time', since different

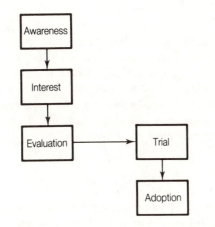

Figure 13.6   The adoption process.

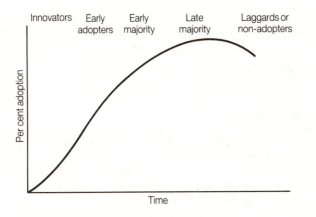

Figure 13.7   The adoption curve.

promotional approaches will need to be targeted at these adopter groups as the product moves through its life cycle. The important characteristics of each group are as follows.

Innovators

They are the first to adopt. For promotion purposes, they tend to rely on impersonal and scientific information sources, or other innovators, rather than personal salespeople.

Early adopters

Research suggests that this group tends to have the greatest contact, of all the groups, with salespeople. Mass media are also important information sources. But perhaps the finding of greatest significance is that there is a higher incidence of opinion leadership among the early adopters. Many in this category will be regarded highly – and with credibility – by others and can be used as a sort of 'pivot' between communicator and target audience. If the opinion leaders are influenced, these often influence the 'followers'.

Early majority

They will usually not consider an innovation until many early adopters have tried it. A long period may elapse between trial and adoption. The early majority has considerable contact with mass media, salespeople and early adopters – thus reinforcing the point about targetting the opinion leaders.

Late majority

The late majority are less likely to follow opinion leaders and early adopters. They make little use of mass media and of salespeople. They tend to be more orientated to other late adopters than to outside sources of information.

Laggards or non-adopters

This group tends to be tradition-bound and it may not pay for marketers to bother with this intransigent group.

This model shows the crucial importance of the early adopters because they influence the early majority – and help spread the word to many others.

This is often also described as the *two-step flow of communications*. See Figure 13.8.

The tendency is for influence to flow from mass media to opinion leaders, who are receptive to the idea presented, and from those opinion leaders to the mass market. There are relatively few active information seekers in the market and a large number of passive information recipients. These information seekers may be different from innovators because they may seek information only about the product or service which interests them.

Figure 13.8 Two-step flow of communications.

Marketing can recognize the prime importance of these interpersonal conversations and recommendations by opinion leaders. If early groups reject the product, it may never get started. But if the early groups accept the product, then what the opinion leaders in each social group say about it may be critical. This reinforces the importance of trying to reach the opinion leaders (communicators) in various social groups. However, opinion leaders are hard to identify and it is important, therefore, to recognize that the mass media can play an important role in getting the message to them.

An alternative approach is to discover more of the characteristics of opinion leaders, perhaps in demographic terms – and then to simulate opinion leaders in promotional campaigns. The use of well-known 'personalities', or even the 'ordinary', but 'believable' person with street-credibility, are relatively common approaches in advertising campaigns.

Another and slightly more comprehensive approach can be found in Delozier (1976) and Evans (1980) and is summarized in Figure 13.9.

These models are helpful in understanding markets as they currently stand and, therefore, in contributing to what promotion should be doing – and how. What is also important is for promotional research to help determine how the promotion element of the mix blends with other mix elements to achieve more general marketing objectives.

Advertisers are perhaps a little slow to set goals in the above areas and to measure progress towards them. Some have set communication and audience

---

Exposure	Individuals' exposure to media is selective, therefore the focus here is on selecting and scheduling promotional media in a way appropriate to the target market (see media research in Figure 13.11.
Attention	Of over 1500 ads each American is exposed to per day in the US, only about 5% are noticed, thus, it is important for research to evaluate ways of gaining attention, such as using a T-Scope for colour and legibility studies (see copy tests in Figure 13.11).
Perception	Messages should also be interpreted (perceived) in the intended way, so research should discover what receivers of messages think the message is trying to communicate.
Retention	Messages are to be remembered in the intended way – conduct recall tests (see copy tests in Figure 13.11), and research the effects of repetition. Also, research any associations that are intended to be conditioned in the response to the brand's message.
Conviction	Favourable emotions and intentions should be developed, so research into attitudes (which are composed of cognitions, emotions and intentions).
Action	Measure scales – trial and repeat purchase. Coupon redemption counts, for sales promotions.
Post purchase	Research into satisfaction levels and any possible doubts due to perceived inconsistencies (cognitive dissonance) between elements of the purchase process by individuals.

Figure 13.9 Model of individuals' response to marketing communications. (*Source*: Adapted from Evans (1980) and Delozier (1976))

goals, and measured copy and media effects, but few have set financial goals and measured sales and profit effects. The result is that advertising appropriations are quite commonly set with extreme laxity, often being based simply on 'past experience' or calculated as a fixed percentage of sales.

Managers generally do not find it much help to be told that their advertising campaign scored plus this or minus that; they want to know why the advertisement or series of advertisements did well or badly. Quite often, management distrusts the validity of either the samples or the test situation. When Mrs Smith fills in the structured questionnaire at a commercial assessment session, does she really put down the things that she would be thinking if she were watching the commercial in her own sitting room? In many cases, the validity of some of the techniques for evaluating advertising effectiveness are distrusted. Probably, of all the problems in advertising, testing advertising effectiveness is perhaps still the biggest.

Daniel Starch (1968) did much research on the evaluation of advertising, which has its roots back in the mid-1930s. His procedure was to conduct research among a sample group of readers of a magazine and then take measurement of the number of that sample who remembered each advertisement in a specific issue. Both spontaneous and prompted awareness were picked up. Average scores could be monitored for black and white advertisements colour advertisements, whole-page advertisements and so on, and eventually similar calculations were made for product fields. This supplied norms against which an advertisement's performance could be compared. This is discussed in more detail date in the chapter.

Areas of study which are difficult to assess include, how many more sales result directly from an advertising campaign, or what level of continuous advertising is directly responsible for a specific sales target? Figures 13.10 and 13.11 summarize the main areas and approaches in promotion research.

Decision required	Type of research needed
What to say	Objectives and theme of platform research
How to say it	Copy research
Where, when, and how often to say it	Media research
How much to spend	Level-of-effort research

Figure 13.10   Advertising research.

ADVERTISING RESEARCH

Advertising objectives

Researching existing awareness, cognitions, emotions, intentions, etc. or image dimensions for the advertiser's product or service, may form the basis of the objectives of a campaign.

For example, misconceptions might be identified and considered desirable to correct. The same dimensions can be re-tested after such a campaign to assess its effectiveness.

See Colley's Dagmar model (1961) 'Defining advertising goals for measured advertising results'.

See also Figure 13.9 which demonstrates a sequential model that also incorporates copy tests and media research.

Copy tests

Testing the advertising message both *before* and after it is released.

Before tests
Group discussions (sometimes referred to as consumer jury tests). Viewing alternative commercials on video tape, or looking through possible press ads in a portfolio are alternative forms of presenting messages. Sometimes a pre-final version is presented as a 'storyboard' of ideas (i.e., before conversion to film). Laboratory tests are sometimes used e.g., eye tracking with infra red beam of light that traces path of eye over an ad, or the use of a lie detector for emotional response, or T-Scope for legibility and colour effectiveness at different speeds of exposure.

The 'Schwerin' method can be used, as can simulated sales tests in mock stores to evaluate POS material.

After tests
Usually involve some form of recall or recognition test, or experimental design which extends the above to before–after method.

Media reesearch

Involves a matching of market profile with readership profile of print media or TV viewing or radio listening – for media selection and schedule purposes. National Readership Survey provides demographic profile of readers of different publications and those read by the intended market segment (again defined in demographic terms) should be considered for selection. BRAD gives costs of selecting publications, and some circulation data. Thus, it may not be the cheapest publication that is selected, but the one with the lowest *cost per thousand* circulation figure.

MEAL gives expenditure figures for advertisements per quarter – could be used as a guide for how much to spend (relative to competitors).

Figure 13.11 Framework for advertising research.

Copy testing

Copy testing is concerned with which copy, headlines, illustrations, or perhaps music, will best communicate the message. Studies answering questions of this sort have traditionally made up the bulk of advertising research and are still called, even in the age of television, copy research.

Verbal investigations into advertising response

There are many popular ways of pre-testing and post-testing copy. Most of them involve some verbal response to interviewer questions by a limited group of consumers (rarely with any attempt to approximate a representative cross-section). The answers indicate the degree of awareness, recognition, recall, liking, preference or conviction aroused in the respondents by the advertising. They measure the progress made towards achieving advertising goals, *not* marketing goals such as sales.

The *limitation* common to these studies is that the respondent's claim of having been exposed to advertising cannot be taken at face value. For years research services have reported the proportion of each sample who, upon being shown an advertisement, claim to have noted it (the recognition method), or who, upon being shown a brand advertised in a magazine they have read can 'play back' enough of the advertisement to indicate that they had in fact seen it (the aided recall method).

The simultaneous popularity and questionability of these studies led in 1959 to the largest purely methodological investigation ever conducted in copy research – the five volume Printed Advertising Rating Methods Study carried out by the US Advertising Research Foundation. The study found, among other things, that recognition scores did not decrease through memory loss with the increase in time since the original reading, as might have been expected. This suggests that respondents were 'recognizing', not the advertisement they had actually seen, but the likelihood that this was the kind of advertisement they would have noted, given the opportunity. Recognition could also result from previous purchases rather than being the cause of later ones. These effects are related to the degree of advertising carry-over and the amount of habitual behaviour in customer brand choice. Carry-over refers to the rate at which the effect of an advertising expenditure wears out with the passage of time. Habitual behaviour indicates how much brand hold-over occurs independent of the level of advertising.

Other studies have found that respondents have claimed noting control advertisements they could not have seen. The extent of misclaiming was directly related to the respondent's reports of past reading behaviour, their interest in the product advertised, and other personal characteristics. Such claims are completely useless as reports of prior exposure.

Verbal studies also appear to be ineffective as predictors of future behaviour. One review of 28 studies has shown that factual recall of advertising changes without corresponding changes in behaviour or attitudes. It concludes that what is retained by respondents may have nothing to do with their subsequent purchases. Such failure of recall or attitude change to predict or coincide with behavioural changes may be a product of the methods used to measure these changes. As suggested in Figure 13.4, advertising may not be the most effective promotion element in the 'action' stage of the buying process.

Non-verbal investigations

As verbal behaviour fell under suspicion, non-verbal behaviour became increasingly popular (though still quite limited) as a measure of copy effectiveness. Laboratory methods, although themselves criticized as artificial, grew in favour as they began to measure relatively involuntary responses to advertising, including visual recognition, skin moisture and pupil dilation. None of these methods has yet been found to predict future purchases, but they do help to provide indices of attention-getting capability and awareness, which, if related to sales goals, might provide a diagnostic basis for improving copy performance.

The most rapidly growing form of copy research is the pre-testing of broadcast commercials. In the US, the Schwerin Research Organization mails invitations to randomly selected households to see a theatrical presentation of films – these are general interest films, with some commercials. Afterwards, a competitive preference test is organized and viewers are offered a year's supply of a product, the brand of which they must choose. This test is said to encourage serious judgement, on the lines of everyday shopping, of the relative merits of competing brands. Some of the brands being advertised during these films are thus viewed in a fairly realistic way by respondents.

Newer TV commercial pre-tests measure:

- The rate at which the viewer will press a pedal to keep the tube lit and the sound audible (the CONPAAD method devised by the Associates for Research on Behaviour).
- The number of women who will choose the brand in a supermarket after seeing its commercial (Tele-research).
- The comments of groups invited to watch a commercial in a TV studio which can make and test a revised commercial on the spot (Telpex, offered by the London Press Exchange).

Less artificial are on-air tests using split-cable facilities, whereby half the viewing households are shown one commercial and half another, and their subsequent purchases are compared. Such tests are also carried out without cables by major agencies who buy a time slot in a few cities (or regions in the UK), usually from one client for another, insert the test commercial, and compare sales in these test areas with sales in the rest of the country.

In practice, some kind of pre-test is performed on most TV advertisements, if not for those in newspapers and magazines. The extent and quality of these efforts vary, but any large agency will provide some measures if the client requests them. Large advertisers generally demand testing, and a few even require that test scores meet some established standard. Few finished commercials, however, are sacrificed because of poor score.

Group discussions are probably the most widely used forum for pre-testing television commercials at present – alternative commercials can be presented on video to respondents in this 'coffee morning' type of research approach.

Media planning

A media planner will need to know the following:

- The advertiser's strategy for their product or service
- The competition
- The advertiser's objective in advertising
- The budget
- The timetable
- The target group
- The seasonality
- The regional spread.

This information will not always be available as desired by the media planner/buyer whose judgement may therefore have to be used in filling in the missing information.

The brief itself may be put together inside the advertising agency, with the client's cooperation, or presented to the client for approval. A media brief, most would agree, needs to cover the objective – this answers the question, '*What* do we expect to achieve?' The target audience also needs to be dealt with, as do the regionality and seasonality of that market. Do we need to change these factors? The balance must therefore be 'right' in terms of impact, frequency and coverage. Impact covers areas such as size, time, length and the use of colour.

Evaluation

In order to plan a campaign, the process must start with an evaluation of all the available media. This evaluation is necessary and its objectives are:

- To see which media are feasible, for example, when colour is important, as with lipsticks, this will automatically exclude certain media, including some of the press.
- To select the principal medium.
- To decide how it should be used.
- To establish any secondary or supporting media, if necessary.

Feasibility

In deciding the feasibility of the media, the following points need to be considered:

- *Experience* It is essential that a particular medium has proved to be effective either in the past or in current, similar situations.
- *Competitive angle* Some may think it prudent to use the same media as the competition, but it may be beneficial to use different media.
- *Creativity* Radio would be unsuitable for, say, cosmetics, as would the black and white press. Colour may therefore be vital for, say, tourism in an exotic location, in order to create the right mood.
- *Regional spread* Advertising may be needed only in certain areas, especially when a regional test market is under way. Regionalization is possible with certain media up to a point, that is, with commercial television, but it is not possible with the national press.
- *Cost* Notably the 'cost per thousand' (that is, how much it costs for every 1000 people that the medium reaches).
- *Target audience and its characteristics* Demographically, psychographically and so on.
- *Availability and lead time* If a campaign is to take place at short notice, then the use of colour magazines, for example, where artwork must be completed a long time in advance of publication date, is not a feasible proposition.

The media schedule

A media schedule indicates precisely how and when the advertisements will appear. A very simple indication of what this would look like is given in Figure 13.12.

	1/6	8/6	15/6	22/6	29/6	6/7	13/7	20/7	27/7
Sunday Telegraph	●		●			●			
The Sunday Times		●		●	●				●
Observer	●		●			●		●	
TV Times	●	●					●		
Radio Times				●	●			●	
Homes and Gardens	●					●			●

Figure 13.12 A media schedule.

In certain cases, rather than concentrate expenditure on a series of short sharp bursts, it may be preferable to spread a campaign to achieve the 'drip' effect. There is no one pattern and research will have to be carried out in each case to establish the best *solution*.

The S-Curve effect

The typical relationship between advertising frequency and sales effect is normally a convex curve, but in the case of new products an S-Curve will apply. The S-Curve effect of a product occurs if the sales rise sharply after its introduction because of a heavy initial promotion effort, then drop as promotional support is reduced, but then rise again as further promotion and possible positive word-of-mouth communication takes place. (See Figure 13.13.)

Selecting the 'best' medium

For effective promotion, specific target customers must be reached. Unfortunately, not all potential customers read all newspapers, listen to all radio stations or read all posters. Not all media are equally effective. There is no simple answer to the question, 'What is the best medium?' Effectiveness depends on how well it fits with the rest of a particular marketing strategy. To be specific here, however, it depends on:

- The company's promotion objectives.
- What the target market is.
- The funds available for advertising.

We have already examined each of these questions; now we have to answer the initial question.

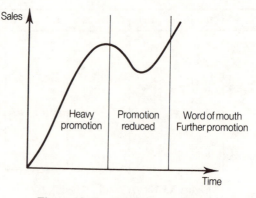

Figure 13.13 The S-Curve effect.

The individual advertising situation largely determines the complexity of media selection. There are, however, no rules-of-thumb or simple formulae for solving these selection problems. Each advertising situation presents its own unique set of circumstances. Each type of medium has its own character, and each specific medium, in turn, differs from the next. *There is no single 'best' medium for all advertising situations*. Each media decision must be made in the light of the particular requirements of a particular situation. Even competitors selling nearly the same products to nearly the same markets employ different media strategies.

Obviously, a limiting factor that always has to be taken into account is the budget available for advertising. There is never enough money to exploit fully all the media opportunities available. Therefore, the advertiser must be selective. He or she seeks to maximize the return on the advertising investment by selecting those media that will deliver the message most efficiently and effectively.

Creative media decision is made, according to Sandage and Fryburger (1975), when all the factors in a particular market situation are combined with 'media experience and sound judgement and imagination' to determine the strategy or the choice of media.

Factors to consider when selecting the medium

The principal factors to be considered when selecting the medium are the following:

- The market
- Extent and character of distribution
- Creative strategy
- Circulation
- The audience
- Media costs
- Editorial content
- Advertiser usage.

The market

Initially, the advertiser must ensure that he or she has a thorough and definite understanding of the market for his or her product. Remember that an advertising medium is a carrier of a message. The sender of the message can select the character with confidence only when he or she knows the type or class of consumer at whom the message is to be directed. So, it is very important that media be selected that will reach the desired group.

Newspapers, magazines and other media are not all alike. One newspaper, for example the *Sun*, will have a different following from another, for example the *Daily Telegraph*. One newspaper may be conservative in its editorial and news policy, for example the *Express*, another liberal, for example the *Guardian*.

Of course, the type of consumer at whom advertising is to be directed is often predetermined by the product's character, for example, farm machinery is not sold to the public in general, so it would be folly to advertise such products in a general household magazine.

Since the real purpose of an advertising medium is that of a messenger, strong emphasis must be placed on the necessity for knowing the direction the messenger takes.

Extent and character of distribution

Advertising will be of little or no value in getting people to buy merchandise unless such products are placed within easy reach. Though an advertiser has national distribution, he or she may wish to work some territories more intensively than others. The results of a market analysis may have revealed some areas as being more lucrative than others, thus meriting more sales effort. In such case, national media may be supplemented by media serving the richer areas only. Local media would therefore suit best.

Creative strategy

If an advertisement is designed to build and sustain a certain brand image or product personality, it should be placed in media having personality traits that complement and reinforce the desired image.

Some media, for example TV, magazines and radio, have distinct personalities that may be described as masculine or feminine, modern or old-fashioned, high-brow or low-brow, homely or worldly, serious or frivolous. Those media that have the kind of personality that is right for the product tend to strengthen the effectiveness of the image-building advertisement.

Copy that is to appear should be written in terms that will be understood by readers of the publication. The advertiser should 'talk' to the audience in its own language. It is probable that greater effectiveness will be obtained if different copy is written for each medium where differences in audience are discernible.

Circulation

The term 'circulation' has been used to describe various dimensions of all types of media and has a different meaning for each type. Nowadays, we tend to restrict 'circulation' to refer to the number of copies of a newspaper or magazine sold. These circulation figures give the advertisers an indication of:

- How many people are reached by the publication.
- Where these people live.
- The degree of interest people have in editorial comment.

However, the advertiser will also want to know the readership, that is, the number of people who read a newspaper or magazine. Readership may be considerably greater – by several factors – than circulation.

Incidentally, since rates charged for space are primarily dependent upon the circulation, it is of value to the advertiser to use the media with the highest, relevant circulations.

Audience

The audience is defined as those people whose minds are reached by the medium carrying the advertiser's message. Circulation is measured in numbers of copies; and audience is measured in numbers of people. Circulation figures are indirect evidence of how many and what kinds of people a medium reaches; audience data is direct evidence obtained from sample surveys of the people themselves. Composition of a medium's audience, however, is often more important than its size.

Media costs

It is important to compare costs with the ability of the medium to render the kind of service desired. Since the advertiser is interested in using a carrier that will deliver his or her message to his or her prospects with a minimum of waste, the first task of selection is that of measuring such abilities. A number of media may qualify as possibilities. Then, when appraising this select group, the advertiser must deal with two basic questions: 'How much will I have to pay for the space or time?' 'What do I get for what I pay?'

A comparison of line rates in a newspaper tells advertisers how much more they will have to pay for space in one newspaper than in another, but it does not reveal the differences in advertising value they will receive, for example the number of readers and their composition. The usual procedure is to compare line rates by reducing the competing rates to a common denominator of one unit, the price per unit. As a rule, the greater the circulation of a newspaper, the lower is its price per unit; the smaller the circulation, the higher is the price per unit. 'Cost per thousand', is a typical measure in this respect.

In the case of TV advertising, rates are quoted in units of time. To compare rates charged by different regional companies, an appropriate standard is the cost-per-commercial-minute per thousand viewers or, in the case of radio, listeners.

Editorial content

This is less easily measured but, nevertheless, it is no less important than other dimensions of a medium.

It is logical to assume that the environment in which an advertiser's message appears has an appreciable influence on the effectiveness of the advertisement itself. It behoves the advertiser to appraise carefully the editorial content of newspapers and magazines before making a selection and to match editorial and advertising 'atmospheres'.

Advertiser usage

The extent to which other advertisers employ a given medium is often used as an indicator of its effectiveness. A medium which consistently carries a greater total volume of advertising is assumed to be the one that advertisers generally consider more effective. However, the total volume carried is less significant to an individual advertiser than is the amount of advertising for his or her type of product.

An advertiser's choice of media should not be governed by his competitors' choices, but where and how competitors place their advertising should be considered. A competitor's marketing strategy and tactics can be rather well determined from records showing the extent to which he or she uses specific media.

Media characteristics

The communicator has a wide selection of media channels from which to choose and within each medium there is available a further selection of alternatives. The publications, stations or sites that survive are those which deliver results.

The advertising business is particularly skilled at selecting those areas of communication that are able to deliver the results at a reasonable cost; this is usually measured in cost per thousand, that is, the cost of reaching each one thousand people in the segment concerned. In most cases, the segment is divided into subgroups according to established classifications, for example the socio-economic groups. The advertiser therefore is able to calculate the comparative costs for any one classified group against another.

Although knowledge of the target audience and strengths of any given channel in reaching that audience are necessary to the copywriter, this quantitative information is not so important as the qualitative factors inherent within each medium. These are the creative elements that enable the copywriter to develop his or her message according to the strengths and weaknesses of a chosen medium. Ideally, the copywriter will be consulted prior to media selection so that creative aspects are taken into account, and before schedules are settled, so that central themes and appropriate storyboards are produced.

Equally, the amount of time available to prepare copy and artwork for a campaign is dependent on media or channel choice. Copy dates may range from three or four days for a national newspaper, to six months for particular television channels.

Media provide opportunities to see or hear. Delivering an audience to advertisers is often their main source of revenue. However, it is up to the advertiser and, in particular, the copywriter and visualizer to create interest in a brand and to stimulate action towards a sale. Media provide a communication network; the advertiser must provide the means of successful and effective communication for its brand.

Mathematical models

Considerable efforts have been made to develop mathematical models from which an advertiser can find the best media mix and pattern to reach a desired audience. Such efforts have cast light on the complex problems latent in making these judgements.

Before a substantially effective model is operational, it must be able to estimate many factors:

- Media and audience overlap, especially between broadcast and print.
- The effects of multiple exposure, of advertisement size, and of time and spacing.
- The relative value of reach and frequency.
- The effects of campaign age.
- The relationships between advertising exposure, perception and communication.

In general, the amount and extent of advertising stimulus can be, and is, measured reasonably effectively. The major gaps continue to lie in measuring consumer response to the stimulus, particularly in distinguishing the contribution of the advertising from that of the medium.

Coupons

Many advertisers try and stimulate 'action' on the part of the consumer by including a coupon in the advertisement. Coupons may entitle their holders to a price reduction, or be returnable to the manufacturer for further information. The number of coupons returned – by retailers or consumers – can be used as a measure of the success or failure of the advertisement to communicate. Coupons therefore enable an accurate measure of response to be made.

It is also possible to compare different advertising approaches using coupons. For example, two different advertisements for the same product could be used, carrying distinguishable coupons; the advertisement that brings in the largest number of enquiries could be said to be the most successful.

One interesting side-effect of coupon advertising, particularly in the industrial goods field, is that coupons can provide the manufacturer with an effective list of potential customers, which, at some future date, can be used for direct mail advertising or for making personal contact.

Interesting research was conducted some time ago into the effects of repetition in advertising, Ray and Sawyer (1973) found that those actually returning coupons were a small proportion of those who could recall the advertisement and even of those who liked and then claimed intention to buy (Figure 13.14).

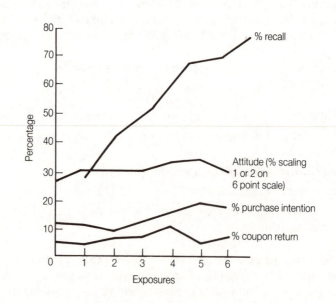

Figure 13.14 Repetition effects in marketing communications. (Adapted by the authors from Ray and Sawyer (1973))

Key numbers

This is a method used to evaluate different advertising media, although *it only applies where the advertisement demands a positive response, such as 'writing in' or returning a coupon*. The advertisement carries an identifying 'key', either on the coupon or in the address line.

This technique is used a great deal in the field of recruitment advertising. For example, suppose a manufacturer were trying to recruit senior computer personnel. In addition to using the computer press, they might consider also advertising in *The Sunday Times* and the *Observer*. The identical advertisements would appear in each newspaper, except for the key number. In *The Sunday Times* this (which would appear in the address line) would probably be ST1, standing for *Sunday Times* first insertion, and in the *Observer* the key number would be O1, meaning *Observer* first insertion. By studying the addresses on applicants' envelopes, the response from each publication can be assessed in terms of quantity and quality, and this information can prove extremely valuable for any further recruiting in that particular field.

Keying advertisements also works in terms of selling products. Thus, a manufacturer selling garden tools could advertise in a number of gardening publications, which he evaluates by keying the advertisements. This can be of great help in the planning of advertising campaigns.

Split run tests

Many newspapers and magazines will stop the printing presses in the middle of a press run. Some national newspapers, for instance, include special folded-in local sections with national editions. Where a newspaper is using different fold-ins for different regions, advertisers can experiment with various advertisements for the same product and judge the results.

By 'splitting the run', the advertiser is able to vary the advertisements going out in the same issue of the publication, with (say) having half the edition using one advertisement and the other half using another advertisement. When geography and other variables can be isolated and accounted for, the actual sales at retail can provide a reasonably reliable indicator as to which advertisement did the best job, assuming everything else is equal.

Consumer jury test

This technique can be used when the advertiser is in a hurry to evaluate advertising copy or headlines. It may be that they cannot wait for the results of a mail, market area or split run test. Instead, a number of advertisements are mounted in a portfolio and shown to a sample of easily reached consumers. The consumers are asked which advertisements they like best, or which would most influence them to buy the product. They may be told to close the portfolio after examining it, and then asked what selling message they received. Sometimes the advertiser may only be testing headlines or copy appeals; these are typed on cards which the respondent is asked to arrange in order of effectiveness.

This rough-and-ready form of research has many detractors, who often refer to it as 'shuffle-card testing'. However, with proper controls and reasonably clear choices, it can produce interesting and sometimes valuable information.

Consumer panels

Another means of checking the movement of goods into consumers' hands is by checking with consumers themselves. In Great Britain, the Atwood Organisation is probably the best known in this field. Members of this firm's panel keep diaries of every purchase they make, with such information as the size bought, the price paid, the store where it was bought, the quantity and so on. The published results show brand share of market, brand share trends, brand switching, channels of distribution and the qualitative characteristics of people buying the products. This data is useful not only for checking the effectiveness of advertising, but for a number of other marketing purposes.

Today, technology has improved the accuracy and ease of collecting this type of data. Some panel operators install bar code readers in members' homes so all they need do is scan the bar codes of the products they have purchased and a code on a card for which store it was from and this avoids the hassles of the old diary method. Often, in addition there will be an electronic set meter installed in the panel homes to record TV channels watched. This – in particular the advertisements shown – can help the advertiser determine the links between advertising exposure and products purchased.

Consumer surveys

Since the actual effects of advertising on sales are so difficult to measure, advertisers have to be satisfied with less direct criteria than sales. The yardsticks of awareness and attitude are receiving increasing attention. It is said that all that can be expected of advertising is that it should increase awareness of a brand's existence and virtues, and build favourable attitudes towards the brand. The assumption is that, if more people learn about the brand and become favourably inclined towards it, increases in sales will automatically follow. This is indeed the logic behind the 'models' of the communications process as outlined earlier, namely, that there is a sequence of events and responses in the process.

Probably the most important type of advertising research is that carried out by such organizations as the Starch Advertising Service of New York. The work of this organization takes the form of surveys – of readership, listening and viewing. The organization is independent, and can therefore be objective in its work. The surveys are based on interviews, using (in the case of newspapers and magazines) a current issue of the publication on which to base questions.

The Starch organization is primarily concerned with who sees and reads the advertisements. Obviously, for people to be influenced by advertising, they must first of all see or read the advertisements. This is the fundamental element in advertising effectiveness studies, and Starch claims to go no further than this. The Starch survey is unpretentious in that it confines itself to advertisements and media and is not concerned with sales.

The Starch method starts by asking the following questions of readers: 'Did you see or read any part of this advertisement?' The responses are percentaged in terms of the number of readers who:

(1) *'Noted'*, that is, saw any part of the advertisement.

(2) *'Seen-associated'*, saw or read anywhere in the advertisement the name of the product or service.

(3) *'Read-most'*, that is, read half or more of the written material in the advertisement.

The researchers then look at the size of each score and the size of the scores in relation to each other. They then examine these scores and their importance in relation to the differing advertising objectives. The three degrees of readership are expressed in percentages.

A drop in the score from 'noted' to 'seen-associated' indicates the number of observers who did not look long enough to learn what product was advertised. A large drop from 'noted' to 'seen-associated' usually indicates that the 'attention-getter' in the advertisement was irrelevant or meaningless, or that the name or picture of the product was inconspicuous.

'Read-most', particularly in relation to the 'noted' or 'seen-associated' scores, indicates whether the 'interest gainer' in the advertisement was strong enough to pull the reader through the rest, and/or whether the text itself had appeal. There are occasions when 'noted' or 'seen-associated' are sufficient to achieve the advertiser's goal, which may sometimes be more modest than actual selling. Some advertisements, moreover, are designed to convey their message visually or in a few words, in which case 'noted' or 'seen-associated' would be considered sufficient. Complicated advertisements full of information obviously need a good 'read-most' rating.

You should remember that the Starch readership studies measure by what is known as the 'recognition method', that is, how many people saw and read a specific advertisement. They do not measure why one campaign or series of advertisements attracts more readers than another. Nor do they measure what the reader retained in his or her mind from having seen or read the advertisement. To probe the 'whys' and 'whats' of advertising we can use impact studies.

Schwerin Research

As introduced earlier in this chapter, this organization is responsible for much of our knowledge on the effectiveness of TV commercials. The main method of operation is to invite audiences to a laboratory or theatre. They are then asked to select certain merchandise to be offered as prizes during the evening. Then a half-hour TV programme is shown, complete with the commercials which are being evaluated (and which are for those products being offered as prizes). The audience afterwards rates the commercials, and is then asked to re-select the prizes. The differences between pre-selection and post-selection of brands are used to measure the effectiveness of the commercial.

The method is also used to evaluate differences in commercial techniques, including the different announcers or personalities performing in the commercials.

Audit Bureau of Circulations

Any coverage of evaluating the effectiveness of advertising would be incomplete without again mentioning the Audit Bureau of Circulations (or ABC). The ABC is the oldest and largest organization for auditing circulation. It is sponsored by advertisers, agencies and publishers, all of whom are anxious to protect themselves against unreliable figures. Only publications with 70% or more paid circulation (that is, paid at not less than half the established basic price of the publication) are eligible for ABC membership and audit.

The ABC's most important service is to provide a reliable standard for reporting the quantity, quality and distribution of circulation. Buyers of space are understandably sceptical of circulation figures not audited by the ABC or some other recognized auditing organization. Consequently, the majority of the large-circulation magazines and most daily newspapers are members.

The ABC is a non-profit-making organization whose object is 'to bring truth to circulation figures upon which all advertising rates are based'. Before organizations like ABC existed, it was all too easy for magazines and newspapers to claim very large circulation figures when trying to sell space to advertisers. Today, the advertiser knows that if a publication is ABC audited, then the circulation figures quoted are extremely accurate.

As has already been indicated, technology is becoming an important force. New improved set meters are being used, as are bar code scanners for consumer panel members. Even the problem of people leaving the room when advertisements are being shown is being addressed and catered for in the latest set meters. We already have the 'people meter' which asks respondents to press a button when they leave/enter the room. This adds more detail to the basic set meter reading – not only whether the TV is 'on' and which channel is 'on', but also whether people are in the room at the time.

There is even the 'passive people meter' which, through a video camera in the respondent's room, digitally records the image of each individual in the household. As soon as someone leaves or enters the room, the machine can automatically record which individual this is – hence overcoming the problem of the people meter, namely that some respondents do not bother to constantly record every departure from and arrival to, their TV room.

With this perhaps futuristic and 'big brother' thought in mind, we now turn from our application of marketing research techniques and approaches within the *mix*, to applications in different sectors of marketing, specifically in international and industrial settings.

APPENDIX

The following are a number of terms in connection with the media.

Audit	This may refer to audited circulations such as: ABC – Audit Bureau of Circulation; or an in-house audit, whereby the household's stock or consumption of goods is counted; or retail audit, where a check is carried out on stock sales, purchases and inventories in store by such organizations as the A. C. Nielson Company.
Circulation	Number of copies of each issue of a publication distributed either by sale or free.
	Controlled circulation: the distribution, free of charge, of a publication to a member of a professional body, or people who are selected because of their position in an organization or their profession.
Cost per thousand	The total cost of reaching a thousand viewers/readers/listeners with a given advertisement.
Coverage	The proportion expressed in percentage terms of a target audience having an opportunity to see/hear the advertising.
Demographics	This refers to changes in population in terms of age, sex, location, socio-economic groups and so forth.
Exposure	The actual exposure of the advertisement to the members of the target audience.

Frequency	The number of times the target audience has an opportunity to see the campaign, expressed over a period of time.
Impact	The actual exposure of the advertisement to a member of the target audience. A publication, for example, in which the advertisement appears has an average issue readership of 500,000 and an average spread traffic of 85%. Therefore, the number of advertisement impacts will be 500,000 × 85% = 425,000 impact.
Net coverage	Proportion of the target audience having the opportunity to see at least one advertisement in a campaign.
Profile	The composition of the readership or audience in terms of demographic or psychographic characteristics (or even geodemographics such as ACORN, referred to in various chapters of this book)
Ratings	This normally refers to television and involves the percentage of the potential TV audience who are viewing at a given time, or the percentage of TV homes with sets switched on at a given time.
Schedule/Media schedule	A matrix of media and dates as well as rates.
Target ratings	The total number of ratings a time buyer aims to achieve by area in a given time.

Useful sources of information

The Audit Bureau of Circulation (ABC)

This provides *audited* net sale figures. Over 1600 ABC publication figures are given by publishers every six months. An ABC figure is an audited net sale figure based on an average number of copies sold per day, week or month, as the case may be, over the preceding six-month period prior to 30 June and 31 December. The work is very closely and accurately controlled.

Joint Industry Committee for National Readership Surveys (JICNARS)

The JICNARS figures given in the National Readership Survey publish the results of some 30,000 interviews per year. More than one hundred national publications are included and sometimes specialist magazines as well.

BARB (Broadcasters Audience Research Board)

BARB, formerly JICTAR (Joint Industry Committee for Television Advertising Research) gives information about the audience figures for the previous week's commercial television programmes. The method used has been to attach a meter to a representative sample of homes throughout the UK. This records the channel and the time at which the television set is switched on and off and with the new people meters, also measures which family members are in the room at the time.

JICRAR (Joint Industry Committee for Radio Audience Research)

This uses diaries to record 'listenership' of commercial radio audiences.

REFERENCES

Booz, Allen and Hamilton (1968). *Management of New Products* 4th edn. New York: Booz, Allen and Hamilton

Colley R. H. (1961). *Defining Advertising Goals for Measured Advertising Results*. Association of National Advertisers of New York

Delozier M. W. (1976). *The Marketing Communications Process*. New York: McGraw-Hill

Evans M. J. (1980). An analysis of customer behaviour. *Retail and Distribution Management* **8** (2), 61–4.

Evans M. J. (1991). *Marketing Communications*. London: CIM/RRC

Ray M. L. and Sawyer, A. G. (1973). Repetition in media models. *Journal of Marketing Research* **10**, 22–8

Sandage C. H. and Fryburger U. (1975). *Advertising Theory and Practice* 94th edn. Illinois: Irwin p. 442

Starch D. (1964). Measuring the effect of advertising on sales. *Printers Ink*, March–May.

14

International Marketing Research

In this and the next chapter we turn to the application of marketing research approaches within specific sectors of marketing activity, namely international and industrial markets.

International marketing research

The role of marketing research is equally important in both domestic and international marketing. The differences in international environments, however, make conducting marketing research more difficult. Consider the research information needed by the following potential international marketers in order for them to make decisions on how to proceed:

- A large British company is contemplating building a factory in continental Europe. Management wonders if its product should be changed to suit the new market.

- A pharmaceutical company has to decide how to price a prescription drug product manufactured in its factory in Brazil for the Latin American market. Should the same pricing schedule as that used in Britain be followed? If not, what criteria should be used to set the price?

- A toiletries company must determine how effective its UK advertising strategy will be in promoting its product mix in South East Asia.

Such situations are examples of international marketing problems that require marketing research. In each case, the company's past experience cannot provide an adequate basis for decision. In fact the information necessary to support management action is more likely to be found outside the organization. Special-ized trade journals, or government studies, or discussions with professional level personnel who have special industry expertise, are likely to be helpful. Or if all of these fail, it may finally become necessary to undertake a customer survey.

The procedures and methods of conducting marketing research are con-ceptually the same for both domestic marketing and international marketing. For example, before collecting data, the researcher must have a clear idea of the research problem. Likewise, only an appropriate sample with yield valuable results. Procedural similarities aside, international marketing research differs from domestic marketing in three major ways:

(1) The effects of the international environment on the whole company as a profit-orientated unit are considered (Thwaits, 1983). For example, the marketing research project concerned with the ramifications of a substantial price increase in a particular foreign country must consider questions that do not apply to the domestic market; for example, will the company's subsidiary be nationalized if prices are increased beyond a certain level?

(2) Many concepts and frameworks (that is, market segmentation), which constitute the core of marketing decision making in the domestic arena, may be unusable in international marketing, not because the concept cannot be transferred, but because the information necessary to make such a transfer is not available. For example, if there is a lack of current income distribution data on a country, any analysis of the demand for a product will assume incorrect income categories and, therefore, cannot mean much for practical purposes.

(3) Finally, the ethnocentric nature of marketing makes cultural differences among nations a significant factor. Thus, culture in a domestic market can be considered to be naturally understood, but in international marketing the culture must be fully investigated.

Cross-cultural factors raise a variety of conceptual, methodological and organizational issues in international marketing research relating to:

(1) The complexity of research design, caused by operation in a multicountry, multicultural and multilinguistic environment.

(2) The lack of secondary data available for many countries and product markets.

(3) The high costs of collecting primary data, particularly in developing countries.

(4) The problems associated with coordinating research and data collection in different countries.

(5) The difficulties of establishing the comparability and equivalence of data and research conducted in different contexts (across countries). For example, the results may imply a cultural difference towards responding to questionnaires.

(6) The intrafunctional character of many international marketing decisions.

(7) The economics of many international investment and marketing decisions (Douglas and Craig, 1983).

Information requirements of international marketers

The nature of marketing decisions does not vary from country to country, but the environments may differ. For this reason, the sort of information required to complete a marketing study may vary from one country to another. For example, in a situation where a marketer is free to set prices based on competition, a detailed analysis of competition should be made. But in a country where the price is set by government, information on governmental cost analysis would be of greater importance. The fact that environment determines what kind of information is needed makes international marketing research efforts quite different from domestic marketing research work.

Market research is required for testing, entering, or leaving a market and deals with market performance, market shares, and sales analysis and forecasting. Marketing performance research involves market measurements, either to compare a company's performance against specified standards or to project a possible future outcome. Market potential refers to the total market demand under optimal conditions; market forecast shows the expected level of market demand under the given conditions. To illustrate, when Heublein Inc. decided to expand its Kentucky Fried Chicken into certain middle eastern countries, like Saudi Arabia, it conducted for five years beforehand market potential research in each country.

Market share refers to a company's proportion of total sales in an industry during a set time, usually a year. The market shares held by competitors shape marketing strategy for a company. The competitor with a respectable market share will have a cost advantage over its rivals. This cost advantage can be passed on to the customers through lower prices, which in term strengthens the company's hold on the market. Because of the strategic importance of market share, companies keep constant watch on its fluctuations. Data supplied by industry associations, if properly analysed, usually shows respective market shares.

Past sales information can be analysed in different ways: by amount of profit from different products, by productivity of sales territories (for example, South East Asia or Scandinavia), or by customer type. Sales analysis can pinpoint problems.

Sales forecasts refer to estimates of future sales of a product during a specific period. Sales forecast is the single most important basis for preparing budgets. No matter which sort of international marketing study is planned, the researchers must take into account the foreign country's environment in all its aspects: legal, political, social, cultural, and attitudinal, as shown by both the buying habits of its consumers and the business practices of its enterprises. Naturally, familiarity with the environment is equally important in domestic marketing, but knowledge of domestic environment can come more easily from personal experience. For example, if a British company is interested in doing business in Colombia, it must learn about a political system that may be different in ways that are taken for granted in the United Kingdom political structure. This suggests the importance of having nationals of the foreign country involved, for even with access to adequate data it may not be possible to culturally decode it.

General research information

All marketing research requires three general groups of overall information in addition to the more specific categories already discussed.

(1) General information about:
   (a) Community-type conditions (for example, political happenings – campaigns, elections; demographic events – special annual ethnic or religious celebrations; national events – holidays and so on).
   (b) Business conditions (for example, business ethics and traditional associations).
   (c) Lifestyles and living conditions, that is, social and cultural customs and taboos (for example, the role of women in society).
   (d) General economic conditions (for example, the standards of living for various groups of people and the economic infrastructure – transportation, communication and so on).

(2) Industry information about governmental decisions affecting the industry; resource availability (for example, labour and land); current or potential competitors (that is, general information about their markets and their problems); competition from British companies, local companies and/or third country companies; industry policy, concerted actions in the industry and so forth.

(3) Study-related information: collateral data generated to complete a specific market research study. For example, a study concerned with market potential needs information on supply and demand in market areas of current and potential interest (that is, capacity, consumption, imports, exports). On the other hand, a study concerned with the introduction of a new product requires information about existing

products, the technical know-how available in the country, sources of raw material, leads for joint ventures and so on.

The amount of information to be gathered in a given case depends on the cost–benefit relationship of such information. For example, let us assume a company has an opportunity to export machinery to Italy. Although the company normally checks on the credit rating of an importer before making a shipment, such a delay might ruin a particular transaction. The company figures out that if the importer does not make the payment as stipulated, it stands to lose £2000 after accounting for the advance from the importer. On the other hand, the company could have a market research firm carry out a study on the credit worthiness of the importer for £3000 in a very short time. In other words, the cost exceeds the benefit and the study is not worth it. This example, while oversimplified, illustrates the importance of relating the cost to benefit, in terms of time and money, before deciding to undertake marketing research.

Finally, the nature of information required will vary based on the objective of research. To illustrate the point, Figure 14.1 lists the type of information a company needs to determine export potential. The company must examine different types of environments as well as undertake market and product research.

Stage one: Preliminary screening

Preliminary screening involves defining the physical, political, economic and cultural environment.

Demographic/physical environment
- Population size, growth, density
- Urban and rural distribution
- Climate and weather variations
- Shipping distance
- Product-significant demographics
- Physical distribution and communication network
- Natural resources

Economic environment
- Overall level of development
- Economic growth: GNP, industrial sector
- Role of foreign trade in the economy
- Currency, inflation rate, availability, controls, stability of exchange rate
- Balance of payments
- Per capita income and distribution
- Disposable income and expenditure patterns

Political environment
- System of government
- Political stability and continuity
- Ideological orientation
- Government involvement in business
- Government involvement in communications
- Attitudes towards foreign business (trade restrictions, tariffs, non-tariff barriers, bilateral trade agreements)
- National economic and developmental priorities

Social/cultural environment
- Literacy rate, educational level
- Existence of middle class
- Similarities and differences in relation to home market
- Language and other cultural considerations

The export marketer will eliminate some foreign markets from further consideration on the basis of this preliminary screening. An example would be the absence of comparable or linking products and services, a deficiency that would hinder the potential for marketing company products.

Stage two: Analysis of industry market potential

Market access
- Limitation on trade: tariff levels, quotas
- Documentation and import regulations
- Local standards, practices, and other non-tariff barriers
- Patents and trademarks
- Preferential treaties
- Legal considerations: investment, taxation, repatriation, employment, code of laws

Product potential
- Customer needs and desires
- Local production, imports, consumption
- Exposure to and acceptance of product
- Availability of linking products
- Industry-specific key indicators of demand
- Attitudes towards products of foreign origin
- Competitive offerings
- Availability of intermediaries
- Regional and local transportation facilities
- Availability of manpower
- Conditions for local manufacture

Stage three: Analysis of company sales potential

The third stage of the screening process involves assessing company sales potential in those countries that prove promising based upon the earlier analyses.

Sales volume forecasting
- Size and concentration of customer segments
- Projected consumption statistics
- Competitive pressures
- Expectations of local distributors/agents

Cost of internal distribution
- Tariffs and duties
- Value added tax
- Local packaging and assembly
- Margins/commissions allowed for the trade
- Local distribution and inventory costs
- Promotional expenditures

Landed cost
- Costing method for exports
- Domestic distribution costs
- International freight and insurance
- Cost of product modification

Other determinants of profitability
- Going price levels
- Competitive strengths and weaknesses
- Credit practices
- Current and projected exchange rates

Figure 14.1 Information needs for determining export potential. (*Source*: Tamer Cavusgil S. (1985). Guidelines for export market research. *Business Horizons* (November/December), 30–31

Collecting secondary data at home

There are two kinds of data as discussed in Part I – primary and secondary. Primary data are gathered by the researcher. Figure 14.2 characterizes the two kinds of data. Research based on secondary data may be conducted either at home or abroad.

Primary data	Secondary data
• From knowledgeable individuals at the professional level.	• From published sources or collected by others.
• May be costly in time and travel.	• Usually free or low cost.
• May tend to be subjective.	• Can be collected quickly.
• Must be pilot-tested.	• May be biased or incomplete.
• Can be very specific to problems at hand.	• May be out-of-date.
• Cannot require disclosure of proprietary information.	• Requires careful analysis of limitations.

Figure 14.2 Characteristics of primary and secondary data.

Sources

There are five main sources of secondary information: international agencies, the government, consulting companies, foreign government offices and banks.

International agencies

The United Nations, the World Bank and the International Monetary Fund gather a variety of economic and social information on different countries of the world. This information is available to the public. For example, the United Nations Statistical Yearbook provides information on worldwide demographics. Also, the World Bank's 'World Tables' summarize information on living patterns via such indicators as televisions, telephones and cars per thousand families. The International Monetary Fund (IMF) provides historical information on national economic indicators – Gross National Product (GNP), industrial production, inflation rate, money supply – of its member countries. This information is available on computer tapes.

The information available from these international organizations, however, has two drawbacks. First, the information is based on data supplied by each member country. It is difficult to determine what criteria and means have been used. In some cases, the reliability of the data should be questioned, because the information compiled has been passed along by various bureaucrats who may have slanted the data for their own purposes. Second, the information is dated. It takes time for an international organization to gather information from all over the world, analyse it and make it available to the public in summary form.

Most university libraries and public libraries in major cities carry the United Nations and the World Bank publications. The IMF information may be available only in more specialized libraries.

Government sources

In the UK, for example, the Department of Trade and Industry (DTI) is the single most important source of secondary information. For instance, if a company wants to find out with whom to deal in an overseas market, the DTI British Overseas Trade Board (BOTB) provides names of distributors/dealers to approach.

The DTI BOTB informs businesses not only about international business conditions abroad, but also about events and happenings and their impact on international business. Some other government organizations (that is, departments and agencies) issue newsletters and other publications. An international marketer could subscribe to those pertinent to particular products or markets.

Consultancy companies

Many management consultancy firms (including accounting firms) specialize in services for British business abroad. Some of these companies conduct original research. Their findings are available to the international marketer. Some consultancy companies put out a number of publications (newsletters issued periodically, studies issued on a regular basis and *ad hoc* studies). Similarly, the large accounting firms issue a variety of finance and accounting related information on different countries of the world. Price Waterhouse, for example, regularly publishes booklets on selected countries, providing perspectives on doing business there.

Foreign government offices

Usually, an embassy has a commercial attaché who may be a valuable source of secondary information on that country. For example, let us assume research is being carried out to prepare a market potential study in order to decide whether a company should assemble televisions in Bulgaria. Import data on television sets in Bulgaria for the past five years is needed. The Bulgarian embassy in London might have a government publication that quickly and easily provides such information.

Other units of a foreign government in Britain can serve as important sources of data. For example, a hotel chain interested in constructing a hotel in Jamaica may find the Jamaican government tourist office in London an important source of information.

Many governments maintain special offices in Britain for the purpose of promoting trade and business with UK companies. These special offices offer all sorts of business-related information.

Multinational banks

Both British banks active worldwide (such as Barclays, Lloyds, National Westminster) and branches of foreign banks in the United Kingdom are additional sources of secondary information. Many of these banks maintain libraries. They usually offer free access to customers, present and prospective. In some instances, however, a bank may have information a researcher seeks in one of its reports, but the data may not be made available. It is worth while, nevertheless, to contact a multinational bank for secondary data.

Advantages of secondary research at home

Secondary research conducted at home is less expensive and less time consuming than research abroad. The research at home keeps commitment to future projects at a low level: no contacts have to made overseas, and no high-level decisions have to be made on exploring markets outside the home country. Research in the home environment affords easy communication with sources of information. In addition, requests for certain kinds of information are often more favourably received by foreign sources located in Britain, where political pressure and business customers do not inhibit response. Research undertaken at home about a foreign environment also gains objectivity. The researcher is not constrained by overseas customs and can apply the same standards of quality and analysis as would be used for a project related to domestic business.

Disadvantages of secondary research at home

Secondary research undertaken at home has various limitations. First, current information may be scarce in the home country. After all, there is a time lag between data gathering in a foreign country and its transmission, say, to Britain. Further, certain information/elements may be uncovered in the foreign environment that will ultimately bear on the project. For example, a company may be exploring the feasibility of establishing a factory in Malaysia to manufacture air conditioners. Research done in Britain is likely to reveal a good potential market for air conditioners based on secondary data such as medium per capita income, hot climate, low rate of air conditioners per hundred households and encouragement by the Malaysian government. However, this data omits an important fact about Malaysian living: there are certain regions without electricity. Such a fact would become immediately obvious to an observer on the spot, but maybe not to a UK-based researcher.

Secondary research abroad

An alternative to carrying out secondary research in the home country is undertaking secondary research abroad. It should be recognized that the abundance of information available, say, in the United States or in the United Kingdom, from both government and private sources, is not found in most countries of the world, including the developed ones. However, interest in collecting socio-economic information has greatly increased. As countries progressed economically, it became important to collect and publish statistical information on commercial matters, on a regular basis. As a matter of fact, it may be claimed that availability of reliable secondary data is directly related to the level of economic development of a country. Even among third world countries, data-gathering activity has greatly improved since the 1970s. This may be attributed partly to United Nations' efforts to impress upon countries the desirability of keeping national statistical information accurate and current (Permut, 1977).

Sources

The following are the major sources of secondary information for an international marketer.

Government sources

The single most important source of secondary information on a country is the national government. The quality and quantity of information will vary from country to country, but in most cases information on population statistics, consumption standards, industrial production, imports and exports, price levels, employment and more, is conveniently available. On the other hand, data on retail and wholesale trade may be found only in certain countries. The government data is usually available through a government agency or major publishers in the country. In many countries, marketing-related information gathered by the government is not separated from other sorts of information. Thus, the researcher must go through a plethora of information to choose what is relevant.

Private sources

In many countries there are private consulting companies which gather and sell commercial information. Information from private sources may in fact have been collected by the government originally, but consulting companies analyse and organize it in such a manner that business executives can more easily make sense of it. For example, International Information Services Ltd (IIS), a global product pick-up service located in Sussex, the United Kingdom, provides information on such specific issues as the most popular pizza flavours in France, and retail pricing structure for shampoos in Venezuela compared with that of its neighbours in Colombia and Brazil. Each day over 400 IIS shoppers visit supermarkets in 120 countries searching for information requested by clients as varied as Coca-Cola, General Foods, Procter and Gamble, Nestlé and Unilever. The information gathered by IIS shoppers is stored, along with data from the company's comprehensive library of foreign trade publications, in a computerized database, enabling IIS to offer clients continuous updates on new food, household and pharmaceutical products introduced worldwide. IIS uses these data to compile bimonthly indexes of the new products.

Research institutes, trade associations, universities and similar sources

Although not every country in the world has trade associations or research institutes (in both developed and developing countries), such institutions could be important sources of secondary data. In some countries they are set up with the help of international agencies and/or the government.

Local businesses

A company may be in contact with one or more businesses in a foreign country. These contacts can serve as important sources of secondary data. Even if these businesses have collected no data on their own, they could gather and communicate data available through other local sources such as those mentioned earlier.

Problems with foreign secondary data

The researcher must be aware of problems and deficiencies when interpreting information. The following brief summaries deal with some of the difficulties with the reliability of foreign secondary data.

The underlying purpose of data collection

As mentioned earlier, the single most important source of marketing-related secondary data in any country is the government. The government as a political institution may not approach data collection with the same objectivity as a business researcher. This problem is particularly severe in developing countries, where governments may enhance the information content in order to improve the picture of economic life in the country. In this way, political considerations overshadow the reliability of the data.

    The researcher must ascertain that the data available is accurate within the limits of its sources and that there are no hidden assumptions that might distort the information from the researcher's point of view.

Currency of information

Information gathering is an expensive activity. When the government has limited resources, data gathering becomes unimportant. Thus, information may not be gathered as frequently as desirable. The researcher needs to be very careful that the information available overseas has not become outdated.

Reliability of data

This is not just an international problem. The reliability of data will be affected by data collection procedures. For example, the sample may not be random, so that the results cannot be assumed to reflect the behaviour of the total population. Even when a good sampling plan has been laid out, it may not be properly adhered to (for example, the interviewers might substitute subjects when those required by the sampling plan cannot be reached). In brief, numerous factors may affect the reliability of data.

It may be difficult for the researchers to judge the reliability of secondary data available in a country, and it would be dysfunctional to try to test that reliability. If the researchers are indeed very concerned with reliability, they would be better off undertaking primary data collection. Researchers should judge for themselves how far to accept that data on the basis of inputs from different contacts in the country about their own experiences with secondary data there. This leads to the idea of 'triangulation' or a kind of consensual validity.

Data classification

Another problem has to do with the classification scheme of the available data. In many countries data reported is too broadly classified for use at the micro level.

Comparability of data

Multinational corporate executives often like to compare information on their host countries about such matters as review of market performance, strategy effectiveness in different environments and so on. Unfortunately, the secondary data obtainable from different countries is not readily comparable. Keegan (1984) reports, for example, that in Germany purchases of televisions are considered expenditures for entertainment, while in the US television purchases are in the category of furniture, furnishing and household equipment. These discrepancies make brand share comparison nearly impossible.

Availability of data

Finally, in many developing nations, secondary data is very scarce. Information on retail and wholesale trade is especially difficult to obtain. In such cases primary data collection becomes vital.

Primary data collection

An alternative to secondary data is primary data collection. Primary data presumably provides more relevant information because it is collected specifically for the purpose in mind. However, the collection of primary data is an expensive proposition in terms of both money and time. Thus, the underlying purpose must justify the effort. For example, when a company has to make a decision about appointing a distributor for the occasional sale of its product in a developing country, it is not necessary to have primary data on the long-term market potential. On the other hand, if the company is considering the establishment of a manufacturing plant in the country, it may be important to undertake a market potential study.

Problems of primary data collection

Primary data collection in a foreign environment poses a variety of problems. These problems are related to social and cultural factors and the level of economic development. They can be grouped under three headings:

(1)   Sampling problems.

(2)   Questionnaire problems.

(3)   The problem of non-response.

Sampling problems

A good piece of research should reflect the perspectives of the entire population. This is feasible, however, only when the sample is randomly drawn. Unfortunately, in some countries it is difficult to find completely representative and detailed information on the socio-economic characteristics of the universal population because such information is lacking, not available on a current basis, or, at best, is inadequate. The researcher then has to estimate characteristics and population parameters, sometimes with little basic data on which to build an accurate estimate (Cateora, 1983). Some samples are still biased in the end. Limitations aside, some directories are available to help the international marketing researcher to draw an adequate sample, especially in the industrial marketing area.

Sometimes data gathering may have to be confined to urban areas due to the inadequate means of transportation available in a specific country. Further, only a small percentage of the population may have telephones (Davis, Douglas and Silk, 1981). The World Bank statistics indicate, for example, that there are only four telephones per thousand population in Eygpt, six in Turkey and thirty-two in Argentina. In many countries the postal system is so inefficient that letters may not be delivered at all or may reach the addressee only after a long delay. In brief, it may be extremely difficult to obtain a proper random sample, especially in developing countries.

Questionnaire problems

In many countries different languages are spoken in different areas. Thus, the questionnaire has to be in different languages for use within the same country. In India, for example, fourteen official languages are spoken in different parts of the country, while most government and business affairs are conducted in English. Similarly, in Switzerland, German is used in some areas, while French and Italian are spoken in others. Unfortunately, translating a questionnaire from one language to another is far from easy. In the translating process many points are entirely eclipsed, because many idioms, phrases and statements mean different things in different cultures. This translation problem may be partially averted with the help of computers, in terms of spell checks, wording and so on.

Problems of non-response

Even if the interviewee is successfully reached, there is no guarantee that he or she will cooperate and furnish the desired information. There are many reasons for non-response. First, cultural habits in many countries virtually prohibit communication with a stranger, particularly for women. For example, a researcher simply may not be able to speak with a Saudi woman on the telephone to find out what she thinks of a particular brand. Second, in many societies such matters as preferences for hygienic products and food products are too personal to be shared with an outsider. In some Latin American countries, a woman may feel ashamed to talk with a researcher about her choice of a brand of sanitary product. Third, respondents in many cases may be unwilling to share their true feelings with interviewers because they suspect the interviewers may be agents of the government, for example, seeking information for imposition of additional taxes. Fourth, middle-class people, in developing countries in particular, are reluctant to accept their status and sometimes may make false claims in order to reflect the lifestyle of wealthier people. For example, in a study on the consumption of tea in India, over 70% of the respondents from middle-income families claimed they used one of the several national brands of tea. This finding could not be substantiated since over 60% of the tea sold nationally in India is unbranded, generic tea, sold unpackaged. Fifth, many respondents willing to cooperate may be illiterate, so that even oral communication may be difficult. In other words, their exposure to the modern world may be so limited, and their outlook so narrow, that the researchers would find it extremely difficult to elicit adequate responses from them. Sixth, in many countries privacy is becoming a big issue. In Japan, for example, the middle-class is showing increasing concern about the protection of personal information. Information that people are most anxious to protect include income, assets, tax payments, family life, and political and religious affiliation. Finally, the lack of established marketing research firms in many countries may force the researcher to count on *ad hoc* help for gathering data. How far such temporary help may be counted on to complete a job systematically can only be guessed (Jain, 1987).

Solving the problems

There are no foolproof methods to take care of all the problems discussed above. The following hints, however, may help to eliminate some of the problems. The international marketing research effort should be undertaken in conjunction with a reputable local company. The resources of the cooperating company will be invaluable; for example, its knowledge of local customs, including areas such as the feasibility of interviewing women while husbands are at work; its familiarity with local environment, including modes of transport available for personal interviews in smaller towns; and its contact in different parts of the country as sources for drawing a sample.

From the beginning, a person fully conversant with both sound marketing research procedures and the local culture should be involved in all phases of the research design. Such a person can recommend the number of languages in which the questionnaire should be printed and what sort of cultural traits, habits, customs and rituals to keep in mind in different phases of the research.

The questionnaire may first be written in English, and then a native fluent in English can translate it into the local language(s). A third person should retranslate it into English. This retranslated version can then be compared with the original English version. The three people involved should work together to eliminate differences in the three versions of the questionnaire by changing phrases, idioms and words. Ultimately, the questionnaire in the local language should accurately reflect the questions in the original English questionnaire.

If feasible, the persons recruited to conduct the interviews should have prior experience. The local cooperating company may be helpful here. In any event, complete instructions and training should be given before the fieldwork starts. The conducting of interviews should be practised. Ways must be found to ensure that the interviewers follow the instructions for proper sampling control. For example, the researcher might accompany the interviewer sporadically.

Finally, the researcher should draw the best possible sample. If the sample is not random, the researcher should employ appropriate statistical techniques in analysing the collected information so that the results reflect the reality of the situation.

Organization for international marketing research

International marketing research can be carried out both at the headquarters in the home country and in the host country. Marketing research at the headquarters will be in two areas: short-term planning and budgeting, and strategy formulation. For example, yearly forecasts of sales for different products in different countries will be a part of the annual budget. But a study undertaken to determine if a new product successfully sold in Britain should be introduced in international markets would have a strategy focus.

Marketing research studies in host countries are concerned mainly with day-to-day operations, tactics to achieve specified goals and short-term marketing planning. For example, a study may examine the factors responsible for poor sales performance in the previous quarter. Similarly, marketing research may be undertaken to decide if a concentrated seven- or ten-week advertising campaign is preferable to spreading advertising over the whole year.

Sales forecasting will naturally be carried out to develop budgets. As mentioned earlier, the headquarters may also make sales forecasts. Thus, for discussion of annual plans and budgets, the host country manager would use his or her forecasts as the basis for resource allocation, while the headquarters' managers use their forecasts to negotiate and approve the country budgets.

Marketing research is unquestionably an important function that must be conducted both at the corporate headquarters and in the host countries. For example, the marketing research function for NCR (National Cash Registers Incorporated) in host countries is performed at different levels, according to the importance of each country to the parent company. In Japan, in the United Kingdom, and in Germany, NCR has a large marketing research department simply because the company is extremely active in these markets. On the other hand, in a country like India where NCR commitment is meagre, a marketing research study might be assigned to an outside consultant.

In addition to undertaking marketing research at the corporate level and in the host countries, in many companies marketing research may also be conducted at the regional level. A company may divide its international operations into regions: for example, Western Europe, Far East, Latin America, Middle East, Africa and South East Asia. Each country manager in a region would report to the regional executive. Under such arrangements the regional executive may seek marketing research information to formulate a regional marketing strategy or to develop the marketing focus of a country within the region. There may be a specific person responsible for marketing research in the region, or one of the salespersons may carry this responsibility.

What is important to recognize is that marketing information is important at all levels. However, the process of gathering, analysing and reporting market-related information may not necessarily be called marketing research. Further, marketing research responsibility may not necessarily be assigned to a marketing person. Of course, the extent of marketing research that a company undertakes would vary according to the style of management and the importance of a particular foreign country for a given product (Jain, 1987).

Another way of categorizing information is suggested by Keegan (1984), and on this basis information may be grouped into five broad areas with twenty-three categories (see Figure 14.3).

In general, the value of international research can be summarized according to Douglas and Craig (1983) as follows:

(1)   To aid in decisions relating to international market expansion, for example, whether new countries are potential candidates for market entry or existing products might be carried into new markets.

(2)   To monitor performance in different countries and product markets based on criteria such as return on investment and market share, so as to diagnose where existing or potential future problems appear to be emerging and, hence, where there is a need to adapt current marketing strategies or tactics.

Category	Coverage
	I MARKET INFORMATION
1. *Market potential*	Information indicating potential demand for products, including the status and prospects of existing company products in existing markets.
2. *Consumer/customer attitudes and behaviour*	Information on attitudes, behaviour and needs of consumers and customers of existing and potential company products. Also included in this category are attitudes of investors towards a company's investment merit.
3. *Channels of distribution*	Availability, effectiveness, attitudes and preferences of channel agents.
4. *Communications media*	Media availability, effectiveness and cost.
5. *Market sources*	Availability, quality and cost.
6. *New products*	Non-technical information concerning new products for a company (this includes products that are already marketed by other companies).
	II COMPETITIVE INFORMATION
7. *Competitive business strategy and plans*	Goals and objectives. Definition of business: the 'design' and rationale of the company.
8. *Competitive functional strategies, plans and programmes*	Marketing: target markets, product, price, place and promotion. Strategy and plans: finance, manufacturing, R&D, and human resource strategy, plans and programmes.

9. *Competitive operations*   Detailed intelligence on competitor operations. Production, shipments, employee transfers, morale, etc.

III PRESCRIPTIVE INFORMATION

10. *Foreign exchanges*   Information concerning changes or expected changes in foreign exchange rates by exchange control authorities and immediate influences upon these authorities.

11. *Foreign taxes*   Information concerning decisions, intentions, and attitudes of foreign authorities regarding taxes upon earnings, dividends and interest.

12. *Other foreign prescriptions*   All information concerning local, regional or international authority guidelines, rulings, laws, decrees, other than foreign exchange and tax matters affecting operations, assets or investments of a company.

13. *Home government prescriptions*   Home government incentives, controls, regulations, restraints etc., affecting a company.

IV RESOURCE INFORMATION

14. *Human resources*   Availability of individuals and groups, employment candidates, sources, strikes etc.

15. *Money*   Availability and cost of money for company uses.

16. *Raw material*   Availability and cost.

17. *Acquisitions and mergers*   Leads or other information concerning potential acquisitions, mergers or joint ventures.

V GENERAL CONDITIONS

18. *Economic factors*   Macroeconomic information dealing with broad factors such as capital movements, rates of growth, inflation, economic structure and economic geography.

19. *Social factors*   Social structure of society, customs, attitudes and preferences.

20. *Political factors*   'Investment climate', meaning of elections and political change.

21. *Scientific and technological factors*   Major development with broad but relatively untested implications.

22. *Management and administrative practices*   Management and administrative practices and procedures concerning such matters as employee compensation and report procedure.

23. *Other information*   Information not assignable to another category.

Figure 14.3 Twenty-three categories for a global business intelligence system. (Adapted from Keegan W. J. (1984). *Multinational Marketing Management* 3rd edn, pp. 215–16. New Jersey: Prentice Hall

(3) To scan the international environment in order to assess future world and country scenarios and to monitor emerging and changing environmental trends.

(4) To assess strategies with regard to the allocation of corporate resources and effort across different countries, product markets, target segments and modes of entry, to determine whether changes in this allocation would maximize long-run profitability.

The following chapter is concerned with industrial marketing and its associated research approaches.

REFERENCES

Anon (1985). Product pick-up firm samples international supermarkets. *Marketing News*, **19**, 10

Cateora P. R. (1983). *International Marketing* 5th edn. Illinois: Irwin, 267–8

Davis H. L., Douglas S. P. and Silk A. J. (1981). Measuring unreliability: A hidden threat to cross national marketing research. *Journal of Marketing*, **45**, 98–108

Douglas S. P. and Craig C. S. (1983). *International Marketing Research*. Englewood Cliffs NJ: Prentice-Hall

Jain S. C. (1987). *International Marketing Management* 2nd edn. Boston, Mass: Kent Publishing Company

Keegan W. J. (1984). *Multinational Marketing Management* 3rd edn. Englewood Cliffs NJ: Prentice-Hall, 224

Permut S. E. (1977). The European view of marketing research. *Columbia Journal of World Business*, **11**, 94

Thwaits J. A. (1983). Global marketing success is contingent on a solid bank of foreign marketing intelligence. *Marketing News*, **17**, 1

FURTHER READING

Cavusgil S. T. (1985). Guidelines for export market research. *Business Horizons*, **28**, 30–31

King W. R. (1985). Information, technology, and corporate growth. *Columbia Journal of World Business*, **19**, 29–34

Mayer C. S. (1978). The lessons of multinational marketing research. *Business Horizons*, **21**, 9–10

15

Industrial Marketing Research

The area of industrial marketing is often overlooked in discussions of research. Yet industrial products constitute a far larger part of the economy than consumer goods, in terms of number of products, volume and value. Industrial marketing can be divided into categories in several ways. One method of categorizing industrial products is based on the complexity of the process of buying the product from the buyer's point of view. Four categories have been identified (Lehmann and O'Shaughnessy, 1974):

(1) Routine products, where both the technical performance features of the product and application procedures are known.

(2) Procedural problem products, where the technical performance is known but application procedures need to be developed.

(3) Performance problem products, where the technical performance of the product is unknown.

(4) Political problem products, where the product is a major buy affecting many organization units and costing a lot of money, and both technical performance and application procedures are unclear.

Numerous other bases exist for categorizing industrial products. Among these are the following:

(1) Price.

(2) Criticalness of the product to the overall operation and appearance of the system as a whole.

(3) Distribution method (direct sales versus industrial distributor/agent).

(4) Amount of custom engineering involved (standard versus special order products).

(5) Number of key customers.

(6) Degree of expertise of purchasing agents.

Given certain combinations of these characteristics, an industrial good can be quite similar to a consumer good, hence the marketing and marketing research problems and methods become very similar. The point is that many consumer goods have characteristics similar to industrial goods. The result of this similarity is that industrial marketing research can use many of the techniques and procedures of consumer marketing research.

Industrial marketing researchers and buyers

Industrial marketing researchers can learn from consumer product marketing research, partly because consumer product marketing has had the benefit of sophisticated techniques being routinely applied. There is a great reluctance to believe that they have anything to learn from consumer product marketers. In fact, there is a certain amount of defensiveness and resentment towards marketing researchers on the part of industrial marketers. Perhaps this defensiveness has something to do with the sales orientation of industrial marketing. Still, such defensiveness seems unfounded since, for example, industrial marketing accounts for a large share of GNP when compared with consumer marketing. Still, there tends to be a fairly conservative attitude that suggests consumer and industrial marketing are completely different. While there are differences, there are at least as many similarities.

One common and overriding fact, however, about industrial or organizational buyers, and the one which also distinguishes between consumer and organizational purchasing, is that they are primarily purchasing for organizational rather than personal motives. With this in mind, many of the differences between consumer and organizational marketing research are ultimately due to differences between consumer and organizational market behaviour.

The fact that buyers are purchasing on behalf of their organization has led some observers to suggest that the organizational buyer is always more rational and better informed than his consumer counterpart. This, in turn, leads to the suggestion that organizational buyers utilize only objective factors such as delivery, service and (predominantly) price, in evaluating potential suppliers. These assertions may be substantially correct in any given buying situation, but they are not necessarily invariably so.

Although purchase motives are the primary distinction between consumer and organizational purchasers, a number of other differences are worthy of note inasmuch as they have implications for marketing research. These differences are as follows.

Setting for buying

For consumers, the buying unit is within the family or household, whereas for an industrial buyer, the setting for buying is within the organization. This means that the industrial marketer must take account of factors such as organizational procedures for buying, levels of authority and so on, which are not relevant to consumer marketing.

Technical/commercial knowledge

Usually, the organizational purchaser will be a trained professional. Such buyers are likely to be much more knowledgeable, both technically and commercially, than, say, the typical purchaser for consumer foods. For example this requires a very different approach in terms of selling to such buyers.

Contact with buyers/channels of distribution

Industrial markets are usually more geographically concentrated than consumer markets. Factors such as proximity to labour markets, raw materials and transportation facilities often dictate an industry's location. In addition, compared to consumer products markets, there are usually fewer buyers in an industrial market. Taken together, these factors mean that the industrial product marketer normally has much more direct and personal contact with his purchasers or potential purchasers. In industrial markets also, distribution channels tend to be shorter with many marketers supplying direct.

Number of people involved in purchase

In a consumer buying decision, the number of people involved will be small ranging from one individual to possibly the household and close friends or relatives. In the industrial buying decision, depending on the size of the organization and the nature of the buying decision, a great number of people may be involved. Research by Buckner (1967) set out in his book, *How British Industry Buys*, confirms this increased size of purchasing unit.

Derived demand

Industrial buyers adjust their purchases according to the projected outlook for their sales, buying more when growth in sales is forecast than when they are not. This can lead to a 'pendulum effect', that is, one buyer may start off with a modest cutback on his or her order, creating a knock-on effect back through the chain of production and marketing and resulting in other buyers making progressively larger cutbacks.

Reciprocal trading

This, in effect, means that two companies can be both buyer and seller at the same time but for different purposes.

Industrial buying decisions – stages and types

As mentioned in Chapter 8, it is useful to think of the buying process, for both industrial and consumer product marketing, as a problem-solving or decision-making process. Once the marketer understands these steps and the factors and forces operating within each of them, he or she is in a position to make more informed, and therefore better, marketing decisions.

A more detailed description of the stages in the decision-making process of the industrial or organizational buyer, developed by Robinson Faris and Wind (1967), is as follows:

(1) Anticipation or recognition of a problem.
(2) Determination of approximate characteristics, and quantity of items required.
(3) Description of specific characteristics and quality of needed items.
(4) Selection of potential sources of supply.
(5) Acquisition and analysis of proposals.
(6) Selection of supplier(s) to provide needed items.
(7) Selection of a system for future ordering.
(8) Performance feedback and evaluation.

Within this generalized, decision process we can recognize three distinct types of industrial purchasing decision, each of which will have different implications with respect to progress through the decision-making sequence. These different types of purchasing decision are outlined as follows:

New task decisions

This involves the purchase of products or services for which little or no previous purchasing experience exists. With this type of purchase decision, the buyer will spend considerable time and effort in the search and evaluation stages of the decision process, and hence the provision of adequate marketing information is essential.

Modified rebuy decisions

This is where the product or service being purchased has been purchased before but where the purchaser is considering an alternative product or supplier.

In this situation, the purchaser will have some knowledge and experience of the product or service in question, but will be looking for information on alternatives.

Straight rebuy decisions

This is where the product or service being purchased is one which has been bought frequently in the past. Managers have extensive purchasing experience on which to rely and purchasing is routine. With this type of purchasing decision, the buyer may move directly from the problem recognition stage to the selection of an order routine.

As mentioned earlier, one of the distinguishing features of organizational buying is that more people may be involved in the decision-making process. It is important for marketing research to identify precisely who is involved and their respective roles. Collectively, these individuals are known as the Decision-Making Unit (DMU) or, as Webster and Wind (1972) have termed it, the 'Buying Centre'.

The size of the DMU may vary from one to literally dozens of individuals depending upon such factors as:

- the size of the organization;
- the value/importance of the purchase; and
- whether the purchase decision is a new task or a modified or straight repeat purchase.

Perhaps of most importance is the need to identify the different roles which individual members of the DMU perform in the purchasing decision. Five roles have been identified in this respect, namely: User – Influencer – Buyer – Decider – Gatekeeper.

In many organizational purchasing situations – using objective measures, for example, price, delivery, quality and so on – competitive offerings are perceived as being very similar. In such situations, the organizational buyer may be just as susceptible to 'non-rational', subjective appeals.

Having argued that industrial marketing (and, therefore, industrial marketing research) is not that different from consumer marketing, we now turn to some of the features of industrial marketing which affect the research carried out. The major problems remain the same: preparing annual plans, assessing market potential, allocating effort to different elements of the marketing programme and so forth. Differences result from the environmental conditions, which affect (a) the amount of different types of research executed and (b) the form of the research. Some of the most important features are purchasing agents and the buying process, identifying the buying centre, direct (personal) sales, custom engineering, few key customers, hard-to-obtain interviews and the specialized nature (or general absence) of test marketing.

Purchasing agents and the buying process

The formal institution of a purchasing agent separates industrial marketing from consumer marketing. Here a manager is charged with making good buys (that is, low price, reliable performance, delivered on time, as well as other decision criteria). The purchasing agent becomes the principal contact point for sellers and suppliers of routine order products (bolts, paper and so on). The agents also have influence in more complex product selection. Moreover, they tend to serve a gatekeeper role, in which they screen vendors from the person or persons who make the actual buying decision. Therefore the important research problems are:

(1) to find out who the purchasing agents are;

(2) to find out what their preferences are; and

(3) to find out whom, if anyone, they are 'fronting'.

Identifying the buying centre

Industrial marketing often involves finding out who has impact on a decision. For example, the selection of new electronic machinery by a company may be influenced by users, engineers, line managers and purchasing agents (the decision-making unit, the DMU). The first task is often to try to locate these people. This is typically achieved by 'snowballing', which consists of asking people in the organization to identify those who are involved in the decision. By asking several different people and comparing responses, a core of key people typically emerges.

In addition to identifying who has influence on a decision, it is useful to understand the kind of influence they have. Returning to the example of the decision-making process related to new electronic machinery, the financial manager is likely to control the budget and, hence, has signature authorization power. Such a person can block a decision but rarely makes a choice unilaterally. On the other hand, users often have strong preferences but no authority. Consequently, it is useful to try to understand who has authority (budget), who has interest/preferences, and who is perceived as being the expert.

Direct (personal) sales

Personal selling is used for many consumer goods and services, for example, cosmetics and insurance. In industrial marketing, however, the salesperson is typically accorded more prestige, power and pay. Also, the salesperson tends to serve more of a technical consulting role to the customer. In fact to many people, industrial marketing is synonymous with sales management. Hence, research related to sales management forms a large part of industrial marketing research. Some of the most common types of research which relate to sales management are:

(1) Overall sales forecasting.
(2) Potential estimation of sales (by sales territory, industry or type of customer).
(3) Sales effectiveness estimation.
(4) Selection of salespersons.
(5) Territory boundaries and salesperson assignments.
(6) Salesperson time allocation scheduling.
(7) Salesperson compensation schedules.

Interestingly, much of the research on these topics takes on an operations research orientation, especially territory boundary, assignment problems, time allocation scheduling, and compensation schedules, which are amenable to mathematical programming approaches.

Custom engineering

Many large industrial products, such as power generators, require custom engineering for each sale. Thus, the technical expertise of the sales (or technical back-up) staff plays a large role in the sales effort. For this reason research focusing on (a) determining the importance of custom engineering, (b) determining the types of custom engineering needed and (c) assessing the perceived competence of the sales staff is common. Similarly, the importance of after-sales service becomes more crucial and perceived competence in this area is also a key area of interest.

Few key customers

For specialized industrial goods, the number of key customers may be in the range of 10 to 30 and can be as small as 1 or 2, so many of the statistical procedures which depend on large samples are not applicable (although there are some possible statistical adjustments that can be applied to determine sample size in industrial settings). The result of this is that analytical techniques to study industrial customers tend to be small-sample orientated, including mainly tabular procedures such as cross-tabulations.

Hard-to-obtain interviews

For consumer products it is relatively easy to find consumers who are willing to provide information about their preferences and usage patterns and to try out products. For many industrial products, it is sometimes hard to decide whom to interview. Once the key individual is uncovered, getting an appointment and uninterrupted responses from busy managers is extremely difficult. Reliable data is also hard to obtain. For example, most executives or purchasing agents correctly perceive that it is to their advantage to have many products available. Consequently, respondents tend to indicate more interest in new products than they may actually have, but once you obtain cooperation you can obtain a great deal of information.

Specialized nature (or general absence) of test marketing

Possibly one of the most obvious distinguishing characteristics of much of industrial marketing research is the specialized nature (or general absence) of test marketing. This can often be explained by the fact that, unlike most frequently purchased products, the costs of developing and making prototypes are usually very high. This makes potential estimates the crucial numbers in 'go–no go' decisions and, hence, places particular emphasis on market potential estimation. The closest analogy to test marketing is the design and sale of a custom designed and manufactured product. Depending on how well it works, this may develop into a specific product line. Still, some industrial companies sometimes decide to undertake a test marketing programme. The four most used methods of market testing for industrial durable goods are as follows.

Product-use tests

The company selects a small group of potential customers who agree to use the new product for a limited period. Then, the researchers observe how the customers use the product. After the test, customers are asked to express purchase intent and other reactions.

Trade shows

These exhibitions draw a large number of buyers who view new products in a few concentrated days. Managers can see how much interest potential customers show in the new product, how they react to various features and terms, and how many express purchase intentions or place orders.

Distributors and dealer display rooms

This method yields preference and pricing information in the normal selling atmosphere for the product.

Controlled or test marketing

Here, the company will produce a limited supply of the product and give it to the salesforce in a limited number of geographical areas, in order to try to sell it. The company also give promotional support, printed catalogue sheets and so on.

Data sources

The sources of data used by industrial marketing researchers tend to lean heavily towards published data held either in government reports or by syndicated services. Besides reliance on secondary data, such as the Census of Manufacturers data and trade association sources, most research relies on interviews of key prospects. This is often carried out informally by sales personnel who, acting as application specialists, are often called upon to diagnose customer problems and recommend solutions. The solutions are often the source of new product ideas. Hence the salesforce often play a role that encompasses sales, market research and new product development. In achieving formal interviews, a common approach is to use salespersons as interviewers. This last section will proceed to discuss some of the pros and cons of this approach.

Salespersons as interviewers

The appropriateness of using salespersons as interviewers depends on a variety of conditions.

Type of research and salespersons

If the research is fairly mundane (for example, penetration studies designed to find out if a particular product is being used, or questions about product line extensions) and the interview is very structured, ordinary salespersons are adequate. When the problem becomes more complex (for example, new product concept tests), however, the salesperson needs to have some special skills to complete the task fruitfully.

Time available

Salespersons will push research to the back of their agenda (commissions are paid on the basis of sales, not completed questionnaires). Hence, super busy (and good) salespersons are generally poor interviewers.

Type of customers – interference of roles

Some customers may resent interviews. When this is the case, the potential lost sales are probably not worth the information obtained, which will be of dubious value at best.

Access to right people

The thought of using salespersons as interviewers is appealing in that it is apparently a cost-saving approach. However, if the people to be interviewed are not regularly contacted by the salespersons, the apparent economies vanish.

Control of sample and interviewer cheating

Assuming a salesperson is given a quota of interviews to collect, he or she may typically (a) talk to friends among the clients and (b) be tempted to cheat by personally filling out the questionnaires. This might also happen with consumer marketing research interviews, but maybe the checking procedures are better in this case. With these points in mind, the following are keys to successful salesperson interviewing:

(1)   Have a good questionnaire (pre-tested).
(2)   Train the salesforce.
(3)   Have only a few surveys per year and limited time per survey.
(4)   Include data-collection as part of the salesperson's job description.

In summary, then, the pros of salespeople interviewing include speed, ease of implementation, and spin-off knowledge, which the salespeople may acquire by being involved in the research. The cons include time diverted from sales calls, potential annoyance to salespeople and customers, and lack of training.

Finally, this section on industrial marketing research is short because the differences are more environmental than analytical. Nonetheless, someone interested in industrial marketing research may want to consult some other sources (for example, Rawnsley, 1978; Cox, 1979; Choffray and Lilien, 1980).

REFERENCES

Buckner H. (1967). *How British Industry Buys*. London: Hutchinson
Choffray J. and Lilien G. L. (1980). *Market Planning for New Industrial Products*. New York: John Wiley & Sons
Cox W. E. Jr. (1979). *Industrial Marketing Research*. New York: John Wiley & Sons

Lehmann D. R. and O'Shaughnessy J. (1974). Difference in attribute importance for different industrial products. *Journal of Marketing*, **38**, 36–42

Rawnsley A., ed. (1978). *Manual of Industrial Marketing Research*. New York: John Wiley & Sons

Robinson P. J., Faris C. W. and Wind Y. (1967). *Industrial Buying and Creative Marketing*. Allyn and Bacon

Webster F. E. and Wind Y. (1972). *Organizational Buying Behaviour*. New Jersey: Prentice-Hall

FURTHER READING

Lehmann D. R. (1989). *Market Research and Analysis* 3rd edn. Illinois: Irwin

16

Marketing Research and Marketing Intelligence

Whereas marketing research is concerned with relatively focused aspects of marketing information, the theme of this chapter is one of 'wider horizons', with the main (though not exclusive) contexts of analysis being both external to the organization and concerned with less immediate decision making.

The context of analysis is, in some senses, the least tangible of a marketing information system because by dealing with the marketing environment through environmental scanning investigation is less focused than marketing research – *what* is studied may be totally irrelevant to the organization.

This chapter discusses *what* to investigate and provides some suggestions as to *how* such investigation might be conducted and organized. First, the context of marketing intelligence – that is, marketing's environment, is reviewed.

The marketing environment

The basis of 'intelligence' informational requirements for marketing is that marketing's environment provides conditions and influences that impinge or potentially impinge upon marketing. Examples include the effects of government economic policy, changes in technology and the implications of societal change.

The importance of the environment comes from the nature of marketing itself, as defined by the Institute of Marketing:

> 'the management process responsible for identifying, anticipating and satisfying customer requirements profitably.'

This importance is based on the word anticipate which requires a degree of forecasting and projection into the future. To (merely) identify customer requirements usually involves specific marketing research programmes, but to anticipate requires a broader perspective – continuously monitoring current trends (not all of which are necessarily obviously relevant) in order to plan ahead.

It is the marketing function in an organization which is primarily responsible for looking outwards. Indeed it is generally the case that this function, being at the interface of the organization and its environment, is at least theoretically in a particularly good position to understand what is happening – and what might happen – outside, in order to initiate appropriate organizational response.

It should be added, however, that marketing's environment is not only concerned with elements external to the organization, but also with those influences internal to it but external to the marketing function, such as the organizational position and relative power of the marketing function *vis à vis* other functions.

Direct and indirect influences on marketing management

Depending on the specific influence, marketing activities might be directly affected (new technology providing alternative methods of conducting the same activities, or legislation governing these). Alternatively, market behaviour might change – due to changes in the social structure or social attitudes, or perhaps due to changed lifestyles resulting from technological and/or economic change – thus with indirect implications for marketing response.

It is the latter which probably provide the greatest challenge because the former, the direct influences, are generally easier to spot and may be more obviously relevant to the organization's marketing activities because they are concerned with marketing activities themselves. However, those influences which are indirect will often be 'further away' from the immediate focus of the organization since they are the 'knock-on' effects of environmental change elsewhere, and in some cases their eventual impact within the marketplace could be relatively obscure.

A further point is the interaction of influences. The combined impact of economic and technological change, for example, might give extra momentum to (say) the home-centred society in certain segments, since in-home entertainment expands with technological development, and leisure time expands with high unemployment or increases in hi-tech production processes.

Marketing environments

It is worth identifying the types of environmental influence concerned – some have already been briefly mentioned and Figure 16.1 provides a framework for considering these and others.

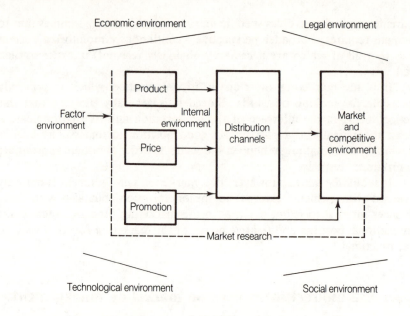

Figure 16.1 The main 'environments'.

This framework of various influences on the marketing process is merely a picture representation of a way of thinking. It should not be analysed much further *per se* because this might misleadingly imply some mutual exclusivity of such influence – 'lists' of influence are prone to imply this, as Glaser (1985) warned.

The previous example of interaction between economic and technological change in a 'Gestalt' or synergistic manner to create societal and market change demonstrates this point, and this might not have been foreseen from monitoring and analysing 'discrete' environmental influences.

If the marketing process is thought of in this way it reinforces the market environment as the focus of marketing activity and, taking its direction from the market, the marketing mix is then the organization's marketing response. The whole process is therefore influenced and affected by changes in economic, technological and societal factors and the changes in levels and types of competition in factor, reseller, consumer markets and so on.

Environmental influence

The market and social environments

The most obvious aspect of the market environment is concerned with a fundamental marketing principle – customer orientation. Marketers should think in terms of what customers are buying rather than what the supplier is selling. Levitt (1964) expounded this when he encouraged organizations to ask themselves the question 'What business are we in?' and to answer with a market orientation such as, in his example of Hollywood, 'in the entertainment business' rather than merely 'making films'.

In one way this is outside the scope of environmental scanning since it is a role of other elements of a marketing information system. Marketing research investigates specific dimensions of market behaviour and marketing models attempt to describe the market behaviour to investigate. However, this whole area is of great importance in understanding the environment. Firstly, it is not only the marketing function which should be so market-orientated, it is also important for this philosophy to pervade the entire organization. Thus, the internal environment of the organization should be understood – and influenced if need be.

Secondly, the market is not static and there will be changes in market behaviour which straightforward 'targeted' market research (even continuous research programmes) will not be even attempting to pick up. Such changes might emanate from other environmental influences – for example, economic or technological in origin – which eventually may be reflected, indirectly, in new and changed market behaviour. For example, highly focused market research into the cinema market might not, in itself, have identified changes in the broader entertainment market (as implied by Levitt).

Thirdly, the competitive environment, as a component of the market, can be included because a greater understanding of the *competitive* nature of the market environment is probably becoming more important, as Unger (1981) has suggested:

> 'knowing what the consumer wants is often not too helpful if a dozen
> other companies also know . . . a company must be competitor
> oriented. It must look for weak points in the positions of its
> competitors and then launch marketing attacks against these . . .'

The Market Research Society's Code of Conduct states that 'any form of espionage' shall not be associated with marketing research. There is, however, perhaps a thin line between some forms of research and some forms of espionage.

Moving to more specific market and social environmental influence, current topical trends include changes in the demographic structure and changes in social attitudes.

The former trends are easily monitored and projected from population statistics such as Social Trends and Regional Trends (both published in government reports) and show the fading 'age bulge' of 16- to 24-year-olds. Indeed, by 1990 the number of 16- to 24-year-olds had declined by 30% compared with the mid-1980s.

In some of these markets, although there is some difficulty in creating brand loyalty among 'young adults' – among other factors because of a scepticism about advertising (Piper, 1978) – once achieved, that loyalty can be quite strong in subsequent years. The extreme example of the large banks' marketing budgets spent on influencing 18-year-olds (especially prior to going to university/college) demonstrates this point.

A related aspect of 'the market' is that these young adults are more conservative and, at the same time, more interested in self-expression than their counterparts in previous generations (Evans, 1981; Shay, 1978; Lazer, 1981). An inference from this is that whereas they may, in general, be less interested in 'newness' *per se*, there are possibly more marketing opportunities because self-expression is manifested as greater societal pluralism. So, there may be many more, though smaller, market segments to identify and cater for.

The economic environment

In many instances it is difficult to separate the economic from the political environment because one is often, to some extent, a manifestation of the other. That is, government philosophy will be reflected in the economic policies adopted. For example, a dramatic demonstration of this occurred in 1979 with the change in government when almost overnight there was a reduction in income tax and an increase in interest rates. The former (income tax) had different effects on different market segments – the base rate was reduced from 33% to 30% (and subsequently even lower) giving such payers a certain amount of extra disposable income, but the top band went from 90% to 60% (again, there has been a subsequent further fall) giving these payers a substantially greater amount of extra disposable income. At the same time it is generally known that these latter have a higher *marginal propensity to save* and the former a higher *marginal propensity to consume*.

Higher interest rates had the effect of eating up more than the extra disposable income of the base rate tax payers, because of higher mortgage and other credit repayments, but those paying higher rates of tax were attracted to the increased dividend returns associated with high interest rates. For 'income segments' it has been shown that only 6% of the population were better off in 1986.

Increases in unemployment have obvious implications for lower spending power in those segments but at the same time there are new buying requirements coming from changed lifestyles and a greater degree of spare time.

This is a simplified example but it does show that economic policy changes do not affect all market segments in the same way. For example, 94% of all jobs lost since 1979 were lost in 'the North' (Employment Census 1984), confirming the popular perception of the two nation concept – important for geographic segmentation in marketing.

The legal environment

This 'environment' concerns legislative changes which may impinge upon the marketing activities of a firm. For example, changes in food labelling and description laws will directly affect packaging and also possibly promotion. There will be implications for international marketing concerning the different rules of various countries.

Laws constraining what can be included in advertising will likewise directly affect this element of marketing mixes. Again, there will be international differences – the interpretation and imposition of some of these will become more interesting in the future as DBS (Direct Broadcasting by Satellite) expands international advertising possibilities.

Consumer protection legislation may fundamentally change what is permissible in terms of product and service features, and indeed the whole area of consumerism may become as persuasive a force as it is in the US.

A continuous monitoring of the press and of the reporting of parliamentary affairs will help spot proposed legislation which might affect marketing operations. In some instances, the organization might, by itself if it is particularly powerful or influential with politicians, or collectively in an industry group, be able to lobby Members of Parliament to influence the nature and wording of such bills. This itself forms a topical debate in ethical practice; whether it is legitimately a part of the democratic process or whether business should not ethically be able to influence law-making in this country. This 'influencing of the environment' is conducted through the use of PR consultants who carefully select MP's who have a personal, as well as, or instead of, a professional interest in the area. These will then be targets of (in some cases) quite lavish hospitality and entertainment budgets – and possibly even more persuasive incentives! The concept of attempting to influence the environment (not only the legal environment) has been discussed by several writers (for example, Thorpe, 1975; Kotler, 1984).

The technological environment

Aspects of this were discussed in Chapter 6, but some further points can be made here. First, reiterating the earlier points, but putting them in a wider marketing context, technological change affects marketing in the three ways outlined earlier (that is, contributing directly to new product marketing because technology can provide new products; contributing to new ways of conducting marketing activities; and contributing to changes in market behaviour, to which marketing should respond).

The Sinclair C5 is an example of technology providing a new product but is also an example of a less than convincing marketing offering in terms of customer satisfaction.

The home computer is a more obvious example of technological change (smaller and cheaper silicon chips and so on) providing something which customers are prepared to purchase.

Secondly, the dynamic nature of technology has provided (and is projected to continue to provide) new ways of conducting marketing activities. Many of these are not actually new marketing *activities* but the *methods* of conducting some of these activities are affected by new technology.

Cable and satellite broadcasting, for example, provide new ways of advertising; the former helps target in a more focused manner ('narrowcasting' as opposed to broadcasting) and the latter has implications for international advertising. 'Cable' has other implications for marketing such as conducting market research surveys directly into consumers' living rooms via the cable, TV screen and key pad. Mail order buying has been given a boost through this as well, and the future is likely to see increased use of Viewdata technology (through cable) in consumer purchasing from home.

The third level of influence of technological change is that, in an indirect way, market behaviour is altered because of the effects on lifestyles which technological developments sometimes bring. The examples here can probably be summarized with reference to Columbus, Ohio where all homes have been cable wired – but not only so that they can receive several TV channels and shop from home, but also to enable them to conduct their financial transactions through the cable link to banks, and also to be able to work from home in some cases. The 'attendance ethic' at a place of work has been replaced with a sort of ultimate 'flexitime'. The home terminal allows people to do their work in their own time and to download results to their employer's central computer.

There are a great many social implications inherent in the tremendous increase in 'home-centredness' that this brings, but from a marketing perspective the changes in lifestyles which result will change the product and service requirements of people affected in this way.

In the UK there have been, for several years now, examples of each of these developments (Prestel for mail order and even for the odd survey conducted by the big catalogue companies; The Royal Bank of Scotland with their Home Banking system (also using Prestel) and some employees at British Aerospace in Hatfield working from home through a modem link between home terminals and the firm's computer).

What is likely to happen in the future is the kind of synergy as exemplified in Ohio – with all the associated consequences for marketing opportunities; but only if the scanning process is capable of not only identifying the trends but also able to project specific market implications for the organization concerned. This is, therefore, a suitable point at which to turn to intelligence models of scanning and techniques, and research approaches for scanning.

Environmental scanning

Scanning has been described concisely by Jain (1981) as:

> 'an early warning system for the environmental forces which may
> impact a company's products and markets in the future.'

In this way scanning enables an organization to 'act upon' rather than to 'react to' opportunities and/or threats. The focus is not on 'the immediate' but rather has a longer term perspective which is necessary for being in a position to plan ahead. Some writers have gone even further, Thorpe (1975) for example, concludes that the whole effectiveness of organizations is to some extent dependent on their abilities to understand – and to use this understanding of – environmental uncertainty.

Thus, as a component of a marketing information system, environmental scanning has a less immediate role than, say, market research and in many ways a less focused field of interest than other elements. One key point is that environmental influence is not static but is continuously changing, hence the need for continuous monitoring of various influences, both internal and external. A danger of not thinking in this way might be analogous to what Toffler (1970) described as 'Future Shock' in his book of the same name, as Johnson and Scholes (1984) point out:

> 'the speed and frequency of change is such that managers and
> management systems often cannot cope; what occurs is a sort of
> internally generated shock which is rooted in managers' inability to
> see the strategic impact of possible changes and therefore make the
> changes necessary to adjust the organization's strategy to its
> environment.'

Along with these writers, Cravens *et al.* (1980), also draw attention to the increasing speed of change.

Another essential consideration in managing the effects of environmental change is that many influences may superficially appear to be constraints on marketing activities, but opportunities should always be sought, and even these supposed constraints where possible should be converted into opportunities. To reinforce this point it has been suggested that marketing should think of positive and *negative* opportunities, rather than merely opportunities and constraints (Book, 1981).

Environmental scanning models

So far the nature of the environment has been outlined, together with some examples of how marketing might be affected, but what of the *way* in which to scan the environment in the first place?

Several models have been suggested as ways of considering and structuring the scanning process, Cravens *et al.* (1980) propose a straightforward sequential model of scanning stages, summarized in Figure 16.2.

A more comprehensive model was suggested by Jain (1981), as can be seen in Figure 16.3.

This model is useful for its integration with corporate planning and strategy decision making.

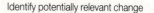

Identify potentially relevant change

Determine direction, magnitude and rate of change

Forecast probability of impact, timing and consequences

Develop strategy response

Figure 16.2   Scanning stages. (*Source*: Cravens, Mills and Woodruff (1980))

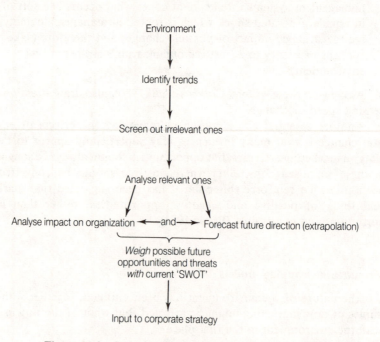

Figure 16.3   Scanning procedures. (*Source*: Jain (1981))

Organizational considerations

Aguilar's (1967) model is similar to the above but incorporates some organizational dimensions of who should be involved in the process, and when this involvement should occur (Figure 16.4). However, the introduction of the human element now raises other issues.

Some writers and researchers point to organizational problems in the practical implementation of scanning procedures. Indeed, as well as more general aspects of marketing decision making, Piercy (1985) argues that the corporate environment's effect on marketing management has been a neglected area of research and understanding. He proposed a model of this process, showing that marketing decisions are taken in the context of internal power struggles, political influences and organizational uncertainty.

Aguilar (1967), for instance, demonstrated that those who most need scanning information (top management) are not those who most deal with the collecting and analysing of such data, and that this is a problem because there is quite a distortion and loss of information before it reaches the decision makers.

Generally, then, because there is reliance on people in the scanning process there can be failure to see the relevance of some information and/or other problems of information distortion in its transmission.

In smaller companies Aguilar found that top management *were* the main scanners, but whereas this might appear to overcome the above problem the information they generally scanned was somewhat narrow and too focused in nature to be considered a true environmental scan. That is, that management

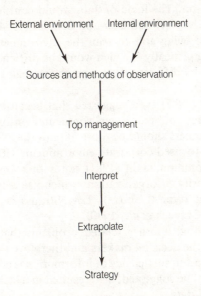

Figure 16.4 The scanning process. (*Source*: Aguilar (1967))

was more concerned with the more immediate state of specific industries and markets than with scanning widely in order to identify longer term trends and effects.

Greenley (1986) also found an emphasis on the appraisal of more immediate aspects of specific product markets and less interest in broader perspectives and trends, and his research (extending Aguilar's original research) covered larger organizations and was of course both more recent and related to the UK.

Three organizational scanning modes were identified by Jain (1981), namely that scanning is conducted by:

(1)   line managers,

(2)   planners, or

(3)   a specific environmental scanning department.

Cravens *et al.* (1980) suggest the main commitment to scanning should be on the part of line managers, but this is possibly a rather narrow view; it is probably appropriate for more than line managers to scan because the former tend to be very, and sometimes too, close to their own spheres so that broader horizons of perspective can be difficult to achieve. This is certainly the view adopted by Jain (1981).

A related consideration is whether scanning should be conducted centrally or decentrally throughout the organization. Cravens *et al.* (1980), for instance, argue in favour of devolving to specialist departments, such that the technological environment is scanned by a technical department within the organization and so on. The logic of Jain would conflict with this and other writers would also disagree. Johnson and Scholes (1984), for example, point to the importance of being able to scan the environment more globally and, therefore, more synergistically – which would be difficult if different environments were scanned by different departments for their own relatively narrow perspectives and uses.

Indeed, Seger (1977) even suggested that because of the obscurity and superficial irrelevancy of many environmental influences, the 'working environment' for scanners should be more akin to the 'ivory tower' than to the more blinkered and focused corporate environment. However, this approach in practice is not common. Jain (1981) notes that General Electric are an example of the minority of organizations which use a specific environmental scanning department (type 3 above). Levi Strauss is another example, as reported elsewhere (Cravens *et al.*, 1980).

Aguilar identified another related problem, that those collecting the information are not the decision makers and therefore there is the problem of whether the right type and sufficiency of information is collected. These aspects (of the same problem) he suggested, also resulted in a lack of integration of the very diverse types of data.

With these problems and dangers in mind some suggestions are now submitted for *how* to scan the marketing environment.

Techniques for scanning

A useful framework integrating the *models* or *stages* of the scanning process with specific *techniques* for conducting the work can be inferred from Jain (1981), whose empirical research resulted in a systematizing of environmental scanning. Figure 16.5 is proposed as a scanning model incorporating this work along with the other points discussed here.

Stage 1

Environmental events are picked up from a continuous literature search (and any other source of information, such as personal contacts and so on).

Scanning 'stage'	Scanning 'techniques'
1 Identify environmental *events*	Literature search by free-thinking teams with representation from planners
2 Delineate relevant *events*	Trend-impact analysis Opportunity threat matrices Delphi panels
3 Analyse impact of relevant current and future organizational events	Cross-impact analysis Opportunity threat matrices Delphi panels/scenarios
4 Relate *events* to organizational strengths and weaknesses to identify opportunities and constraints	SWOT analysis
5 Convey information to planners	
6 Planners involved in repetition of scenario building	Delphi panels with planners
7 Incorporation in corporate strategy	

Figure 16.5 An environmental scanning model.

Information collection should be conducted not 'by area' according to specialist departments, but rather by freer-thinking teams (preferably including representation from the decision-making planners).

Stage 2

Relevant trends may be screened using *trend–impact analysis* (Figure 16.6). For this (indeed for cross-impact analysis and opportunity–threat matrices) *Delphi* panels are set up, in the case of trend–impact analysis here, to identify for each environmental event:

(1) The *desirability* of the event.
(2) The organization's technical feasibility of using or coping with the event.
(3) The probability of the event occurring.
(4) The likely time (within the next few years) of the event occurring.

These may be assessed quantitatively, for example from '0' through '0.5' to '1.0'.

It is also likely that the team discusses the nature of organizational impact in terms of areas of marketing affected such as, direct implications for advertising or market research procedures, or implications for changes in market behaviour to which marketing should respond.

Because the problem essentially is to identify change and trends and then to determine likely impact on the organization in the future, Kotler (1984) describes a matrix for evaluating environmental influence in terms of threats and opportunities. This uses two main criteria – the degree of probability of the influence happening at all, and secondly the degree of impact it will have on

	EVENT	
	No. 1	No. 2
Desirability	(say) 0.8	0.5
Feasibility	0.5	0.3
Probability of occurrence	0.5	0.1
Time of occurrence	1998	1995
Area of impact	Consumer market segments	Industrial market segments Marketing research techniques

Figure 16.6 Trend–impact analysis. (Refers to non-specified 'events' and demonstrates the subjective analysis based on estimated probabilities) (Adapted by the authors from Jain (1981)).

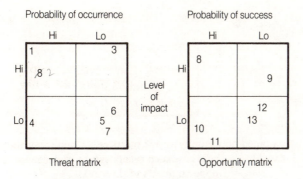

Figure 16.7 Opportunity–threat matrices.

the organization if it does happen. This is suggested as a useful approach for projecting probabilities of events occurring and their level of organizational impact. Thus, it may be a possible additional approach for determining those events on which to concentrate and those to leave for the moment. It could lead to the construction of opportunity–threat matrices as exemplified by Figure 16.7.

According to the priorities identified in this way, the organization should presumably concentrate on '1' and '2' because these are the most likely threats to occur and are also likely to affect the organization most. Presumably, '8' is the first opportunity to aim for since it would not only help the organization the most, but is the most likely to succeed.

Stage 3

This next stage is to analyse the current and future organizational impact of relevant events and this requires more detailed consideration of the selected events, and analysis of effects 'between' events. Cross-impact analysis can help here. A grid plotting events against themselves is constructed, thereby forcing analysis of the interaction of events (Figure 16.8).

Event	Probability of occurrence	Impact					
		No. 1	No. 2	No. 3	No. 4	No. 5	No. 6
No. 1	0.6						
No. 2	0.3					0.4	
No. 3	0.5	0.8					
No. 4	0.1			0.4			
No. 5	0.4						
No. 6	0.3						

Figure 16.8 Cross-impact analysis.

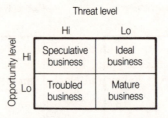

Figure 16.9   Combined opportunity–threat matrices. (Again, refer to non-specified 'events' – 1 to 13 – to show how such events can be evaluated in terms of opportunities and threats.)

Perhaps opportunity–threat matrices could help provide probabilities and the analysis would then go on to show that (say) *if* event No. 3 does occur (probability of 0.5) then the probability of event No. 1 occurring increases from 0.6 to 0.8. If No. 2 occurs, it has no effect on the 0.4 probability of event No. 5 occurring and so on.

If opportunity–threat matrices are combined, a picture of the organization's general state may emerge (Figure 16.9), and as Kotler suggests, the organization can respond to its environment by:

(1)   *Opposition*, it can fight the constraints.
(2)   *Modification*, it can change its market segments or mixes.
(3)   *Relocation*, it can change to another market.

Scenarios, again probably created and analysed by Delphi expert panels, extrapolate how these events, interacting with each other, might impact marketing (directly or indirectly).

Stage 4

These results can be fed into more conventional SWOT analysis (as concisely described in McDonald (1984)) to relate events and their implications to the organization's strengths and weaknesses.

Stage 5

The planners may also be involved in the reworking of scenario-building for the marketing impact of these events.

This was a recommendation made by Aguilar (1967) because of the problem he identified of the information collectors not being the decision makers, resulting in poor use and integration of information (points made under the heading 'Organizational considerations').

Stage 6

From here there will be further progression as an input to corporate strategy planning. However good the scanning may be, the results should be properly used. This again highlights the points made under 'Stage 5' above, and further reinforcement comes from Fahey and Narayanan (1986):

> 'Perhaps the most significant problem in many organizations is inadequate linkage between environmental analysis and strategy analysis.'

Strategy implications

Response to 'the environment' has been categorized by Galbraith (1979) as

(1) Independent.
(2) Cooperative.
(3) Manoeuvring.

'Independent' strategy response is probably the most likely (though not always the most appropriate). This is where the organization changes some dimensions of its marketing mix in order to respond to environmental change.

'Cooperative' strategy response is where the organization, together with other(s) – implicitly, explicitly or through some other form of cooperation or coalition – initiates some form of group response.

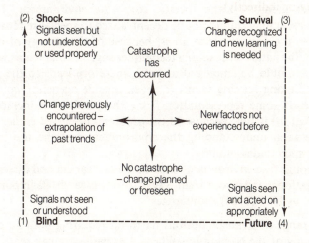

Figure 16.10 Strategy responses.

The third of Galbraith's strategy responses is 'manoeuvring', where the organization attempts to shape the environment, rather than respond more passively.

In a study of the public sector in Hong Kong, Mushkat and Roberts (1986) used this framework and found that the 'independent' strategy response was by far the most employed.

In another study, Binsted (1986) produced a model of the effectiveness of organizational strategy response, showing that organizations need not only to identify change, but also to understand and use this knowledge of change, and indeed to learn and *re*-learn responses. Figure 16.10 describes these considerations and implies a possible sequence of organizational learning with respect to responding to the environment.

A 'learning curve' taking the organization, in sequence, from '1' to '4' is a likelihood for some organizations, but others may progress directly from '1' to '4', avoiding the difficult area between '2' and '3' where many will simply not survive if further progression is too slow.

Conclusion

Understanding the marketing environment (and *using* this understanding for decision-making purposes) requires more than being armed with lists of environmental influences. A synergistic perspective of 'events' is less limiting, and a systematic process of scanning for 'events' is more helpful in providing relevant and important inputs to strategy decision making. The proposed environmental scanning model (Figure 16.10) incorporates these considerations.

In terms of organizational design for scanning, the picture is not clear and depends greatly on the specific corporate environment. However, it appears that scanning should not be decentralized to specialist departments for these to scan their own interest areas, because of the synergy of influences.

Also, the nature of scanning techniques suggests that teams with broader perspectives should be employed and this therefore leads to the proposition that freer-thinking scaning teams (or even outside agencies) would be more appropriate. If some representation from 'the planners' is included at some stage here, all the better, because of the problems discussed earlier concerning the gap between understanding the environment and the use in corporate strategy of such understanding.

Although 'the environment' may be a less clear cut and discernible focus for organizational endeavour than, say, market research, its importance could be decisive, as Hall (1980) summarizes:

> 'the range of strategic options narrows, requiring both an early
> warning of the coming hostility and as early strategy repositioning for
> a company to survive and prosper'.

Although 'marketing management' is not the focus of this book, we feel that the incursion in this chapter into the more strategic issues of marketing is an important and relevant reminder of the necessary linkages between *what* is researched, *how* and for *what purpose*.

We have now covered marketing research and its applications within various areas of marketing, together with this review of marketing intelligence and environmental scanning. Our final chapter provides an overview of the marketing research industry itself, together with some views concerning the future and future developments within the industry.

REFERENCES

Aguilar F. J. (1967). *Scanning the Business Environment*. Macmillan

Binsted D. (1986). Learning to cope with change. *Management Decision*, **24** (3)

Book A. (1981). A Look into the Future. Presentation at Newcastle upon Tyne Polytechnic on behalf of American Express

Cravens D. W., Hills G. E. and Woodruff R. B. (1980). *Marketing Decision Making: Concepts and Strategy*. Illinois: Irwin

Employment Census 1984

Evans M. J. (1981). So who's a dedicated follower of fashion? A perspective of the behaviour of fashion consumers, SSRC/MEG Presentation

Fahey L. and Narayanan V. K. (1986). *Macroenvironmental Analysis for Strategic Management*. West Publishing

Galbraith J. R. (1979) *Organizational Design*. Reading Mass: Addison-Wesley

Glaser S. (1985). The marketing system and the environment. *European Journal of Marketing*, **19** (4)

Greenley G. E. (1986). The strategic and operational planning of marketing. McGraw-Hill

Hall W. K. (1980). Survival strategies in a hostile environment. *Harvard Business Review*, **58** (5)

Henley Centre for Forecasting *Planning Consumer Markets and Leisure Futures* (quarterly)

Institute for Fiscal Policy Studies (1986)

Institute of Marketing (1975). Moor Hall, Cookham

Jain S. C. (1981). *Marketing Planning and Strategy*. South Western Publishing

Johnson G. and Scholes K. (1984). *Exploring Corporate Strategy*, Englewood Cliffs NJ: Prentice-Hall

Kotler P. (1984). *Marketing Management, Planning, Control and Evaluation*. Englewood Cliffs NJ: Prentice-Hall

Lazer W. (1981). Lucrative marketing opportunities will abound in the upbeat 1980's. In McCarthy *et al.* eds. *Readings in Basic Marketing*. Illinois: Irwin

Levitt T. (1964). Marketing myopia. In Bursk and Chapman eds. *Modern Marketing Strategy*. Cambridge Mass: Harvard University Press

McDonald M. (1984). *Marketing Plans: How to prepare them, how to use them*. Heinemann

Mushkat M. and Roberts E. (1986). Environmental adaptation in Hong Kong public enterprise. *European Management Journal*, spring

Piercy N. F. (1985). The corporate environment for marketing management: an information – structure – power theory of marketing, marketing planning and intelligence. *Marketing Intelligence and Planning*, **3** (1)

Piper J. (1978). The teeming teenage market place. *Marketing*, Feb.

Regional Trends (annually), Central Office of Information

Social Trends (annually), Central Office of Information

Seger E. (1977). How to use environmental analysis in strategy making. *Management Review*, March

Shay P. A. (1978). Consumer revolution is coming. *Marketing*, Sept.

Thorpe R. M. (1975). *The External Environment of Organisations*. Management Bibliographies, MCB

Toffler A. (1970). *Future Shock*. London: Bodley Head

Unger L. (1981). Consumer marketing trends in the 1980's when growth slows. *European Research*, **9**

17

The Marketing Research Industry and the Future

In this final chapter we take a look at the state of the marketing research industry itself. We review the key players and look at how to liaise with the industry and analyse the changing environment within which the industry operates. Attention is especially given to technological changes. The final section makes, what at times are bold, suggestions as to how the industry might develop over the next few years - we'll see.

The marketing research industry

Organizations carrying out marketing research

The industry may be divided into several types of organization which carry out research. First, there are manufacturers' market research departments, which range from those that have responsibility for every stage of the research process, including the planning, implementation and analysis of research programmes, to those that may utilize some secondary sources of data, but have little more than a liaison role with outside agencies when primary data is involved.

Second, more and more distributors - especially retailers - are not just users of research but now have their own market research departments.

Third, there are specialized marketing research agencies, of which over 200 are listed in the Market Research Society in their 1988 Yearbook, compared with less than 50 in 1963.

In addition to the above, other organizations conducting marketing research include the specialist press, the education sector in business school and college student projects and staff consultancy advertising agencies, which

Table 17.1   Top ten agencies.

1979	*Top ten agencies by year* *1986*	*1990*
AGB	AGB (including RSGB)	AGB
Nielsen	Nielsen	Nielson
Research Bureau Ltd	Research Bureau Ltd	MAI UK*
NOP	NOP	Millward Brown
BMRB	MIL	Research International
Research Services	BMRB (including Mass Observation)	Taylor Nelson
Marplan	Millward Brown	BMRB
MAS	Taylor Nelson	Research Business Gp
Louis Harris	Burke Research Group	RSL
Taylor Nelson	RSGB	MORI

*MAI UK was founded in 1990, incorporating NOP and MIL
(*Source*: AMSO, 1980, 1987, 1991)

research markets for clients and undertake copy and media research. There are also local organizations such as Chambers of Trade and Local Authorities which may produce regular reports which can be accessed.

Structure of the industry

Approximately 14 major companies have group shareholding relationships with over 50 agencies. A listing of agency turnover according to AMSO (Association of Market Survey Organizations) in the 1979, 1986 and 1991 Handbooks (Table 17.1) shows that for 1979 the acquisition during that year of Attwoods by AGB gave that group not only the largest turnover, but also the greatest profitability (in terms of pre-tax profit as a percentage of turnover). This excludes the effects of the other big acquisition of that year: Mass Observation by the J. Walter Thompson Advertising Agency empire, which already owned BMRB (JWT is now owned by WWP).

Finally, it is worth mentioning that the industry is represented through various institutions. Among these are the Market Research Society (MRS), the Industrial Market Research Association (IMRA), the Association of Market Survey Organisations (AMSO), the Association of Users of Research Agencies (AURA), and the European Society for Opinion and Marketing Research (ESOMAR).

This list indicates at least two types of research focus, namely industrial and consumer research. Additionally, there is the grey, but growing, area of

Table 17.2 Source of total (%) revénue for AMSO members.

Research buying sector	Total revenue (%)	
	1978	1989
Food and soft drinks	18.8	15.9
Media	7.2	9.3
Health and beauty	6.9	6.7
Public services	–	6.9
Advertising agencies	3.7	5.5
Alcoholic drinks	5.6	7.2
Financial services	1.7	5.6
Pharmaceutical companies	5.1	5.3
Vehicle manufacturers	4.5	5.6
Business and industrial companies	2.0	5.9
Government	7.1	3.9
Retailers	2.9	2.9
Tourism	1.8	2.9
Household durables	1.7	2.6
Household products	4.4	2.2
Tobacco	5.6	1.6
Agricultural products	1.4	–
Oil	–	1.3
Others	14.1	8.7

(*Source*: AMSO statistics, as reported in *Market Research Society Newsletter*, April 1982 and April 1990)

research for non-profit-making sectors such as political parties, fund raising organizations and other 'services'.

Central and local government commission research in order to identify levels of demand for their services and attitudes toward these services – as well as image studies for political campaigning purposes.

Table 17.2 summarizes changes in the main research buying sectors in the UK over a decade or so.

The breadth of services offered by agencies varies considerably – and has been growing and changing in recent years. Some provide a complete range, while others specialize in continuous research, and some offer specialized services like fieldwork or data analysis or the research of 'sectors' – pharmaceutical markets, financial markets and so on. The financial and public sectors are particular examples of relatively recent growth in research activity, especially in the early to mid-1980s (and indeed in advertising activity).

Client–agency relationships

Having looked at the marketing research industry, it is useful to consider the relationship between the industry and its clients.

Perhaps the most critical issues are confidentiality and the use of background statistics to allow the main data to be evaluated for validity and reliability. While arrangements vary, and the relationship between the research agency and the user remains problematic in some cases, one attempt to propose standard terms and conditions is provided by the Market Research Society and is summarized in Figure 17.1.

This Code of Conduct specified various mutual responsibilities, but particularly the right of the client to receive enough information to properly evaluate the research. It provides a basis for a sound agency–user relationship, (Figure 17.2).

Before proceeding with more detailed analysis of some of the components, procedures and techniques of the research process, it is worth devoting some attention to the nature and structure of the marketing research industry, together with a review of organizations providing research services.

The Market Research Society, for example, requires the following (among other requirements):

(a) Members should refrain from any activity likely to impair the confidence of the business community and of the general public.

(b) Members can be expelled if work falls short of reasonable professional standards (e.g., misrepresentation, disclosure of confidential results).

(c) Complaints against members will be investigated.

(d) Respondents should not be embarrassed or hindered or adversely affected.

(e) Respondents must be allowed to withdraw from an interview at any time.

Furthermore, the client should expect from the research organization:

(a) Data analysis forms, cards, punched tape; questionnaires shall be the property of the agency. It can destroy these records two years after the survey.

(b) After submission of the report to the client, the client shall be entitled to obtain from the agency: copies of questionnaires, punched cards, etc.

(c) Every report of a sample survey should contain information on who the survey was for, who compiled it, aims of the survey, data collection methods, findings, and a copy of questionnaires used.

The full Code of Conduct actually runs to as many as 16 pages in the '*Yearbook*' (MRS, 1982).

An additional 'safeguard' for the public is the MRS 'Interviewer Card Scheme' (MRS, 1982), this is to combat, among other problems, the practice of using market research as a guise for personal selling. Only MRS approved interviewers (who have satisfied the Society that they are competent and have been sufficiently trained and supervised) are provided with the MRS identity card of a *bona fide* interviewer.

Figure 17.1   Code of Conduct.

Suggested standard conditions between marketing research agency and client

(1) Research designs remain the property of the originator (client or agency) until paid for.

(2) Research agencies normally should not reveal the client's identity.

(3) Research agencies should keep as confidential any information held about the client (including the fact of the client's research).

(4) If an agency sub-contracts fieldwork to another agency, or combines projects in a single set of interviews, the client should be told.

(5) The research agency should provide the following information to the client:

   (a) a copy of the questionnaire:
   (b) a description of: for whom and by when the survey was done;
                  the objects of the study;
                  the details of the sample, including its actual size and composition;
                  the methods of recruiting informants;
                  the bases for tables of figures;
                  response rates and possible biases;
                  the data collection method;
                  any incentives/rewards offered to informants;
                  the timing of the fieldwork;
                  the nature of the fieldforce and controls used;
                  the names of sub-contractors used, and sources used in desk research.

(6) The client should normally be allowed to attend some interviews.

(7) The client should normally be allowed to receive research records, if required (though not revealing informants' identities).

(8) The agency should not, without permission, reveal research findings to others.

(9) Circulating results by the client outside his own organization should not bear the agency's name, unless this has been agreed.

*Suggested 'Good practices'**

(10) The research specification should be precise regarding the items noted above.

(11) The agency should safeguard the security of confidential material.

(12) The agency should describe background factors like the bases of statistical tables, the effects of sample size and design, possible biases in the results, reliability of desk research sources, the name of the responsible executive.

(13) The researchers should distinguish between results and opinion/recommendations.

(14) The agency should be informed if the client plans to circulate research results more widely and suggest the necessary qualification to be included.

Figure 17.2 Marketing research agency–client relationships. (* *Source*: Adapted by the authors from the Market Research Society Code of Conduct)

Marketing research and its own 'marketing environment'

The environment within which any industry operates is constantly changing and the marketing research industry is no exception.

The political environment

It has already been implied that the political environment has changed recently in that market research has become an expected part of political marketing, in the same way that party political broadcasts have merged into more general and explicit advertising campaigns. This appears to have opened the door for other 'non-business' market research programmes. The changes to the National Health Service during the late 1980s and early 1990s are further evidence of this.

Related to this is the increase in specialist agencies – or agencies with specialist subsidiaries – providing research tailored to financial service markets, tourism markets, pharmaceutical markets and so on.

It is often difficult to separate the political environment from the economic and legal environments and these last two areas provide more examples of change for the marketing research industry.

The economic environment

Perhaps as one result of the economic recession of the early to mid-eighties there were pressures on the research budgets of marketers and this might contribute, in part, to the increase seen through that period in the use of small-scale surveys employing qualitative techniques such as group discussions. These may be expensive per respondent, but if an entire research programme is based on a few 'groups' then the overall cost is often less than if larger, structured (though less expensive per respondent) surveys were employed.

Other cost savings come from sharing surveys with others, and there has also been an increase in the use of 'omnibus surveys', which are regularly conducted surveys of fixed (usually) sample design and reporting procedures, which several clients can buy into in order to place a few questions specific to their own problems – resulting, therefore, in economics of scale derived from the research being shared.

The legal environment

In terms of legislation and marketing research, this is likely to evolve as social attitudes change – for example from the progress, or otherwise, of 'consumerism'.

As long ago as 1964 in the US, Blankenship was calling for more lower socio-economic group respondents to be included in research programmes; for less misleading research (that disguised techniques should not be used); and for research to generally be more in the interests of consumers (rather than for, for example, product tests to lead to the targetting of inferior products at consumers on the basis of them being less distinguishable from the 'genuine' article).

The British Market Research Society has long included in its Code of Conduct activity such as 'selling' or 'persuasion' or 'espionage' which 'shall not be misrepresented as research'. Some of these issues are extended later, but for the present discussion they are included as examples of the controlling evironment relating to marketing research – one which can change with changing social attitudes and experiences, and one which may even lead to changes in the (as yet relatively sparse) law concerning marketing research.

The 1984 Data Protection Act concerns data fed into computers, or otherwise held on databanks, and aims to allow access to such data by those affected. As the Market Research Society itself agrees, this is less relevant in market research because the data of respondents so stored is not important in itself so much as the wider population it represents. The MRS has produced guidelines for its members on the implications of this Act.

The technological environment

Technological change is currently especially topical. This affects marketing research in three main ways. Firstly it contributes directly to new product development programmes because technology itself sometimes provides new products which customers might demand if they are shown to satisfy needs. Secondly, there may be new ways of conducting marketing research activities. Thirdly, technology may change lifestyles and as a result market behaviour. Indirectly, therefore, marketing research would have to respond by measuring different behaviours, interests and concerns.

The following lists some examples of technological change and marketing research:

Cable TV

In addition to its 'narrowcasting' role, it can be used in an interactive way to conduct surveys with respondents using their TV keypads to give pre-coded responses to questions appearing on their screens.

Viewdata

This operates in a similar way in that respondents use their keypads to respond to screen questions. Here, however, the interactive link is made through the connection between the TV and the telephone. A telephone call is effectively being made to the Viewdata computer concerned (for example, Prestel is British Telecom's 'brand' of Viewdata – there are currently over 200 other brands in the UK).

MRT (Market Research Terminals)

These are hand held recorders and in effect act as electronic clipboards. Previously the interviewer needed a different questionnaire for each respondent and the answers so recorded would have to be coded later and physically typed into a computer statistical package. The electronic clipboard, however, allows each respondent's replies to be entered already coded and stored for later direct downloading to the main analysis computer.

Laser scanning

Allows the 'bar codes' printed on packs to be 'read' at the checkout. This not only provides a quick way of processing customers' purchases, it can also be linked with computer stock level databases in-store, which will be automatically updated as purchases are made. A specific marketing research implication of this process is for the retail audit – rather than regular physical stock checks of stores in the 'audit' sample by researchers, the sales of specific brands and pack sizes in the categories being researched can be stored for each day's trading. If desired, these can be downloaded to the research agency's computer over night via a telephone link with the store's computer. All this leads to more rapid and accurate statistics on which retail audit data can be processed. The compilation of the record charts used to be a contract held by the BMRB, but the old system of physically filling in a diary and posting this to BMRB lost out to Gallup's newer technology, based on the above type of system. Such techniques are increasing in use throughout the industry.

Improved instruments

For example, the SET meter for monitoring which TV channels those households in the TV audience research consumer panel are tuned to; the psycho-galvanometer – this measures physical responses which are a manifestation of an emotional response and has been used as part of advertising pre-tests; the eye camera which traces the path the eye takes over a pre-set space onto which photos of advertisements, shelf displays and so on, can be projected, and the tachistoscope which flashes pictures (of, for example, advertisements, pack designs, alternative logotypes and so on) for fractions of a second – this can help identify those designs, colour combinations and typefaces which might be more readily observed and understood.

Video synthesized posters for pre-testing

This allows test posters to be pre-tested. The problem before the advent of video technology was that it was not possible to simulate convincingly a test poster in a real high street location before the campaign was launched. Now it is possible to video record a high street scene – one with the billboard site, of course – and then to superimpose the test poster on the billboard in the film. The poster does not 'fall off the edge' of the billboard frame and appears most convincingly to be the one that is actually being shown in the high street concerned. This enables pre-testing questioning in a much more realistic simulation of reality than was previously possible.

Computer data analysis

There is nothing new about this in principle, but recently more and more statistical packages have become available for use on desk top micros, as well as for minis and mainframes, such as SPSS-X, SPSS and PC+ and MINITAB. Also, there is an increasing variety of analysis packages which are specific to market research, such as SNAP and MARQUIS, and not just to more general statistical analysis. Another fairly recent development has been computer analysis of open-ended questions via key-word searching programmes – and, of course, word processing helps in questionnaire design.

CATI

'Computer Assisted Telephoning Interviewing' has enabled interviewers to watch their VDUs while questioning respondents. The questionnaire is displayed on the screen and as responses are given the predetermined code can be typed in by the interviewer there and then, thus avoiding the time delays and errors associated with coding and entering data after interviews. Then, the next appropriate question appears on the screen on the basis of which answer was previously given – that is, the 'routing' through the questionnaire is automatically provided – thus avoiding sequencing errors. Also possible is random or cyclical presentation of multiple response options.

Undoubtedly, one of the newest additions to the portfolio of market research techniques has been telemarketing. Telemarketing has been described as a 'marketing communication system which utilises telecommunications technology and trained personnel to conduct planned, measurable marketing activities directed at target groups of consumers' (Voorhees and Coppett, 1983). It is a means to provide a quick and effective way of gathering research data, either on an *ad hoc* or a continuous basis. This method affords greater control over research activities by eliminating outside agencies, and provides a quick and cost-effective way of gathering data from present and future markets (Voorhees and Coppett, 1983).

Saris and Pijper (1986) initially developed this interview procedure to improve response measurement of personal interviews – by using continuous scales, by correcting random error measurement and by checking answer consistency. But they postulate future applications with regards to portable face-to-face interviews.

Portable face-to-face interviews

The volume of controls, coding and punching can be reduced in large-scale surveys. The data can be automatically stored in a form which is immediately available for analysis. Likewise, products can be tested along with advertising effectiveness evaluation. Random samples of the population can be issued with a product, or shown an advertising concept by means of digital photography, then questioned about their reactions. Further, the results of pilot studies can more easily be incorporated into the survey with greater speed.

Computer geodemographic databases

These provide links between the National Census data and, for example, the postcode system, databases on bad debt and so on. ACORN, MOSAIC and others make it possible to identify specific types of household and to contact samples of these, by name and address, through such a link.

It has enabled companies to take these large, geodemographically organized databases, for example census statistics, and link them to other sets of data. Market research of this nature provides new insights and better targeted advertising, promotional and merchandising activities (Whitehead, 1986). Database manipulation along these lines already exists in the form of ACORN (produced by CACI), more recently PIN (Pinpoint Identified Neighbourhoods) and Geoplan (produced by Market Profiles).

The Geoplan mapping system will provide manufacturers, retailers and advertising agencies with the capability to convert national survey research, and their own databases, into marketing action maps. They are able, for example, to identify current product penetration, potential target markets for products and services, sites for new outlets and media coverage of identified target audiences.

Any data which is postcode-related can be mapped. Thus, customer files, purchase lists, direct mail respondents, promotion entrants and so on, can all be mapped on the Geoplan postcode sector boundary file. National survey data which utilizes any of the geodemographic systems can be linked by that system to postcode sectors.

Demographic manipulation in this way permits local market sizes to be quantified with a precision which was previously impossible. Databases detailing the size and distribution of retail competitors can then build a more complete picture of the marketplace. Developments in IT encourage the proliferation of increasingly sophisticated marketing databases and geodemographic market segmentation systems.

Marketing research and the future

Trends in marketing research

The world of marketing research is changing rapidly and becoming much more technical in nature, affecting the very scope of marketing research as we enter the 1990s. Job responsibilities and availabilities, research focus and information use are all experiencing evolutionary developments (Schlossberg, 1990a, b).

Slow-growth consumer markets make marketing research even more important in the 1990s. As competition becomes increasingly intense, marketing research will be called upon to set the stage for product and service decisions. Today, there are already about 25,000 people employed professionally in European market research, with well over 100,000 interviewers, according to ESOMAR (Demby, 1990).

Marketing and marketing research approaches are increasingly being employed within those sectors not hitherto considered prime areas for such application. Examples include non-profit-making sectors, such as charities, religious institutions and the National Health Service, which have been adopting these approaches as well. In a general sense, also, the service sector is coming of age and there has been an explosion of interest in marketing and marketing research here.

Today, the future of marketing research hinges on its ability to:

(1) make real contributions to marketing strategy.
(2) provide effective, low-cost, tactical decision support.
(3) separate itself from the pressures of brand management.

The future of research lies not only in determining what colour the package should be, but what product lines deserve the bulk of the company's efforts and resources. Marketing research's future also depends upon its ability to give top management convincing proof that it can contribute in strategic areas.

Marketing research will improve its relationship with management as it becomes more operational. It will move up in its reporting relationships as the research becomes more strategic – as well as tactically orientated.

Marketing research needs to keep its innovative experimental nature. Routine clerical jobs in marketing research will decline and will be replaced by the need for technically skilled, electronically-orientated personnel.

As marketing research becomes more involved with scanning and other technical advances, capital investment tends to replace smaller companies with companies now investing in software and hardware. In the future, emphasis will be on more objective and lower-cost information collecting. But with the tightening of resources, marketing research must answer hard questions. Management too often feels research is neither innovative nor productive. The growth of marketing research depends on how it demonstrates its contribution to other strategic needs.

An explosion in available data, increased retailer sophistication and advances in marketing technology have created an information revolution. As a result, corporate marketing, marketing information systems, market research, and sales departments are re-evaluating goals and strategies for dealing with imminent changes. The first of the changes, and perhaps the most obvious, is the increase of data available for marketing and sales analysis. Today, accurate new measures which describe almost every aspect of marketing mix variables are available, and marketing and sales managers need to manipulate this data on a daily basis.

Although not all companies have embraced scanner data, most have become aware of its potential for creating problems. The familiar three-ring binder has been replaced by a wheelbarrow of hard-copy reports, generated every month. There are no longer enough people in organizations to absorb these massive amounts of data. The information must be made available, in digestible form, electronically.

A little less conspicuous, but potentially more compelling, are the changes which retailers are currently undergoing. The consolidation of retailers is paralleling the frenzy of manufacturer mergers and acquisitions.

With data growth greatly exceeding personnel growth, marketers need systems to bear more of the load by pointing out significant 'events' in the data. This implies a strong need for exception-based selection capabilities, 'rules' for data inclusion and aggregation, and analytic pathways which can be stored and easily modified. 'Drill-down reporting', which allows one-button views of supporting detail, is rapidly becoming a necessity (Overhultz, 1990).

Drill-down reporting is related to the marketing information system's ability to reflect the bottom line. This typically translates into a system's ability to help generate new insights, faster decisions, and/or extend the business knowledge based throughout a company. At the risk of over-simplification, these benefits are derived from a system's ability to think 'like marketers' (that is to understand marketing jargon, data nuances and analysis teams).

Changes in the marketing research planning process

Marketing research will continue to become more integrated in the strategic planning process. In fact, marketing research can be viewed as the external intelligence function of a company. Given such a view, marketing research can be seen as a service function supporting both long-run decisions (for example, five-year plans, new product development through R&D), and short-term (operating) decisions (for example, promotions).

Research and management functions will become more integrated. An increasingly complex world makes increased technical sophistication a likely requirement of managers. Similarly, researchers have been found to occasionally have an idea as well as a number. Hence, more of a team relationship is likely to evolve. Similarly, more rotational assignments between management and research are likely to occur.

The marketing research department will survive, but with caveats on its role and performance that will cover everything from measuring its value and contribution, to its very name and structure. Some large companies in some industries are expanding their departments, fuelling them with greater revenues, and asking them for more and better information.

Marketing research will get caught up in the total quality movement, helping set benchmark measures for companies to measure competitor activity and customer satisfaction performance. Marketing research departments will strengthen their position as the 'window to the competitive environment'.

The marketing research professional may be looking at a scenario that includes quality-orientated types of research in a setting of staff cuts and data explosions, while management demands may dictate more of a role to provide insights, not just data and analysis.

Partnership relations, inside and outside, will be key to marketing research performance. ERAs (external research associates and IRAs (internal research associates) will be the marketing researchers of the future, externals being outside consultants and internals being in-house employees. Marketing research deparments, by the same token, will probably be labelled 'market intelligence', 'consumer insights' or 'business research' in the future. These labels will be derived from the need for more and better integrated information between corporate disciplines and corporate partners, internal and external.

Marketing research professionals will become members of various corporate business teams – these will include people from different disciplines around the company, driven by corporate management asking every department to become more externally (customer and marketplace) focused on its daily operations.

The term 'marketing research' is used today to mean the overall management of market-related information. The result of this change will likely increase the speed of management decision making and shift much of the focus of marketing research from planning to control.

The challenge to marketing researchers is how to design research properly, and analyse data and interpret results in ways that will maximize the benefit of the research to corporate management and yield profitable results (Wilson, 1989). The business climate of mergers and acquisitions has increased the need for short-term profit strategies and, thus, the need to justify marketing research expenditures more than ever before.

Research is now gradually spreading more evenly over all business sectors. National retailers are actively entering marketing research. The concentration of marketing research among a small number of large national advertisers will decline. In the years ahead, manufacturer-sponsored research will be replaced by supplier-sponsored research. In the past, management has tended to ask for data rather than solutions. Suppliers will emerge as the movers and shakers in *ad hoc* research.

In the future, the corporate research group will tend towards becoming an intelligence centre.

New product research will remain a major area because new developments involve high risk, high costs of failure and high uncertainty. Systematic monitoring of new product ideas is already becoming standard practice in many major consumer goods companies.

Research can be a key contributor to productivity by reducing marketing and production costs that come from incorrect marketing decisions. Marketing research remains a magnificent tool for reducing the failure rate of new products and for avoiding inefficient marketing expenses (Hardin, 1983).

It is important for marketing research firms to be innovative in their approach to solving client problems in areas such as new product design, concept testing, pricing sensitivity and data-collection technology. While there continues to be a great deal of interest in customized research projects, new databases, as well as forecasting and modelling techniques, are expected to become substantially more important during the next few years.

Computer-based decision support systems and simulation models will be used to evaluate marketing programmes prior to real-world introductions. Databases and evaluation systems will be integrated into larger, more useful, information systems. New systems are needed which can powerfully link databases together in ways which vastly increase their value to management decision making.

Expert systems and knowledge-based systems will be used to devise competitive marketing strategies. While these specialized intelligence systems are now in their early phases of use, they will become much more commonplace during this decade and have a huge impact on marketing thinking and action. The high-tech developments now employed in marketing research are speeding up and improving quality.

There is also a need for careful tracking research in the areas of consumer awareness, perceptions, attitudes and behaviour over the course of a brand's history. Tracking research can play an instrumental role in understanding brand performance and developing offensive or defensive marketing strategies.

Some of these points should he seen as speculations of expected trends in the field.

Quantitative research

That research will be more quantitative seems to be the general trend of all disciplines, and marketing is no more likely to be an exception than were physics or sociology.

Still, group discussions will be used in ways that are not broadly applied today. Groups will be conducted after the results of quantitative research are tabulated to provide insight into why the results were achieved. This is a shift from the traditional use of focus groups as a way to define and refine *beforehand* the input to be placed into the quantitative studies.

Group discussions will expand to industries that have not previously used them extensively. These will include non-profit organizations, government and segments of the industrial sector that have historically followed a manufacturing orientation, but have now come to recognize the need to focus on the customer or end-user for long-term growth. Videotaping will become standard, as audiotaping is today, and will be built into the cost of groups (Greenbaum, 1990). Three-way electronic focus groups will be more widely used as a powerful enhancement to multi-audience quality discussions.

Societal and technological changes affecting research methods

The following changes in society affect the development of marketing research:

- A population steadily growing less accessible to interviews. Households containing an adult not working full-time and therefore likely to be home for an interview have declined dramatically.

- Less willingness to be interviewed. People, no longer interested in research interviews as a novel experience, are more suspicious and less responsive. As a result, traditional in-home interviewing is becoming more difficult to carry out. The telephone has become a dominant way of reaching a usable sample.

- Rapidly-developing electronic technology is having a profound effect on data collection – permitting tighter control and greater accuracy. WATS (Wide Area Telephone Service) centres and cathode ray tube interviewing machines in shopping malls are reducing questioning errors, dishonest interviewing and poor execution of field interviews.

The face-to-face interview, once the mainstay of research, remains essential for open exploratory questioning – where exhibits measure reactions to storyboards and television films. Many shopping malls in the future will have a marketing research 'store' incorporated in their physical layout design. In-person, at-home interviews can become increasingly non-representative. More accurate responses can be obtained in the controlled environment of shopping malls and it is more practical to apply cathode ray tube interviewing in a shopping mall than in homes.

In tune with needs for tight control (accurate sampling and high-speed data processing), the WATS interview has arrived. It provides:

(1)   More accurate sampling.

(2)   Better control of call-backs.

(3)   More effective interviewer training and control.

(4)   Quicker, better validation.

(5)   Easier interview observation.

WATS interviewing, once more expensive than locally conducted surveys, is today less expensive because of higher productivity. CRT interviewing equipment, which automatically processes data, is today only practical for larger samples. Soon programming efficiencies will make it useful for smaller samples as well.

Higher labour costs are encouraging use of pre-recruited mail panels and shared omnibus interviews. The utilization of national mail panels, where labour is supplied by the respondent and information is dropped off and picked up at a low-cost postal rate, will become more prevalent.

Innovations such as two-way cable TV will make a new type of in-home personal interview (without an interviewer physically present) possible. Similarly, automated checkout systems provide an extremely useful source of information.

The increasing availability of data will lead to:

(1)   More analysis of disaggregated data (only pertaining to specific areas of investigation).

(2)   More integrated databases, as the trend towards 'single-source' data suppliers suggests.

(3)   More research which is decision support system orientated than purely analytical number crunching.

Legal considerations will increase. On one hand, more research will be required for various regulatory purposes. On the other hand, new constraints in areas such as privacy protection will affect the type of research which can be carried out.

With new sources of data, larger databases, expanded computer software, and more emphasis on direct responses in the marketplace, the role of the marketing researcher is likely to become even more important in the business world of the later 1990s than it is today.

REFERENCES

AMSO Association of Market Survey Organisations Yearbooks, 1979, 1986, 1987, 1991

Blankenship A. B. (1964). *Marketing Research Management*. New York: American Marketing Association

Blankenship A. B. (1971). Point of view: Consumerism and consumer research. *Journal of Advertising Research* **11**, 44–7

Data Protection Act (1984). HMSO

Demby Emanuel H. (1990). ESOMAR urges changes in reporting demographics, issues worldwide report. *Marketing News*, **24**, 24–5

Greenbaum Thomas L. (1990). Focus group spurt predicted for the '90s. *Marketing News*, **24**, 21–2

Hardin David K. (1983). Research state-of-art: Today and tomorrow. *Marketing Times* (March–April)

Market Research Society Newsletters, April 1982, April 1991

Market Research Society Yearbooks, 1982, 1988

MINITAB – the authors acknowledge the cooperation and help of MINITAB Inc, of 3081 Enterprise Drive, State College, PA 16801 USA

Overhultz G. (1990). How to have an information revolution without chaos. *Marketing News*, **24**, 27

Saris W. E. and Pijper W. M. (1986). Computer assisted interviewing using home computers. *European Research*, **14** (3), 144–50.

Schlossberg H. (1990a). Don't toll the bell yet: Marketing research is merely evolving, not dying. *Marketing News*, **24**, 1, 2, 13

Schlossberg H. (1990b). Major changes forecast for marketing research. *Marketing News*, **24**, 25, 27

Voorhees R. and Coppett J. (1983). Telemarketing in distribution channels. *Industrial Marketing Management*, **12**

Whitehead J. (1986). Keying in to new data. *Marketing*, 6 March

Wilson R. D. (1989). New trends and issues in marketing research. *Marketing Educator*, **8**, 1, 3, 4

18

Problems and Cases

Problem 1: Marketing performance control – Brand share research

Introductory comments

Retail audits and consumer panels (or both types of data sources) can be used to monitor brand shares. In a test area it may well be necessary to enlarge the regular, ongoing samples of retail outlets or of consumers, or to set up special *ad hoc* ones. It depends on the choice and the size of the test area. In addition, the standard reporting interval may be shortened, but the data collection procedures are standard.

Figure 18.1 compares the data yield of these two types of syndicated service, whose main *raison d'être* is, of course, the continuous monitoring of marketing performance. Figure 18.1 shows the strengths and, by implication, the weaknesses of the two data sources.

The procedures used to predict national or broad-scale shares from area tests are similar whichever form of panel is used, but the consumer panel has certain advantages in brand share prediction. However, before comparing predictive procedures there are some further details to be filled in:

- In both cases the client (company) specifies the brands they want to see recorded, usually major competitors plus an 'all others' group, together with the client's brand.

- The brand characteristics to be classified individually in the regular report are also agreed in advance – type of pack, size, flavour and so on.

Retail audit
Consumer sales and brand shares:

- Units
- Sterling/Dollar
* Average per shop handling

Consumer panel
Consumer purchases and brand shares

- Units
- Sterling/Dollar
- Brand penetration
- Consumer typology (quarterly or special)
  – demographic characteristics
  – Psychographic characteristics
- Buying behaviour
  – x amount bought
  – x loyalty/switching

Retailer purchases

- Units (not Sterling/Dollar)
- Brand shares

Where purchase was made

- Type of outlet

Source of delivery

- Direct/via depot/other

Retailer stocks and brand shares

- Units
- Average per shop handling

Stock cover

- Days, weeks, months

Prices

- Average retail selling prices at the time of audit

Prices

- Average purchase price

Promotion

- Display at point of sale (POS)
- Special offers

Promotion

- Offers associated with purchases

Advertising

(quarterly or special)
- Media consumption by panel members ('single source' data, i.e., via the Target Group Index)

By Type of Retail Outlet
By ITV Area/SMSA (Standard Metropolitan Statistical Area)

- Reports:
- Bi-monthly

By ITV Area/SMSA (Standard Metropolitan Statistical Area)

- Reports:
- Four-weekly

Figure 18.1 Data yield of retail audit and consumer panels compared.

We are now going to consider how retail audit and consumer panel data may be used to indicate what the effect of the experimental treatment would be if it were applied to the national or broader market. We first need to distinguish between *projections*, which assume that all other things remain equal, and *predictions*, which attempt to take account of factors which vary between the experimental area and the broader market.

The retail audit is based on samples of retail outlets which represent the volume of business going through different categories of outlet, not the number of shops in each category. The sample may represent one type of outlet such as grocers or chemists (as in the Nielsen Food Index and the Nielsen Drug Index) or, where distribution is through a variety of outlets (as with razor blades or soft drinks), the sample may be constructed to represent this variety.

The consumer panel will represent either private households with data collection via the housewife, or individuals. In addition to panels representing consumers in general, there are a number of specialist panels such as the Motorists Diary Panel, operated by Forecast (Market Research).

The retail audit is a demanding but straightforward operation:

Past stocks + deliveries − present stocks = sales

'Past stock' is stock left for sale at the close of the last audit, usually two months ago; 'deliveries' means stock coming in since the last audit. This is the simplest form of expressing a retail audit, other factors which might be included are obsolescence (write-offs), returned goods (from customers or to suppliers), wastage (thefts and so on). The formula is simple, but the procedure is infinitely detailed.

The consumer panel data derive either from a diary, designed as a pre-coded checklist, or from an audit of household stores. The retail audit is valuable in the experimental situation because in addition to recording retail sales and brand shares, it monitors distribution achieved and signals the danger of 'stockout' (a particular risk in an experimental launch dependent on pilot plant production). The consumer panel describes the types of consumer responding to the experimental treatment and makes possible the calculation of repeat purchase rates.

Prediction by standardizing brand shares

Taking a simplified example, if a new brand were to achieve £100 consumer sales in an experimental area where sales of all brands in the product field totalled £1000, it would be naive to assume that, on going national, the new brand would achieve £10,000 in a national market worth £100,000. Simple projection of the 10% brand share from experimental area to total market is to be avoided, because even nationally distributed and consumed brands show regional variation. The field as a whole may show little variation, but individual brand shares are the product of past achievement on a number of fronts –

selling and sales promotion, distribution, advertising – and it is unlikely that the marketing histories of the brands in the field will have followed, in each case, a uniform course in all areas.

The effect of marketing history up to and during the experiment is taken into account by standardizing brand shares, a technique developed by Davis (1970), and Crimp (1985). When a new brand is introduced into an area market, achievement in brand share is made at the expense of other brands already *in situ*. Assuming a positive result for the new entry, some brands will resist more successfully than others. If the experiment is allowed to run long enough to allow for . . .

- the experimental treatment to begin eliciting a response (penetration);

- the assessment of how quickly brand loyalty and switching patterns can be expected to develop (repeat purchase); and

- the taking into account of the degree of precision required in the estimate of effects;

. . . and provided that a competitor does not succeed in muddying the water,

- an estimate of national share is arrived at by applying the changes to brand shares observed in the experimental area to the shares held by competing brands in the national market.

The procedure is spelt out in the following statistician's formula: if XEo, YEo and so on, are brand shares in the experimental area prior to the introduction of Brand T, and if T_1, X_1, Y_1, and so on, are the brand shares after the introduction; and if XNo, YNo, and so on, are the brand shares in the wider market prior to the launch, the projected share of Brand T nationally will be T_1, where:

$$T_1 = 100 - \left\{ XEo \cdot \frac{X_1}{X_o} + YEo \cdot \frac{Y_1}{Y_o} + \ldots \right\} \%$$

This example relates to an experimental launch. The standardization procedure could also be used when predicting the effect of changes to the marketing of an existing brand, but the impact on market testing of individual elements in the mix is likely to be less noticeable than the impact of an experimental launch. It will be more difficult to achieve statistically significant results. The AMTES (Area Marketing Test Evaluation System) econometric model is designed to meet this problem.

Brand shares are the product of the historic working of the marketing mix variables at certain fixed points in time, that is, when the observations are taken. These data may show the relationship between area brand sales and national sales to be a volatile one. In this case the underlying relationship is revealed by averaging the readings over a period before and after the introduction of the treatment. The length of this period will depend on the frequency with which the product is bought.

Problem

Hauser Pharmaceutical Company has just ended the experimental launch of its new brand *'Liprotect'* into a product field of four brands (A–D). The company had set a target share of 12% for its new brand. The final results of the experimental market testing phase (which lasted nine months) are shown below in Table 18.1.

Table 18.1   Experimental market results.

	Brand share (%)		Lost to	Loss as % of
	Before	After	Liprotect	pre-test share
A	30	27	−3	−10
B	15	10	−5	−33.3
C	25	25	–	–
D	30	27	−3	−10
Liprotect	–	11	11	
	100	100		

The shares of the four competing brands in the wider market prior to the launch of *'Liprotect'* were as follows:

Brand	Brand share % (before launch of new brand)
A	35
B	9
C	31
D	25

Questions

(1) Calculate the projected market share of *'Liprotect'* nationally.

(2) Calculate the projected national market shares of the competing brands, A, B, C and D, after the launch of *'Liprotect'*.

(3) Comment on the projected position of *'Liprotect'* in the national market.

Problem 2: Estimating salesforce size

Introductory comments

The decision made most frequently with respect to distribution channels concerns the *number and location of sales representatives.*

How many sales representatives should there be in a given market area? There are three general research methods for answering this question. The first, the sales effort approach, is applicable when the product line is first introduced and there is no operating history to provide sales data. The second involves the statistical analysis of sales data and can be used after the sales programme is under way. The third involves a field experiment and is also applicable only after the sales programme has begun.

Sales effort approach

A logical, straightforward approach to estimating the number of sales representatives required for a given market area is to:

(1) Estimate the number of sales calls required to sell to and to service prospective customers in an area for a year. This will be the sum of the number of visits required per year – Vi – to each prospect/customer – Pi – in the territory, or

$$\sum_{i=1}^{n} ViPi \qquad\qquad (18.1)$$

where n is the number of prospects/customers.

(2) Estimate the average number of sales calls per representative that can be made in that territory in a year – c.

(3) Divide the estimate in statement (1) by the estimate in statement (2) to obtain the number of sales representatives required, R. That is

$$R = \frac{\sum_{i=1}^{n} ViPi}{\bar{c}} \qquad\qquad (18.2)$$

The research required for this approach is that of compiling lists of prospective customers, with sufficient information about each customer to permit an assignment to be made of the desired call frequency. Prospect lists can be developed using trade association directories, chamber of commerce listings, registrations with state and local governments, listings in the *Yellow Pages* and other secondary sources. As a general rule, the lists developed from these sources will not contain all of the prospective customers in the area; some will inevitably be missed. Canvassing on the part of the sales representatives who are assigned to the area can be required to supplement the list developed from secondary sources. A later adjustment in the number of sales representatives (or in the size of the sales territory) may also be required.

Problem

The following case illustrates this procedure. Downey Industrial Cleaning Products Limited is opening a sales territory which marketing research has indicated has 230 prospective customers. Some of these prospects will need to be called upon once a month (12 times per year), others once every two months (6 times per year), and still others once each quarter (4 times per year). Assume that the distribution of firms per number of sales calls per year is as shown in columns (1) and (2) of Table 18.2.

Table 18.2   Required number of calls per prospect per year and number of prospects in a new sales territory – Downey Industrial Cleaning Products Limited.

Column 1 Calls per prospect per year	Column 2 Number of prospects
12	50
6	80
4	100
	230

Downey Industrial Cleaning Products Limited estimated that the average number of calls to be made by each sales representative per year is 720.

Questions

(1) Calculate the total number of calls required per year and the number of calls required per year for each prospect category.

(2) Calculate the number of sales representatives needed in the new sales territory which has been targeted by Downey Industrial Cleaning Products Limited.

(3) After having applied the formula, suggest any specific adjustments that might be required with regard to the allocation of the sales representatives.

Problem 3: Broadcast media research

Introductory comments

There are numerous terms that rating services and media planners use to define a television or radio station's audience, penetration and efficiency. We will discuss some of these before examining some procedures used to buy television or radio time. TV households (TVHH) refers to the number of households that own television sets. For example, in the United States approximately 70 million households (over 98% of all households) own television sets. By looking at the number of households that own TVs in a particular market, we can gain a sense of the size of that market. Likewise, by looking at the number of TV households tuned in to a particular programme, we can gain a sense of how popular the programme is and how many people our commercial is likely to reach.

The percentage of homes in a given area that have one or more TV sets turned on at any particular time is expressed as households using TV (HUT). If there are 1000 TV sets in the survey area and 500 are turned on, the HUT figure is 50%.

We are all familiar with TV shows that have been cancelled because their ratings slipped. What does that really mean? The percentage of TV households in an area that are tuned in to a specific programme is called the *programme rating* :

$$\text{Rating} = \frac{\text{Number tuned to specific station}}{\text{TVHH}}$$

The networks are interested in high ratings because that is a measure of a show's popularity. If a show is not popular, advertisers will not want to advertise on it and a network's revenue will fall. Similarly, local stations often make changes in their local news shows in order to increase their popularity, and, thereby, their ratings.

The percentage of homes that have sets in use (HUT) tuned in to a specific programme is called the programme's share of audience. A programme with only 50 viewers could have a 50% share if only 100 sets are turned on. For that reason the programme ratings figures are important because they measure the audience as a percentage of all TV households in the area, regardless of whether the TV set is on or off.

The total number of homes reached by some portion of a programme is referred to as total audience. This figure is normally broken down to determine audience composition (the distribution of audience into demographic categories).

Gross rating points (GRPs)

In television, gross rating points are the total weight of a media schedule against TV households. For example, a weekly schedule of 5 commercials with an average household rating of 20 would yield 100 GRPs, or a total audience equivalent to the total number of TV households in the area.

To give another example, a company determined that a schedule of 50 GRPs per week would be sufficient at the beginning of its television campaign. This might have been accomplished by buying 10 spots with an average rating of 5, or only 2 spots with an average rating of 25. The latter might have been feasible by using a highly rated primetime programme, but then the frequency would have been very low. So the company opted to use the late evening newscasts, which had lower ratings against total TV households, but higher shares of those adults watching; it also afforded the company the ability to gain frequency.

The results of the company's decision demonstrated the wisdom of its choice. In key markets where the commercials ran, surveys were taken, and the number of respondents who looked on the company as an attractive investment alternative increased by 20% – to more than 60% total. In control markets where the company's commercials did not air, the company's image remained virtually unchanged.

Selecting programmes for buys

To determine which shows to buy, the media buyer must select those most efficient in relation to the target audience. To do this, a simple computation is made of the cost per rating point (CPP) and the cost per thousand (CPT) for each programme, as follows:

$$\frac{\text{Cost}}{\text{Rating}} = \text{CPP} \qquad \frac{\text{Cost}}{\text{Thousands of people}} = \text{CPT}$$

Obviously, the lower the cost per thousand, the more efficient the show is against the target audience. The media buyer's task, therefore, is to compare the packages of each station, substituting stronger programmes for less efficient ones. The media buyer tries to use the best areas each station has to offer to construct suitable packages.

Buying radio time requires a basic understanding of radio terminology. Naturally, much of the language used for radio advertising is the same as that used for other media. But radio also has numerous terms that are either peculiar to it or have a special meaning when applied to radio advertising. The most common of these are the concepts of dayparts, average quarter-hour audiences and cumes (cumulative audiences).

Dayparts

The radio day is divided into five basic dayparts:

  6 a.m. to 10 a.m. – Morning drive
10 a.m. to 3 p.m. – Daytime

3 p.m. to 7 p.m. – Afternoon (or evening) drive
7 p.m. to 12 a.m. – Nightime
12 a.m. to 6 a.m. – All night

The rating services measure the audiences for only the first four of these dayparts, because all-night listening is very limited and not highly competitive.

The heaviest radio use occurs during drive times (6–10 a.m. and 3–7 p.m.) during the week (Monday–Friday). One exception to this is that easy listening (or 'good' music) stations traditionally have their heaviest use during daytime (10 a.m.–3 p.m.). Otherwise, drive time is radio's primetime. This is important to advertisers because usage and consumption vary for different products. Television advertising in primetime, for example, is seen when viewers are least likely to consume coffee. On the other hand, radio's morning drive time coincides perfectly with most people's desire for a steaming, fresh cup of coffee.

Radio stations base their rates on the time of day the advertiser wants commercials aired. To achieve the lowest rate, an advertiser can order spots on a run of station (ROS) basis, similar to ROP in newspaper advertising. ROP advertising rates entitle a newspaper to place a given advertisement on any newspaper page or in any position it desires – in other words, where space permits. However, this leaves total control of spot placement up to the station. Most stations, therefore, offer a total audience plan (TAP) package rate, which guarantees a certain percentage of spots in the better dayparts if the advertiser buys the total package of time.

Naturally, the subject of daypart advantages can be exhausting for the sophisticated advertiser who has the time, resources and facilities to study it in depth.

Average quarter-hour

This term is used to identify the average number of people who are listening to a specific station during any 15-minute period of any given daypart. Following is an example of an average quarter-hour listening estimate:

Station	*Average $\frac{1}{4}$ hour* *Mon–Sun, 6 a.m.–midnight;* *Persons over 12 years old*
Radio Clyde–Glasgow–Scotland Scotland	4200

This means that any day, Monday–Sunday, during any 15-minute period between 6 a.m. and midnight, it is probable (more than likely) that 4200 people over 12 years old are tuned in to the Radio Clyde station.

This same idea can be expressed in terms of 'share' if the station's audience is shown as a percentage of the total listening audience in the area.

Rating points

By extending our computations a little further, this same audience could be expressed in terms of rating points if we showed it as a percentage of the population. Determining the gross rating points of a radio schedule, therefore, simply requires multiplying the average quarter-hour rating by the number of spots. Likewise, the GRPs could also be determined by multiplying the average quarter-hour audience by the number of spots and dividing by the population.

Cume audience

This capsule term for 'Cumulative Audience' describes the total number of different people listening to a radio station for at least one 15-minute segment over the course of a given week, day or daypart.

For example, we can generate 50,400 gross impressions with our schedule on a particular radio station, but that does not mean that 50,400 different people heard our commercials. Many people might have heard our commercial three, four or five times, depending on how long they stayed tuned to that particular radio station.

By measuring the cumulative number of different people listening to a radio station, the rating services can give us an idea of the reach potential of our radio schedule. Thus, cume and average quarter-hour are important concepts. A high cume figure means that a lot of different people are tuning in to the station for at least 15 minutes. A high average quarter-hour figure usually means that people are listening and staying tuned in.

It is important to remember one basic concept about these radio audience measurements. They are derived from the manipulation of statistical data, which involves a complex weighting of various members of the station's surveyed audience. These manipulations produce an important result: generating the average quarter-hour audience figure is dependent on the length of listening. The longer the survey respondent listens, the larger the average quarter-hour audience will be. The cumulative audience is dependent on numerous different people tuning in to the radio station. The more respondents that tune in, the higher the cume will be.

Thus, the most stable (accurate) number for estimating the size, scope and depth of a radio station is the cume. This is because, in the rating service's survey, the cume number is based on a larger sample size!

Problem

Hairlines, a hairdressing franchise chain in Scotland, is planning to air a concentrated advertising campaign using broadcast media. The advertising agency handling their account want to place the company's advertising spots next to highly popular programmes destined to reach the same target audience. The company is particularly interested in targeting the City of Glasgow area, with an advertising media plan based on local radio and local television.

Questions

(1) Assume that the local television programme 'On-the-Spot' game show has a rating of 25, reaches 200,000 people in the primary target audience and costs £2000 for a 30-second spot on Scottish Television. Calculate the CPP and the CPT.

(2) *Hairlines* wants to use radio advertising in the Glasgow area through the placement of spots in Radio Clyde, which has an average quarter-hour listening estimate (Mon–Sun, 6 a.m.–midnight, persons over 12 years old) of 4200 people. The advertising agency handling the company's account found that the total average quarter-hour listening audience for all stations in the Glasgow catchment area is 48,900. Calculate the average quarter-hour audience of Radio Clyde as expressed as an average quarter-hour 'share'.

(3) Since Radio Clyde is located in Glasgow (population: 800,000), we can now express and calculate its average quarter-hour audience as an average quarter-hour rating. Calculate.

(4) *Hairlines* wants to run 25 spots in Radio Clyde during a two-week period. Determine the gross rating points (GRPs) which would result as a consequence of this radio schedule.

(*Note*: Although Radio Clyde is a real radio station, data in this example is imaginary and used for illustrative purposes.)

Case 1 – Phonelink

Several companies used customer expectation surveys to estimate sales for cellular mobile phones. These new phones can be used in cars. As a result of technological advances, they will be available to many more users than previously. Several companies (Cellnet, NEC and others) assessed demand for these phones in several major metropolitan areas.

One of these competing companies, Phonelink, used an approach involving telephone surveys of households earning £20,000 or more, annually. Other firms interviewed businesses only. Phonelink surveyed households because it felt that expected use for business and personal reasons could be measured. Each household head was asked his or her level of interest in this type of product (see Figure 18.2).

Level of interest
If cost were not a factor, how much interest would you have in using this new mobile telephone service? Would that be:

- A great deal of interest?
- Some interest?
- Little interest?
- No interest at all?
- Don't know?

Purchase expectations
If the new mobile telephone service and equipment were available at a total cost of about £45 per month, how likely is it that you or your firm would subscribe to the service for your use? Would you or your firm:

- Definitely subscribe?
- Probably subscribe?
- Probably not subscribe?
- Definitely not subscribe?

Figure 18.2 Customer expectation measure for mobile phones.

The key question asked respondents their likelihood of purchase (Table 18.3) at each of three price levels (£25, £35, £45 per month). Additional questions focused on locations of use (commuting to work or home, during business travel), desirable features (call waiting, call forwarding) and the amount of business versus personal use.

Market sales were estimated from answers to the intent-to-subscribe question. Asking questions at each price level permitted a schedule reflecting the elasticity of demand. To take into account errors by respondents in estimating their probabilities, the percentage of the market subscribing at each price level was estimated as follows:

Table 18.3 Customer expectations forecast of mobile phone sales.

Price level	Strength of interest	% responding
£25	Definitely will	10.2
	Probably will	22.3
	Probably will not	22.1
£35	Definitely will	3.0
	Probably will	14.8
	Probably will not	29.8
£45	Definitely will	1.4
	Probably will	11.7
	Probably will not	31.0

(% definitely subscribe × 0.60) + (% probably subscribe × 0.30)
+ (% probably not subscribe × 0.05) + (% definitely not
subscribe × 0) = % of target market representing potential
subscribers.

These adjustments assume that many people who say they will subscribe
actually will not and that a few who say they will not actually will.

Table 18.3 summarizes the findings at each price level for one major
market area. Total unit sales at each price level can then be estimated by
Phonelink by applying the market percentage to the total number of target
market households in the geographic area. The optimal price would be
determined by estimating net revenue at each price level based on sales and
costs.

Figure 18.3 shows the demand curve associated with price variations.

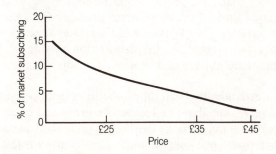

Figure 18.3 Demand schedule for mobile phones.

Questions

(1) Evaluate the advantages and disadvantages associated with the use of
the survey of customer expectations method.

(2) Taking into account the different levels of strength of interest, the
per cent responding in each category and the adjustment factors set
by Phonelink, calculate the estimated per cent of the market likely to
subscribe to the new mobile phone service at each of the price levels.

Case 2 – Ice Delight

To help spread the word about its new light ice cream product, the popular
Hatfield-based firm, with a near cult following for its all-natural product, ran
a promotion campaign called '1000 pints of light' in 1990. It awarded 1000 pints
of light ice cream in a tie-in promotion with the Giraffe Project people, who

recognize special achievers in cities and other localities who 'stick their necks out' for community causes.

The promotion campaign ran in seven major urban and suburban areas and scored points for both groups in terms of identifying prospects interested in 'Ice Delight' and recognizing positive community activists. Ice Delight ran advertisements in York, Sheffield, Newcastle upon Tyne, Birmingham, London, Southampton, and Bristol, calling for nominations for local 'Special long-necked persons', people whose stories are subsequently turned into mini-media events by the Giraffe Project members in Maidenhead, Berkshire.

Ice Delight set up a special 800 telephone number to receive taped nominations, the callers leaving their names, addresses and phone numbers (along with the phone number of their nominee). The caller received an official nomination form and a coupon for a free pint of light ice cream as an inducement to product trial. 'We got so many responses, we wore out the tapes a few times', said Susan Morris, assistant manager for special events at Ice Delight. 'We certainly got overwhelmed.' Ice Delight sent out some 10,000 coupons during the promotion, the distribution varying by market. About 100–150 people called in from each market. The advertisements ran for a week only.

Susan Morris admitted that the promotion did not generate an absolutely pure list of Giraffe candidates or Ice Delight prospects, because some people called in more than once, thinking they would get more than one free ice cream certificate (there was a one-coupon limit). The Giraffe Project made the final decision on who would win the 1000 pints of light, one winner designated for each major market.

The project was 'definitely an experiment', said Susan Morris, adding that final disposition of the names collected has not yet been determined by Ice Delight, other than analysing that the promotional tie-in definitely elicited a solid response, thus telling the company it had the right tie-in and the power to pull in names of prospective (community do-gooder) customers.

Questions

(1) The company did not engage itself in pre-testing the promotion offer based on processing consumer response, but Ice Delight is planning a pre-testing phase for future promotions. What are the main considerations involved in the pre-testing process?

(2) What alternatives are available to the company to develop a post-testing plan for the '1000 pints of light' campaign?

(3) How could Ice Delight calculate the return on future sales promotion programmes?

(4) The company is also planning to evaluate the effectiveness of its advertising campaign by using communication–effects research. What

are the key determinants and measures involved in advertising communication–effects research?

Case 3 – Kamen Food Products Limited

Kamen Food Products Limited planned to introduce *Salada*, a product line of salad dressing, nationally. This was its first entry into the salad dressing category market. The product range consists of ten different types of salad dressing, ranging from the French and blue cheese to thousand island and herb types. The units are encased in a triangle-shaped container, with a shell for protection and stability.

Salad dressing is a new product, with an expected growth rate of 1.5% a year in units consumed. Housewives are the prime purchasers, and the product is consumed in all socio-economic groups.

Supermarkets sell 89% of all salad dressings and are the dominant channel of distribution. *Salada* comes in an innovative package that can be used directly on the dinner table. Ten units are packaged in each container. A case of 12 containers sells to the retailer for £9.25. The suggested retail price is £1.80 per container. Costs as a percentage of factory sales were estimated as follows: fixed costs, 38%; variable costs, 12%; media/production costs, 15%; sampling/couponing, 4%; trade allowances, 4%; other promotion, 2%; salesforce, 6%; distribution costs, 4%; and administration and market research, 2%. Sales are forecast at 2.6 million cases.

The *Salada* product manager is required to present an annual marketing plan to the group product manager. Kamen Food Products Limited uses a standardized format containing the following items:

(1) The brand's current (expected) performance.
(2) Recommendations.
(3) Effect of the recommendations on income.
(4) Situation analysis.
(5) Opportunities and problems.
(6) Marketing strategies.
(7) Tests and marketing research.

John Segura, the product manager in charge of *Salada*, knew some of the questions that must be asked at each stage of the planning process. He was concerned though about the frequency for reviewing these planning questions, which in turn would indicate how frequently the marketing information system must supply data at each stage of the marketing planning process. He was also wondering about the sources of information and the methods of analysis that should be used. Of course, the informational needs of planners and the

Planning stage	Examples of critical question
Environmental analysis	
Organizational values/objectives and policies	• What are the values and objectives of those persons who are in control?
Marketing organization	• How are resources, responsibility and authority organized?
Situation analysis	• What are the unmet needs of the market?
	• What are the profiles of users and non-users?
	• What are the segments for the product type?
	• What are the trends with regard to competitors?
	• What are our brand benefits?
Competition	• What are the industry success factors, capacities and competitive structures?
	• What are our strengths and weaknesses?
Public policy	• How do environmental concerns affect our strategies?
Strategy worksheet (Marketing mix strategies)	
Product	• Can costs be reduced?
	• Does it meet needs adequately?
Price	• What is the price elasticity?
	• What price must we charge to break even?
	• What are competitors' costs and prices?
Channels of distribution	• Which channels are the most productive?
Advertising	• What copy theme should be used?
	• Which media should we use? How frequently?
Personal selling	• How should we recruit, train, motivate and compensate the salesforce?
	• How should sales territories be determined?
Marketing research	• Are the data worth the cost of research?
Profit plan	• What are our forecasted sales and costs?
	• Do learning and experience curves apply?
	• What is the payback period?
Evaluation	• Are we achieving our corporate strategic objectives?
	• Are we achieving our marketing tactical goals?
Control	• How do we implement and control the performance of the marketing plan?

Figure 18.4 **Planning stages.**

sources of data vary so widely across products, services and industries that generalizations are impossible.

John has decided to prepare a list of planning stages with some critical questions that needed to be answered (Figure 18.4).

Questions

(1) What other planning questions should the *Salada* product manager consider as his most important informational needs for the marketing planning process?

(2) Define the appropriate frequency of review that John Segura should consider for each critical planning question

(3) Describe the most appropriate sources of information to be used for each planning question.

(4) What methods of data analysis should the product manager apply in order to answer each marketing planning question?

REFERENCES

Crimp M. (1985). *The Marketing Research Process* 2nd edn. London: Prentice-Hall International

Davis E. J. (1970). *Experimental Marketing*. London: Nelson

Clippings from the Press

Clipping 1 Market Research Society Newsletter, March 1991.

FIELDWORK – THE FUTURE

Charles Ilsley, Director, FDS Market Research Group Ltd, writes

There has been much debate in the market research world about the crisis facing personal interviewing. The industry has traditionally relied on teams of part-time interviewers to go out in all weathers and collect the information that is so valuable to their clients. Despite the growth in telephone research, face-to-face interviews still account for over 70% of all interviews carried out (source: AMSO 1989).

Over the recent past, research agencies have experienced difficulties in attracting and keeping interviewers. The problem has been particularly acute in London and in the other major conurbations. There are many areas at both ends of the social spectrum where interviewing is very difficult, if not impossible, to carry out. Money has been cited as the solution to these problems. Pay the interviewers more and the problems will go away!

FDS Market Research Group Ltd runs one of the larger fieldforces in Great Britain. The company was founded 18 years ago and prides itself on providing high quality fieldwork. However, FDS has experienced the same difficulties as other agencies in recruiting and retaining interviewers and therefore decided to survey its fieldforce to find out what the problems were and how they might be overcome. The agency mailed a questionnaire to the 637 interviewers on its books and received back 333 completed questionnaires, a response rate of 52%.

Factors other than pay need to be addressed

The results were illuminating since they revealed a lot of what was already known about interviewers, but it also showed that there were factors other than pay that need to be addressed.

The majority of FDS's interviewers are married women (only 3% are men) and the age profile is relatively old; 60% being 45 or older (Figure 1).

Initial attractions of the job, namely flexibility, the interesting nature of the work and the opportunity to meet people are more than fulfilled since they are

Figure 1 Age of interviewers

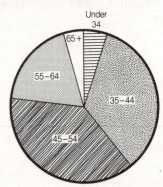

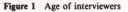

Figure 2 Interviewing – expectation and reality

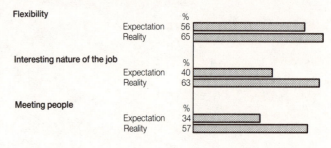

		%
Flexibility	Expectation	56
	Reality	65
Interesting nature of the job	Expectation	40
	Reality	63
Meeting people	Expectation	34
	Reality	57

the main things liked about interviewing (Figure 2).

The things that interviewers dislike about the job divide into three factors; the nature of the job, research elements and employment conditions (Figure 3).

Their unwillingness to work at evenings or weekends, precisely when a high proportion of interviewing needs to take place, stems not just from disruption of family life but from the fact that they (and their family) are not happy to be interviewing after dark. Fifty-seven per cent stated that they were frightened of going out after dark and 49% said that their family worried about them doing this. Fear of crime has been well documented by Home Office and police surveys, and the fact that the majority of interviewers are

women makes this finding no great surprise.

'there are clearly a number of things that can make the interviewer's job more attractive'

There are clearly a number of things that can be done to make the market research interviewer's job more attractive and appealing.

The nature of the job has changed. The rise in the number of working women means that there is now a requirement for the majority of interviewing to be carried out in the evenings and at weekends. However, the anxiety and fear factor could be greatly reduced by allowing interviewers to work in pairs, particularly in the evenings. Needless to say, the cost implications would be considerable.

Complex quotas and tight

deadlines are probably here to stay, but long, boring questionnaires with batteries of rating scales could be simplified and made more acceptable to interviewers and respondents alike. Undoubtedly clients, and indeed research executives, need to be reminded of this and perhaps encouraged to pilot their questionnaires whenever this is possible. Certainly, it would be illuminating for clients to accompany interviewers on their jobs.

'the industry needs to face up to the problems that interviewers experience'

The problems relating to interviewing are such that unless the whole research industry recognises them, its ability to organise surveys and collect data via face-to-face interviews will become increasingly difficult. The industry needs to face up to the problems that interviewers experience in the field. Their job needs to be made more acceptable by the production of well written, logical and interesting questionnaires.

Finally pay and conditions must be kept under review, for although money is not the only cause for complaint it is nevertheless important. We expect our interviewers to be professional and we should be prepared to pay them accordingly.

Figure 3 Interviewer dislikes

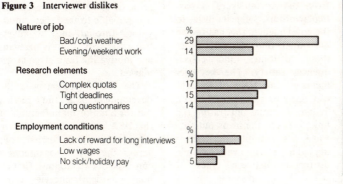

Nature of job
- Bad/cold weather — 29%
- Evening/weekend work — 14%

Research elements
- Complex quotas — 17%
- Tight deadlines — 15%
- Long questionnaires — 14%

Employment conditions
- Lack of reward for long interviews — 11%
- Low wages — 7%
- No sick/holiday pay — 5%

Fieldwork – the future

Key issues

- Interviewing
- Interviewers
- Fieldwork

Questions

(1) Recruiting and retaining interviewers is an increasing problem in the industry. Do we simply need to pay them more?

(2) What are the implications (if any) of the fact that the majority of fieldwork interviewers are women aged 35 and over? How may it affect the manner in which fieldwork is conducted?

Clipping 2   Market Research Society Newsletter, April 1991.

LADDERING INTERVIEWING IN THE UK

April Hogan, Focus on Research, reports

Focus on Research, in conjunction with the Dallas Research Center, recently carried out the first UK laddering project.

Laddering is a new interviewing technique developed and established in the USA and widely used to gain an understanding of market places and issues as varied as that for snack chips and the Pro-life movement.

The technique has its base in 'Means end' theory which suggests that there are links between products (the 'means') and the consequences these provide for the consumer, dependent on the personal values of that individual (the 'ends'). It is these end values, rarely consciously considered, that play a major part in determining consumer choice within any given area.

The in-depth laddering interview elicits these personal motivations by encouraging respondents 'to revisit everyday, common place experiences and to examine the assumptions and desires driving seemingly simple choice behaviour'; exploring in detail consumer's relationships with and response to, particular products and markets.

In practice this requires a great deal of sensitivity and a high level of empathy on the part of the interviewer. The whole process asks respondents to probe quite deeply into themselves, to question their reasons for behaving in certain ways.

Through the use of careful and sympathetic probing the interviewer is able to reach forward from the attributes of a particular product, e.g. its taste, to the consequences this has for an individual, onto the values that these attributes and consequences satisfy. The key elements of this train of thought can easily be summarised into a 'ladder diagram' illustrating the links between the ideas put forward. For example, the following ladder, starting with a simple distinction between types of snack chips, represents part of the data from a US study into the salty snack market.

(Value)	Self esteem
	↓
(Consequence)	Better figure
	↓
(Consequence)	Don't get fat
	↓
(Consequence)	Eat less
	↓
(Attribute)	Strong taste
	↓
(Attribute)	Flavoured chip

Examined as a whole, the responses give a clear, direct and useful understanding of the consumer which has, in the past, proved to be of great use in the development of advertising strategies.

By gaining an understanding of those personal values that are of importance in determining choice, for example, the ability to help one to cope with one's busy day or to contribute to a sense of pride and achievement, it is possible to feed these 'motivators' through into an advertising strategy that is relevant and motivating for a given target market.

The recent project was the development of a study carried out for a major manufacturer in the USA. Nearly 300 executive interviews were carried out across the UK. The interview consisted of two sections: first an hour long depth interview using laddering techniques to build up a picture of consumers' attitudes and motivations; secondly, a structured half hour, computer assisted interview that assessed the relationship between consumers' values and existing advertising.

'Laddering' is particularly useful for international brands and markets as it focuses not on the product but on the values and input consumers bring to that product. The flexibility of the technique is that it follows the lead and direction of individual consumers, by asking them to respond, then to react to that response, rather than questioning in relation to predetermined theories that may have little relevance for that country.

Laddering varies from other depth interviewing techniques, not only in the practical process, but also in the quantitative methods used in analysis.

Content analysis of the links between the product attributes, consequences and personal values is used to produce a hierarchical value map which illustrates the direct and indirect connection between the qualitative concepts elicited during the laddering interview. Analysis of the relationship and level of interconnection between the different elements on the map highlights those values which are of most impact for consumers; turning the laddering process into an important tool for marketing decision-making.

Laddering proved a new and challenging task for the Focus team. As with all good ideas, the basic root of laddering is quite simple. However, the practice proved far more complex. The entire team attended a three day training course, with the Dallas Research Center, to learn how to master the new technique. There was also an extra day's training to explain the software program for the shorter advertising interview.

Coupled with the field task of arranging nearly 300 1½ hour depths across two weeks the job offered a challenge for the whole company.

However, the new insights we were able to gain into a complex market place, justified every effort that had been made to ensure the project ran smoothly and efficiently. Laddering is a new and fascinating technique that we believe takes the depth of consumer understanding one step further.

Laddering interviewing in the UK

Key issues

- Laddering
- Means end theory
- Motivation research
- Benefit research

Questions

(1) Why don't we just ask people if they like the product or brand, rather than this latest version of psychoanalysis?

(2) Work through some laddering interviewing, by extending brand attributes into their consumer consequences, and evaluate the findings in terms of their marketing utility.

Clipping 3 Survey, Spring 1987.

THE MINI-TEST MARKET

Brian Pymont, Joint Managing Director, RBL (Research International Ltd), describes RBL's approach to new product testing

Towards the end of 1985 an issue of *Marketing Week* carried an article, featured on the front cover, wich demanded to know 'Whatever happened to test marketing?' Not a particularly controversial proposition you may think, particularly those of you who are actively engaged in the business of developing new products and trying to get them established in the national market place. And yet it is a measure of the speed of change in the world of marketing consumer products that ten years earlier even to pose the question would have been unthinkable and ten years before that the test market had only recently become part of the orthodox canon.

The crucial decisions along the road from the conception of a new product idea to an eventual national launch are all about evaluating *opportunity* against *risk* and, internal politics apart, the final decision whether or not to push the 'go' button depends on an estimate of the incremental effect on the company's sales volume. When the advent of regional TV made it possible to carry out an almost completely realistic test in one area of the country this was the first point in the development programme when it was possible to quantify a new product opportunity with an actual sales estimate.

Not that the quality of estimating in the early days was much to write home about. The standard approach was to monitor the new product's sales in the test area by means of a shop audit and assume that it would perform in a similar way when it

went national. It soon became obvious that, because market conditions tend to vary from one area to another, test market sales could be a poor predictor of what was likely to happen nationally. The fact that everyone at head office with a vested interest in the new product's success frequently camped out in the test area for weeks at a time just to help things along a little only made a national sales estimate more difficult.

The first real breakthrough came in the late 1960's when Parfitt and Collins of the Attwood Consumer Panel showed that the quality of estimating, both of where the new product would settle down in the test area and from there to national performance, could be much improved by examining individual consumer *purchases* rather than aggregated *sales*. They showed that at any point in time the *sales* of a new product were a combination of first time or *trial* purchases and *repeat* purchases and that its long-term status in the market would largely be determined by this repeat purchase level.

The fact that repeat purchasing tends to depend on factors which are within the control of the manufacturer – product, price, packaging and so on – increases the probability of a constant influence in the test area and the national market (although by no means the certainty of it) and this adds weight to the importance of a measure of repeat purchasing to reliable sales estimating.

From then on consumer panel

data became virtually indispensable to reliable test marketing. But it was about that time too that anxiety among manufacturers about the down-side risks of the TV area test market itself reached the point at which they were prompted to look for alternative, less risky ways of quantifying potential sales volume. Because the test market was the first opportunity to measure sales, right at the end of a development programme, far too many products were getting that far and failing.

In those days RBL was owned by Unilever which tended to be in the forefront of marketing developments and, under its basic research programme, was briefed to find a solution to the problem of estimating the sales of a new product in a realistic way but short of a public test market. Today RBL is no longer owned by Unilever – and numbers many of its competitors among its clients – but the commitment to technical development remains, illustrated by our latest new technique *MicroTest* which is providing accurate sales volume estimates from very little more than normal concept/ product test data.

But back in the late 1960's the task was to develop a full dress rehearsal system – or as near to it as we could get – without exposing a new product to the risks of the test market – the risk of losing a lot of money, of giving competitors about nine month's advance warning of one's intentions, of not being able to optimise the product mix because of the basic inflexibility of a TV area.

The first thing we had to decide was what it was about the test market which made it different from all the other tests to which a new product might be exposed during its development. The answer was pretty simple. The test market is about observing actual *sales* over *time* in a *competitive environment* – none of which is normally a feature of conventional market mix tests. We needed to give a representative sample of consumers the opportunity to purchase the test product with their own money, in as normal a retail environment as possible, over as long a time period as was necessary for the pattern of sales to reflect the crucial repeat purchasing and with an equal opportunity to buy competitive products if they wanted to.

But we had to do it in a way which would limit the financial risk, avoid competitors finding out what we were up to and, above all, learn from the lesson so recently taught by Parfitt and Collins that, if we wanted to make reliable sales estimates, we had to provide good quality *consumer panel* data.

The result of all this was the *RBL Mini-Test Market* and perhaps the most fundamental decision which we had to take in building a system which would really deliver the goods was actually to get into the retail business ourselves. A system based on someone else's stores would leave us short of the control we felt we needed and, anyway, would mean that our clients' competitors would immediately be alerted to the new products on test.

We decided that the population we wanted to represent was UK *housewives* and that the retail operation would sell as many as possible of the products the housewife would find in her local supermarket. Because we wanted to base the operation on a consumer panel, which meant being able to identify individual customers, we decided to opt for a mobile retail operation which would enable the housewives to do their shopping to all intents and purposes at their own front doors. This type of retail outlet enables us to collect excellent panel data because we can easily identify every individual housewife and what she buys.

Whether this is a realistic way of selling products to consumers depends not so much on the characteristics of the retail environment as on whether the panel housewives really use the mobile shop to do their weekly grocery shopping rather than just as an interim top-up. Fortunately it is easy to check out any product field against AGB panel data and this usually shows a remarkably good representation of the national market. Professor Ehrenberg and colleagues at the London Business School also carried out a study of the panel's purchasing dynamics and this showed a good representation of known national patterns.

Once we had set up a balanced consumer panel and a realistic retail operation, the use of the system for test marketing became relatively simple. All we had to do was to find a representative way of stimulating trial of a new product and then sit back and see what happened next. Whether a triallist became a repeat purchaser was as much up to her as it is in the national market.

The final problem was how to induce trial in a representative way. TV was obviously out of the question and we finally opted for a self-contained magazine-type medium which carried high quality press advertisements for test products. This has the advantage of restricting the advertising to the panel housewives and had proved to be a remarkably representative way of stimulating new product trial.

We believe that the *RBL Mini-Test Market* system fulfils the requirements of a valid test market in providing a measurement of *sales* over *time* in a *competitive environment* and it is interesting to look back on some of the famous brand names which have passed through on their way to test market or national launch. Shield, Jif, Bisto Gravy Granules, Birds Coffee, Wispa, Harvest Crunch Bars, Jacobs Farmhouse Crackers, Frish, Wisk – the list is a long one. The list of those which failed to make it is a lot longer.

But back to *Marketing Week* and 'Whatever happened to test marketing?' What the headline was alluding to was the fact that over the years all the old test marketing risks have gradually become more risky and that nowadays a major new risk – a failure to achieve adequate distribution – has appeared on the scene. The fact is that a highly organised multiple retail trade finds restricting a product to one TV area less than convenient and is often only prepared to list it when it is fully national. So it is genuinely the case that for many manufacturers the conventional test market is no longer a feasible option.

This development has given the *RBI Mini-Test Market* a new lease of life. Rather than being merely a way of ensuring that a fundamentally bad product never gets as far as a test market, many well known manufacturers now use it as the final test of their new or improved products. The next stop is the national launch. TV area test marketing may have declined but the *Mini-Test* is as strong as ever.

The *Mini-Test Market*

Key issues

- Test marketing
- New product development

Questions

(1) It was only a decade ago that test marketing became almost the norm for appropriate products. Why has this changed?

(2) Analyse and evaluate the *Mini-Test Market* approach as described in this clipping.

Clipping 4 The Independent on Sunday, 24 March 1991.

AN ALTERNATIVE TO JUNK MAIL IS AT THE DOOR

Demographic databases are letting marketers reach those most likely to buy, reports Anne Ferguson

My neighbours do their grocery shopping at Safeway, with a top-up at Marks & Spencer. The vast majority of us are single flat dwellers with a smattering of go-getting council tenants. We're not big on driving Volvos or playing golf, but the folks round my way are 'cultural travellers', 'young affluentials' or sociable types who are into 'crisps and videos' or 'pubs, pools & bingo'.

I know all this because I have lived in Hammersmith for several years. But some of Britain's biggest retailers and producers of household products know all about me and my neighbours too, because they use a company called Circular Distributors to put things through my door, and CD told them.

CD is one of a growing band of companies that provide direct marketing services, in this case

by distributing promotional material, samples and coupons door-to-door, which CD calls letterbox marketing. The company, which is based in Maidenhead, is also the largest distributor of free newspapers in the UK.

The art of direct marketing is to reach the people most likely to be interested in the products, and not waste time and money on those who will never buy. Consequently, CD performs a much more sophisticated function than simply shoving things through doors at random.

First, it finds out whom the client sees as potential customers, where they live, and then does its best to ensure that every door in the areas selected receives a visit. It uses information from databases of demographic and market research information.

These include Mosaic, a geo-demographic database, Persona, which identifies and locates consumers by their lifestyle, and Checkout, the National Shoppers Survey's analysis of retail grocery and DIY catchment areas.

Impact Plus, CD's latest consumer targeting system, which uses all this information, can reach 18.7 million homes, 85 per cent of Britain's households. A computer printout and map show the client exactly where CD proposes to distribute its promotional material, and the increased penetration of its target market achieved, compared with a random distribution.

Despite the popular view that 'junk mail' is universally loathed, a survey from Millward Brown, commissioned by CD, showed that 57 per cent of the respondents usually look through what they receive and read things that interest them, and 39 per cent like getting things through the door. Of the remainder, most were neutral rather than hostile.

Sophisticated door-to-door distribution such as this is closing the gap between direct mail, which sends increasingly focused promotions through the post to specific addresses, and door-to-door distribution. Indeed, it may even give door-to-door the edge in future.

The European Commission is considering restrictions on direct mail. While the UK operates an opt-out system, where consumers who do not want to receive direct mail must say so, the bias in Europe is towards an opt-in system, where companies may only send promotional material to people who have actually volunteered to receive it.

If the draft legislation in Brussels becomes law, companies like CD, which have found ways to target potential customers without storing information on individuals in their computers, will get a real boost.

An alternative to junk mail is at the door

Key issues

- Database marketing
- Geodemographics
- Psychographic segmentation
- Direct marketing

Questions

(1) Define the role of data analysis in a segmentation study and provide examples of statistical techniques that could be employed in such a study.

(2) Define direct marketing and comment on its inter-relationship with database marketing.

(3) What are the benefits of database marketing?

(4) Define and comment on the concept of 'geodemographics'.

(5) How would you assess the use of psychographic segmentation?

Clipping 5 The Sunday Times Magazine – Business World, 1990.

JAPAN – POLITENESS FOILS MARKET RESEARCH

Phillip Oppenheim's forthcoming book, *The New Masters: Can the West match Japan?*, sets out to debunk Western myths about Japan's rise to its current economic status, and particularly about the reasons why British and US companies seem to have such difficulty selling anything there. To be published in January by Hutchinson Business Books (£18.99), it is full of wonderful anecdotes, of which one of the best concerns a French company's effort to sell yoghurt to the Japanese:

'It goes without saying that market research has to be carefully interpreted through eyes sensitive to Japanese cultural habits. Even then, the eye can sometimes miss certain Japanese idiosyncrasies with disastrous – or, as it happens, sometimes excellent – results. In 1980, BSN, the giant French food group, thought that it could emulate the success in Japan of some Western convenience food products, such as hamburgers and pizzas, with its Danone brand yoghurt. A decade later, the company's original ambitions had disappeared in losses which have exceeded the original investment. For BSN, to its cost, belatedly discovered that Japan is frequently the exception to the theory which teaches that as consumers' lives in developed countries follow increasingly similar patterns, so does their taste in goods.

'I agree with the globalisation, but it's very much more difficult to carry out than it sounds,' said Robert Dahan, BSN's chief representative in Japan, ruefully. Ironically, BSN did many things right. It approached the Japanese market steadily, making its first studies back in 1979, and carefully chose as its local partner a diverse food company called Ajinomoto, which had previous experience of joint ventures.

BSN's crucial mistake, however, was to misinterpret its market research. The company hoped to tempt the Japanese with new types of yoghurt, especially yoghurt-based desserts and fruit-flavoured Petit Suisse cheese. So for six months, the company air-freighted in supplies from France for a careful market survey. The results were superb, with research showing that Japanese customers loved the products. On the basis of this, BSN forecast sales growth ranging from a low of 20 to 30 per cent a year to well over 100 per cent, and the venture was expected to be in the black after a mere three and a half years.

But within 12 months the dream had turned sour, for sales were running at only a fifth of projections. According to Dahan, the initial market surveys, following the theory of global marketing, posed questions to Japanese consumers which were identical to those asked in other countries. The answers were then assessed by the same, European-designed criteria. What they ignored, however, was the inbred politeness of the Japanese. 'They'll say they like a product, even if they think it's bullshit. But they won't buy it again,' said Dahan.

Japan – Politeness foils market research

Key issues

- Global marketing
- International marketing research
- Blunders in international marketing research
- International research design
- Questionnaire design
- Implementation of findings and market forecasting

Questions

(1) Explain some of the key reasons why some companies are becoming more and more engaged in global marketing.

(2) Why is the accurate analysis of environmental information so important in international marketing research?

(3) How would you relate the 'problem definition' stage with possible mistakes to be made when developing an international marketing research project?

(4) What are the three most important problem areas involved in the collection of primary data in a foreign environment?

(5) Comment on some usually encountered difficulties associated with questionnaire design in international marketing research. Provide examples of some steps that can be undertaken to minimize the risk of having a less-effective research instrument.

(6) Comment on some critical issues related to the analysis, interpretation and report preparation within an international marketing research context.

Clipping 6 Business Week, 11 February 1991.

THE 'BLOODBATH' IN MARKET RESEARCH

Staffs have been cut by as much as 50% as skeptical clients retreat

By Mark Landler in New York

It has been a while since market researchers had something to gloat about. Asked to recount a great moment, many still tell the tale of Pillsbury's cake mix. In the late 1950s, Pillsbury Co. developed a recipe that required the consumer to add only milk. The product bombed, so researchers rounded up housewives for interviews. They concluded that the mix made the women feel useless by giving them too little to do. Pillsbury added an egg to the recipe and sales took off.

Such methods may seem hopelessly outmoded in an age when researchers use high-powered computers and complex surveys to plumb the consumer psyche. But these days, all that gadgetry isn't doing much to help business. After growing at an 8% average annual rate in the 1980s, inflation-adjusted revenues for the $2.4 billion research industry declined 1% in 1990, says Jack Honomichl, publisher of the trade newsletter *Inside Research*. And he predicts a similar decline this year.

Pillsbury and other packaged-goods giants, ad agencies such as J. Walter Thompson, and independents such as the Gallup Organization have been slashing research staffs and budgets by as much as 50%. Says Honomichl: 'There has been an absolute bloodbath.' Profits are also down at big research firms such as A. C. Nielsen Co. and Arbitron Co. Control Data Corp., which owns Arbitron, recently announced that the researcher's weak earnings will dampen its overall performance in 1991. And Nielsen's parent, Dun & Bradstreet Corp., attributes some of its 11% decline in 1990 operating income to slimmer margins at its subsidiary.

What worries researchers is that the slowdown is more than just corporate parsimony. They fear a growing skepticism among marketing executives about their craft. One of the biggest problems is the mind-numbing complexity of modern research: Many top executives are bewildered by scanner technology, computer models, and the proliferation of consumer surveys.

Technically minded researchers do little to dispel the confusion. 'Too many of my counterparts are green-eye-shade types,' says Larry Constantineau, director of research at S. C. Johnson & Son Inc. As a result, some marketing executives now regard research the way diplomats describe Argentina: It's the wave of the future – and always will be.

Even more troubling are questions about the industry's track record. Many marketers say that despite all the advances, researchers often do an inadequate job of identifying their clients' customers. 'Market research just hasn't delivered,' says Jim Figura, vice-president of research at Colgate-Palmolive Co. 'It has been an embarrassment.'

Sure, there's still lots of it going on. Indianapolis-based Walker Research Inc. estimates that 72 million Americans were interviewed last year in surveys. But several trends have coalesced to undermine research's reputation.

No answer

First, the validity of surveys is being jeopardized by the growing refusal of Americans to participate. Annoyed by the instrusiveness, 36% of consumers declined to answer a phone query in 1990 – a 12% increase over

1986, according to Walker Research. That skews results by leaving out a sizeable chunk of the market. Yet Gallup and other researchers still rely heavily on phone interviews to get a fix on consumer preferences. And last year, the TV networks cited lack of participation to explain why Nielsen's 'people meter' – which requires consumers to press buttons – recorded a sudden sharp drop in audience for their programs.

More sophisticated research methods have had their share of problems as well. Since the early 1980s, researchers have been making more recommendations for new products based on the results of surveys and computer-generated scenarios for different marketing strategies. The trouble is, these scenarios don't always take all the crucial factors into account.

Colgate, for example, bungled its launch of Fab 1 Shot, a combined laundry detergent and fabric softener, in 1987. Executives familiar with the product say Colgate's simulated market test contained a key error. It proceeded on the faulty assumption that 1 Shot's buyers would be mostly families. But because it comes in individual packets, 1 Shot appeals more to convenience-minded single people than to families with big laundry loads. Thus, the simulation may have been accurate, but Fab 1

Shot missed its audience. Now, its market share is barely 0.1%.

Researchers are also squabbling more than ever about how to measure consumer emotions, which are tough to gauge but critical to buying decisions. In the late 1970s, Selection Research Inc. won many converts to its VALS (values, attitudes, lifestyle) system. SRI developed a set of questions that sorted Americans into segments based on psychological and demographic traits. Clients then bought the 'psychographic' survey to determine the makeup of their own markets. But now, most ad agencies have decided that VALS is not detailed enough. SRI is now pushing a more complex successor to VALS. Still, the agencies have developed their own arcane systems with names such as the Emotional Lexicon and Benefit Chain.

'Never saw it work'

Some marketers argue that with the demise of VALS, the influence of all psychographics has waned. 'These studies were able to segment the consumer market,' says Clay S. Timon, Colgate's former worldwide advertising director. 'But I never saw it work its way into Colgate's advertising.'

To restore their influence and win back the attention of glassy-

eyed senior executives, many researchers are trying to simplify their craft. 'There's a return to fundamentals,' says Colgate's Figura. He and others are deemphasizing fancy psychographics and computer scenarios. Instead, they're trying to fuse traditional survey research such as focus groups with scanner data to make more reliable marketing proposals.

In launching its Prego spaghetti sauce, Campbell Soup Co. stressed simple personal interviews to develop the brand's positioning. Then it hired Nielsen to track purchases and consumer response to its advertising and promotion efforts. Johnson Wax's Constantineau says he and others are jazzing up their presentations and cutting out the jargon in explaining their research.

Meanwhile, the big researchers are looking overseas for growth. Nielsen has targeted Europe for its supermarket scanners and already derives 60% of its revenue from outside the US 'Whether you're a corporate or independent researcher, globalization is a key challenge.' says John H. Costello, president of A. C. Nielsen USA.

But the biggest challenge for researchers is to get a fix on the US market. To do that, they may have to dust off more old-fashioned weapons to beef up their high-tech arsenal.

The 'bloodbath' in market research

Key issues

- The future of marketing research
- IT and marketing research
- Pitfalls and limitations of marketing research

- Public refusal to participate in surveys and data reliability
- Nielsen's 'people meters'
- Simulated test markets
- Measurement of consumer attitudes
- Tracking research
- Global marketing research
- Focus groups revisited

Questions

(1) What will be the major changes expected in relation to the use of focus groups?

(2) Provide some reasons for the high proportion of public refusal to participate in surveys.

(3) Provide some examples of the impact of information technology (IT) on marketing research.

(4) Why is the need for tracking research becoming increasingly important?

(5) Provide examples of some critical trends expected to have an impact on the role of marketing research.

(6) Define 'marketing research' and attempt to uncover some of its pitfalls and limitations.

(7) What is a 'people meter'?

(8) Comment on some key issues involved in consumer attitude measurement.

(9) What is a simulated test market?

(10) Explain some of the principles behind the trend towards a worldwide marketing information system.

Index